L·A·Y
M·I·N·I·S·T·R·Y

L·A·Y
M·I·N·I·S·T·R·Y

A Theological, Spiritual, and Pastoral Handbook

William J. Rademacher

CROSSROAD • NEW YORK

1991

The Crossroad Publishing Company
370 Lexington Avenue, New York, NY 10017

Copyright © 1991 by William J. Rademacher

Printed in the United States of America
Typesetting output: TEXSource, Houston

Library of Congress Cataloging-in-Publication Data

Rademacher, William J., 1928–
    Lay ministry : a theological, spiritual, and pastoral handbook /
by William J. Rademacher.
        p.   cm.
    Includes bibliographical references and index.
    ISBN 0-8245-1086-0
    1. Lay ministry—Catholic Church.   2. Pastoral theology—Catholic
Church.   3. Catholic Church—Doctrines.   4. Women in the Catholic
Church.   I. Title.
BX1920.R29   1991
253—dc20   90-23648
                                                                CIP

Contents

TO

MONSIGNOR JOHN A. GABRIELS

PASTOR

CHURCH OF THE RESURRECTION
LANSING, MICHIGAN
1922–1960

Thirty-five years ago, in his own inimitable style,
he taught me the fine art of pastoral ministry.

May he rest in peace.

Foreword

It was, I think, the end of the 1970s.

The priest had been pastor, principal, and father figure to me for long years. Now that I had finally grown into responsibilities of my own, independent of the diocesan school where he had mentored me for many years, he had become friend and colleague as well. I respected him mightily as good man, fine priest, and fierce intellectual. That's why I was so unprepared for what he said to me that day.

It had gotten to the stage in our two busy schedules where we had to make it a point to meet once a year — a dinner at his rectory, a night at the college of which his sister, also a woman religious, was president, a short conversation at a local jubilee, a little time together at a family event. The conversations were always the same: what had happened in our respective parts of the church since the last time we'd met, what we each felt was coming soon, what matters of ministry we were engrossed in now. This particular conversation was over a hamburger in a cheap restaurant half-way between his parish and our monastery. He wanted a religious education director for the parish; I was the prioress of the local Benedictine community from which he'd had an application.

There was a school in the parish, he explained, but the children who weren't in it, even in this Eastern city with its ethnic ghettoes, far outnumbered those who were. There were new needs for which no priest was really trained: care of the elderly, ministry to the divorced, long-range planning to maintain the physical plant, financial development of inner city resources.

"And what is the diocese doing to address all of that?" I asked.

The answer was a long, deep sigh. He looked away from me and said, "Well, we just finished a study. I'll be giving the priests' senate the figures tomorrow, in fact. By the year 2000," he said, "if the present death and retirement rate continues, we'll have thirty fewer priests in this diocese. They'll have to decide either to give up the diocesan high school or to give up the college. We have thirty priests in each."

"Father," I said with a tone of incredulity thick enough to slice, "those figures can't be correct if all you're counting is attrition from death and retirement." I was astounded at the inadequacy of the report from this brilliant man. "You're taking no account whatsoever of the decline in vocations or the number of dispensations or the rise in the number of the Catholic population to be served."

"I know," he said quietly, "but if I give them those figures, too, they'll never believe them. So I'm starting with the only numbers they'll accept. Death and age."

It was a hard moment. I began to see the frustrating point to which a deficient theology of ministry had brought us.

Down the road at our monastery, married priests and their families came to Mass regularly, young sisters got theology and divinity degrees, lay associates begged to be part of our prayer life and ministry in order to make up for what was wanting in parishes that were hardly operating enough to offer a minimum of liturgies per week — and those quick, lean, and impersonal — let alone the stuff on which a vibrant spiritual life is built. They were all people devoted to the church and the life of its people, but the church never bothered to notice because a "clear and constant tradition" demanded, apparently, that when faced with a loss of the male priesthood, the loss of the sacraments, and the demise of the Christian community that it was good Catholic theology to choose maleness over Eucharist. The weight of the scandal was already becoming almost too much to bear.

William Rademacher's book *Lay Ministry* unmasks the notion for the average Catholic that the constancy of the tradition is also unquestionably clear. He routes us from Moses to Paul, from Ignatius to Gregory VII to John Paul II, tracing both the theology and the practices that underlie contemporary ministry in the church. The trail is one that few Catholics have ever had the chance to walk, and the end point is far different from the one to which we have become accustomed.

Rademacher makes points that must be understood and discussed at every level of the church if the church is to remain vibrant in our own times. The limiting definition of the seven sacraments, the restriction on lay participation in the church, the loss of the scriptural meaning of ministry, the clericalization of the church, the effects of sexism on sacramentality, and an inadequate understanding of the nature of the Christian call are all stones across the door of the tomb that block the resurrection of the church to the fullness of life. Rademacher faces them all, forthrightly and courageously. What's more, he makes us face them, too.

This book questions the unquestionable and finds questions aplenty to pursue. If Rademacher is to be believed — and why not since he uses the most basic teachings of the church to question the accretions of centuries — then fiats from Rome do not always satisfy as answers for the great questions of the faith: How is it that Jesus himself did not come from a clerical line if churches are to be about clerics? Is the point of the Incarnation that Jesus became flesh or that Jesus became male? Is the grace of God really powerless in the face of a woman? Is the priestly ministry the only real, the consumingly total, the final and compellingly official ministry of the church of Christ? And, if so, what about Mary and the married Peter and the community-organized Greek churches? And what about the effect of the political twists and turns on the ecclesiastical world of the societies around them and the coming to new insights along the way about the nature of simony and slavery and racism, and now, perhaps, even sexism?

The story of ministry in the church is simply not a "clear and constant" tradition, and to attempt to make it so is a basic error in a society with an educated laity demanding lay involvement in ministry. The story of ministry in the church is at most a convoluted attempt to maintain the mystery in the moment. To close off that search now in the middle of a changing world may be the final act of infidelity.

The basic question, of course, is whether or not a sacramental church has the right to the sacraments. If not, are we saying by our present prescriptions and controls, lay Eucharists and unpaid personnel, that the sacraments are the preserve of male clerics who hoard and regulate and dispense them at their own pleasure rather than at the pleasure of a people reaching for grace?

Rademacher brings us up close to all these questions at a time when the replacement rate of priests is lower than at any other comparable period in history. We have little time left to theorize about our situation before our children have no experience of Eucharist to learn to love it and our elderly are buried without the sacraments and our souls have gone dry in a wasteland of circuit rider "pastors" whose only function is to deliver our monthly ration of God.

For a people who have grown up with multiple Masses on Sunday and teemingly large Catholic schools that can no longer be afforded and catechism answers that no longer address the current questions and a mobile population for whom the stability of the family is no longer the basis of growth and conversion and a world where Moslems and Buddhists are now near neighbors, the life of Jesus and the spiritual tradition of the church are the only bedrock that have eternal meaning. But who will mediate them to a priestless community?

Rademacher treats the theology of ministry, the history of ministry, the current questions in ministry, and the present opportunities in ministry.

He has done the church a great favor. All may not call it so. The fearful and the rigid and the unseeing will, perhaps, even chafe under it. But for those who take this book seriously, who study it with others, who use it as a measure of their present situation, and who fling it as some kind of standard against the future, it brings hope and liberation and tools with which to talk about the subject to others.

Do I recommend it? I would assign it. It is inclusive and readable, irritating and hopeful, honest and refreshing. Too bad my priest friend didn't have it to submit with his report a decade ago. Then maybe the real figures would have been acceptable, even comprehensible. Then maybe, by this time, we would have been able to come further together in our common search for answers to an ecclesiastical question and a changed culture that is simply not going to go away, either now or in the future.

JOAN CHITTISTER, O.S.B.

Preface

As we begin the last decade of the twentieth century we are witnessing changes of truly historic proportions. One country after another in the Soviet bloc is going through a wrenching transformation from communism to democracy. So far, these revolutions are happening without war and with a minimum of bloodshed. Armed only with candles and homemade signs, the little people, the average citizens, are stopping the tanks, the bombs, and the missiles. With nonviolent people power, they are bringing about peaceful change in their systems of government. Marching through the streets and gathering in the public squares, they are showing the world that average citizens can make a difference. They can bring down Berlin walls and topple governments. They can assume responsibility for their own lives and for their own forms of government.

In the churches too we see the average citizens, the little people, on the move. From the barrio to the highrise, we see the emergence of vast numbers of the baptized as they offer their gifts as ministers in the local churches and in the world. While this grassroots revolution is more gradual, it too represents a change of historic proportions in our way of being church. It shows that the Spirit of Pentecost is energizing the little people of God with a new outpouring of gifts.

While cold winds seem to be blowing down from the top of the hierarchic pyramid, the fire of renewal kindled by Vatican II continues to spread in the pastoral trenches. The growing numbers of baptismal ministers kindle new tongues of fire in the local churches. This Christian people's movement has its own life and momentum. It is a sign of hope, a cause for joy and celebration.

But it is also a cause for concern. It creates tensions and crises. It can be an opportunity for growth or a possibility for disaster. It is a challenge to the whole church to respond to this new wave of ministries in the churches. Will church leaders provide a supportive environment in which these gifts can grow and contribute to the upbuilding of the churches? Will the vision of the universal church be large enough to accommodate this power of the Spirit? Will the churches have the faith to let go of the old institutional forms so they can be free to welcome the new? Will the churches really see and hear the signs of the times and respond accordingly?

With *Lay Ministry* I am trying to do my small part to provide theological, spiritual, and pastoral support for today's emerging ministries. While there are already many good books on ministry, I feel there is still a need for a book with a spiritual and pastoral emphasis.

This book, therefore, is written especially with an eye to the many ministers serving in the pastoral trenches. They may be religion teachers, health care workers, ministers of service, directors of religious education, or numerous other still undefined ministers. Many of these laborers in the vineyard do not have the time or the money to study pastoral theology at a university or seminary. I hope these pages will bring them the spiritual, intellectual, and theological enrichment they need to grow in their ministries. At the same time, I hope my reflections will stimulate lively discussions that will lead to a better knowledge of God's will.

As this book goes to press, I want to express a large debt of gratitude to many people who have ministered to me in bringing this project to a conclusion. I am grateful, first of all, to the librarians at the Catholic University of America, Washington, D.C., at the Benedictine Monastery in Latrobe, Pa., and at the Pittsburgh Theological Seminary. I am particularly grateful to the librarians at Duquesne University who responded graciously to my numerous requests for books through the Inter-Library Loan.

I want to thank Michelle Farabaugh, O.S.B., Joanne Fedewa, S.L.W., Ronald Modras, and William Thompson. They performed an invaluable service in reading the first draft of the manuscript and offering extremely helpful comments to clarify various points of theology and improve the style for easier reading.

I am deeply grateful to Joan Chittister, O.S.B., noted author and lecturer, for taking the time from her busy schedule to write the Foreword.

My thanks to Ann Clifford, C.S.J., and George Worgul for their helpful critique of the chapter on the ministry of women. I am especially indebted to my colleagues at Duquesne University for their support and encouragement to continue my research. I am grateful to my students both at Gonzaga University, Spokane, Wash., and at Duquesne University, Pittsburgh, Pa. By questioning and challenging my ideas they helped me clarify and refine them. Finally, I want to thank Meg Ashcroft, who carefully typed the first draft and then, with great attention to detail, offered theological critique and numerous editorial suggestions to improve the final copy. Without her computer skills, this book would be nothing more than an idea in my head.

Regarding the use of nonsexist language, I have followed the classic work *The Handbook of Nonsexist Writing* by Miller and Swift. This accounts for the frequent use of the plural, which yields a nonsexist "them" or "their" instead of "him" or "his." At the same time, it avoids the cumbersome "he/she." I have not, however, changed the sexist language in direct quotations. While I regret the use of such language even in quotations, I did not feel I could, without permission of the authors, change the wording of their text.

Also, I have not changed the sexist language of the Scriptures, even though I am aware that new translations with inclusive language exist. While I am open to conversion, I feel the Scriptures are revelatory in and through a particular period of history with all its sins and virtues. They proclaim the good news that God in Christ embraced the sinful human condition as sinful in a particular historical period. The New Testament, for instance, honestly reveals the sins of greed, slavery, prostitution, Peter's denial, Judas's betrayal, and, finally, *patriarchy*. The historical Jesus, being especially sensitive to evil, suffered from all these sins, including the sin of patriarchy. If we remove the sin of patriarchy from the Scriptures, it seems to me, we would also have to remove the sins of Peter's denial, Judas's betrayal, and slavery. Removing the historical sinfulness of the human condition from the Scriptures would rob Jesus of much the daily pain and suffering of his incarnate life. At the same time, it would deprive Jesus' love of its uniquely divine characteristic, namely, loving and accepting humans unconditionally in their sins, including the sin of patriarchy.

I have referred to Jesus with male pronouns, believing that the Jesus of history belonged to the male sex. "Christ" and "Lord," however, transcend gender since these are titles for the Risen One. I have used these latter titles whenever they reflected the faith of believers.

For Scripture quotations I have used both the Revised Standard Version/Catholic Edition (1965) and the New American Bible (1970). Many times the RSV seemed to be a more accurate translation of the Greek. Then too, I felt that readers who do not belong to the Catholic faith would be more comfortable with the Revised Standard Version.

As this book goes out into the vineyard, I pray with Pope John XXIII that the Holy Spirit may "strengthen our minds in the truth" and renew her "wonders in this our day, as by a new Pentecost."

When autumn leaves blow over my grave, may these words still bring life to the ministers in the churches.

WILLIAM J. RADEMACHER

Pittsburgh, Pa.
Pentecost 1990

Introduction

What a variety in the history of Christian ministry! What a difference between Cardinal Richelieu conducting the affairs of state as prime minister of France in 1624 and St. Peter Claver bringing medicine, candy, and clothing to the slaves in Cartagena in 1610; between St. Bridget of Sweden telling Pope Gregory XI to get out of Avignon in 1373 and St. Theresa, "the little flower," quietly writing her famous *Story of a Soul* in Lisieux in 1895; between St. Joan of Arc, in full armor, leading the French troops to victory in Orleans, France, in 1492 and St. Martin of Tours, imprisoned as a conscientious objector in Amiens in 250; between St. Margaret of Scotland washing the feet of the poor in 1093 and Bishop Anthony Claret directing a major publishing firm in Spain in 1868; between St. Charles Borromeo administering the papal states in 1560 and St. Martin de Porres nursing the sick in Lima, Peru, in 1630.

The church in the past has experienced a tremendous variety in the forms of its ministry. In our own time, however, many of us are still very familiar with a narrow, clericalized form. The history of this narrowing process is quite complex, but we can surely point to the Council of Trent (1545–63) as the low point in the history of diversity. With the Protestant Reformation threatening its teaching, the Catholic Church concentrated on *official*, ordained ministers. After Trent these ministers were trained under tight control in special seminaries under the watchful eye of the diocesan bishop. Shaped by the defensive theology of the council, these ordained ministries were closely identified with the bishops' own ministry of teaching, ruling, and sanctifying. In actual practice these ministries were even more narrowly defined by the need to administer the seven sacraments, also defined by Trent. This meant that "real" ministries functioned primarily in the church building, the arena of the sacred.

After Trent Protestants continued to move in the direction of the more fluid ministries to the Word, while Catholics moved in the opposite direction of narrowly defined, *ordained* ministries to sacraments. Before Trent, for example, laypersons had administered the sacrament of the

1

anointing of the sick.[1] After Trent only ordained priests were allowed to administer this sacrament.

Now in our own time, inspired by the fresh air of Vatican II, ministry is once again going through a process of diversification. In one large parish there may be nine different full- or part-time "lay" ministries: family life minister, youth minister, pastoral counsellor, minister of liturgy, business manager, parish secretary, director of religious education, the lay principal of the school, and, finally, a health care minister for the sick. To this parish staff could be added the numerous part-time ministers serving on the parish council or ministering on a volunteer basis through various parish committees and organizations. The *Notre Dame Study of Catholic Parish Life* (1984–89) reports that "83% of the leadership within Catholic parishes, paid or unpaid, are laypersons."[2] The diverse forms of ministry increase daily.

This unprecedented growth of ministries is due to a wide variety of factors: the growing shortage of priests; the greater awareness of the Vatican II teaching that the Holy Spirit "distributes special graces among the faithful of every rank"; the new phenomenon in our U.S. culture of second and, indeed, third careers; a greater appreciation of baptism as a ministerial sacrament, conferring a share in the priestly, prophetic, and kingly mission of Christ; the movement of religious women into social ministries.

Both in the church and in the North American culture we are experiencing "a great and yeasty time, filled with opportunity.... In stable eras, everything has a name and everything knows its place, and we can leverage very little. But in a time of parenthesis we have extraordinary leverage and influence — individually, professionally, and institutionally — if we can only get a clear sense, a clear conception, a clear vision, of the road ahead."[3]

As we witness the church's rapid and "yeasty" expansion of ministry, there is, understandably, a growing confusion about what Christian ministry really is. Some are quick to label every good deed as ministry. They tend to inflate the word to such an extent that it loses all meaning. On the other hand, some feel they are doing ministry only when they are doing what the priest has traditionally done, serving as lectors or ministers of the Eucharist during the liturgy. Others, such as directors of religious education and C.C.D. teachers, feel they are doing ministry because they have been delegated by the pastor in some kind of "commissioning" ceremony. For them ministry still comes through some kind of "charge" or mandate from above.

As more ministries evolve, the question is posed more frequently: Is there any kind of *norm* to determine what is and what is not ministry? Who interprets and applies that norm? How does this evolution of new ministries avoid the dangers of individualism and subjectivism where all ministers are their own interpreters of the norm and appoint themselves to ministry through private discernment? Are the form and authenticity of the ministry determined by the pastor, by the bishop, by individual charism, or by the prayerful discernment of the believing community?

Do these new ministers need to be *called* by the community? Or *sent* by someone in authority? Or a little of both? Is ministry defined solely by *need:* the sick, the poor, the ignorant? Or is it defined primarily by *place:* the sanctuary, the parish, the diocese, the hospital, the university? Or is it defined primarily by *function:* teaching, praying, healing, counselling? Does ministry need some kind of certification, installation, or ordination? What is the difference between "service" and "ministry?" Are there official and nonofficial ministries? What is the difference? What does "official" add to, or subtract from, ministry?

As this list of questions grows, so does the need to return to the sources to find some guidance in naming and defining the new ministries of the future. For Christians, the Scriptures proclaimed every Sunday remain an extremely important norm. We may not, however, apply them in a fundamentalist or literal way to our church of today. Besides, Catholics believe not only in the written word of the Scriptures, but also in the oral word of tradition, not only in the Jesus of history, but also in the Christ of faith. The Spirit, promised to us by Jesus, continues to guide the church, including the whole people of God.

So if we are searching for answers for the ministries of today's church, we have to follow the footprints of the Spirit in the sands of history, beginning with the New Testament and then moving on through the rich tradition of the Christian churches. Our journey may take some unexpected turns. Sometimes we will be surprised by the beauty and the grandeur. The scenes may leave us breathless. Other times we will have to make our way through the fog, storms, and debris of the centuries. But the search for truth will bring its own reward. And fortunately, we do have an unfailing light to guide us: "When the Spirit of truth comes, he will guide you into all the truth" (Jn 16:13).

CHAPTER ONE

From Moses to Jesus

"But some seed fell on rich soil, and produced fruit . . . " (Mt 13:8).

We have many new questions about ministry swirling all around us. The search for answers takes us back to our beginnings. We need to rediscover the original dream. What was it about ministry that kindled the fire of early Christianity? What inspired those first laborers in the vineyard? What did Jesus and the Spirit bequeath to the treasury of the church?

We must return, then, to the Bible, the authentic testament to the birth of Christianity. We do so not simply to *imitate* the ministries we find there, to transport them, as it were, across the centuries to answer today's questions about ministry. That would be unfair to the authors of the sacred texts, who were responding to the problems of their own times. (For instance, the Greek-speaking widows were being neglected in the daily distribution, Acts 6:1). However, with the help of the Spirit and community discernment we may find the beginnings of some answers. While we are not looking for preformed models, like divine cookie cutters, to shape today's ministries, we do expect to find some kinds of general and flexible norms, some inspiration, which may guide us in the development of new ministries to respond to the needs of the modern world. We have our own form of "Greek-speaking widows" who are "murmuring" to draw attention to their needs. They are challenging the church to support them in their response to God's call.

As we begin our journey into the Bible, we need to be careful not to carry along any of our modern baggage. We need to guard against "laying a trip" on the sacred writers. In particular, we need to leave behind all our "churchy" expectations about ministry. Most of our modern church simply did not exist in New Testament times. We will do best on this trip if we first die, at least temporarily, to our own experience of church and ministry, so that we come to the threshold of the New Testament completely open to whatever we find there. We need to clear our minds of all our images of priesthood, episcopacy, papacy, and deaconate. Leaving these pictures and experiences behind will, in fact, require a real death. None of us will actually achieve it. But, out of reverence for the truth of the New Testament, we have to try.

So let's enter the world of the New Testament. Let's breathe its warm subtropical air; touch the lepers, smell the stench (Is this the one who returned to say, "Thank you"?); watch the Greek triremes plowing through the Mediterranean Sea (170 rowers — all in sync!); help the slaves wash the feet of the guests (Is this woman the one who washed the feet of Jesus?); hear the Samaritans curse the Jews on their way to the Passover (Is this one on her way to Jacob's well?); hear the soldiers beating, cursing, and kicking the thief through the streets (Is this the Good One on the way to Calvary?); watch the shepherd lifting the wounded sheep to his shoulders (Is this the one who saw Him in Bethlehem?); hear the fishermen throw their empty nets on the shores of the Sea of Galilee (Are these the ones who will be called fishers of men?); chat with the lonely tax collector fiddling with his abacus (Is this Levi who will leave it all to become a disciple?).

The Reign of God

As we continue our journey through the lands of the Bible, we see a certain Jesus preaching from the hillsides of Galilee. We are surprised to hear him proclaim, not the church, but the *reign of God*. And so we must pause to reflect. While a complete review of all aspects of the reign of God in the New Testament is beyond the scope of this work, we need, nevertheless, to stand humbly before this dynamic reality and invite it to speak to us, on its own terms, in its own profound mystery. Especially, we need to hear what it says to us about ministry, first in Jesus' time and then in our own time.

The reign of God proclaimed by Jesus is a familiar concept to the Jews in Jesus' audience. Their understanding comes at least partly from the Old Testament experience with David's kingdom. The real King David was a bandit, an adulterer, and a murderer. Violence was the dominant feature of his life. As king, however, he laid the foundation of a kingdom by capturing Jerusalem and defeating the Philistines. Then, with excellent political instincts, he brought the Ark of the Covenant, that ancient symbol of Israel's unity, into Jerusalem, the new capital of his kingdom. It would only be a matter of time now that the beautiful temple of Solomon would be built. Then David's son would have a sacred shrine and a holy city to sacralize an earthly and still very political kingdom.

History tells us that the Israelites came to understand David's reign in idealistic terms. And there were reasons why that happened: David did unite the disparate tribes of Israel; his military victories brought relative peace; then too, there was Nathan's oracle through which the Jews came to believe that his kingdom would be eternal (2 Sam 7:16). So it's easy to understand that the Jews of Jesus' time were ready to accept a Davidic Messiah, proclaiming the presence of that eternal kingdom. Even though they were expecting a political kingdom, at least they had some ideas about kingdom.

Without going into all the complicated details of the historical development of this idealized and politicized Davidic kingdom, we can outline what meanings the word "kingdom" may have evoked in the minds of the Jews when Jesus announced: "The kingdom of God is at hand" (Mk 1:15).

Throughout their Old Testament history, the terms "king" and "kingdom" are revelatory of God's reigning and saving activity. Before the arrival of an earthly king, God is the shepherd of the chosen people, who takes care of those in need, especially the outcasts of society. When an earthly king does arrive, he is God's vicegerent, not a tyrant like those of neighboring lands. The reign, however, is not limited to the Israelites. God's protective reign is universal. Significantly, the announcement of the reign's presence comes more through the words of the prophet than through the sacrifices of the Temple. Finally, God's reigning and saving activity will have periods of triumph and periods of failure.

As the Messianic reign became idealized, it included both earthly and spiritual blessings.[1] Throughout the Old Testament the earthly and the spiritual realities were a unity — they were a part of the one reality, i.e., the reign of God.

The earthly blessings included the fertility of the land. They "shall plant vineyards and drink the wine, set out gardens and eat the fruits" (Am 9:14). "Along both banks of the river, fruit trees of every kind shall grow: their leaves shall not fade, nor their fruit fail. Every month they shall bear fresh fruit" (Ez 47:12). These earthly blessings included countless descendants: "The number of the Israelites shall be like the sand of the sea, which can be neither measured nor counted" (Hos 3:6).

Freedom from physical evils was also very much part of the blessings of the reign: "Then will the eyes of the blind be opened, the ears of the deaf be cleared; then will the lame leap like a stag, then the tongue of the dumb will sing" (Is 35:5–6).

Yet another blessing would be earthly riches: "I lay your pavements in carnelians and your foundations in sapphires; I will make your battlements of rubies, your gates of carbuncles and all your walls of precious stones" (Is 54:11–12).

Before Jesus, the reign is not a spiritualized, otherworldly reality.

It is not understood as an escape from this earth. There are not two separate worlds: one temporal, the other eternal; one material, the other spiritual; one visible, the other invisible. This aspect of the reign will have an important bearing on any tendencies to overspiritualize the church's ministry, or to confine it to the domain of the sacred or, even more exclusively, to the seven sacraments.

The reign does, of course, include spiritual blessings. First and foremost is God's love, which is revealed to God's people in many forms. The shepherd image says it clearly: "I will gather you, O Jacob, each and every one, I will assemble all the remnant of Israel: I will group them like a flock in the fold, like a herd in the midst of its corral" (Mi 2:12).

Holiness is another spiritual blessing bestowed on the people of the reign: "You yourselves shall be named priests of the Lord, ministers of our God you shall be called" (Is 61:6). And again: "Your people shall all be just;... they are the bud of my planting, my handiwork to show my glory" (Is 60:21). "Sanctify yourselves, then, and be holy; for I, the Lord, your God, am holy" (Lv 20:7).

The reign, as Nathan had proclaimed, will be everlasting: "His dominion is vast and forever peaceful, from David's throne, and over his Kingdom, which he confirms and sustains, by judgement and justice, both now and forever" (Is 9:6). "And the Lord shall be king over them on Mount Zion from now on forever" (Mi 4–7).

A final spiritual blessing is joy in God. "Those whom the Lord has ransomed will return and enter Zion singing, crowned with everlasting joy; they will meet with joy and gladness; sorrow and mourning shall flee" (Is 35:10). "On this mountain the Lord of hosts will provide for all peoples a feast of rich food and choice wines, juicy, rich food and pure choice wines" (Is 25:6).[2]

Thus as we listen to Jesus proclaiming the reign of God near the Sea of Galilee, "reign" already conveys a rich meaning for the Jews. Jesus, in his words and actions, would add new meaning to that word and purify it of its Davidic political connotation. But we need to understand how the first announcement of the reign was received by those who, as Christ's first disciples, would in turn proclaim that reign by their own words and witness.

Reign in the New Testament

As we immerse ourselves in the New Testament and listen more carefully to Jesus, we need to leave behind certain false ideas about the reign. Since most of us have grown up in some kind of democracy, we may have inherited a few unreal, even fictional, images about the reign.

First of all, the reign is not spatial; it is not a place, like the magic kingdom of Disney World. It is not the happy hunting grounds of the Indians or some earthly "utopia" like New Harmony or the Oneida Community.

While the reign contains material, earthly elements, it is not materialistic. The essence of the reign is not found in temporal things. It does not consist in having or not having. This does not imply a moral judgment on possessing material things. It simply means that the reign of God is of a different order.

Reign is not static or stationary. It is never a question of arriving at an unchanging state that is already circumscribed by recognizable boundaries. It is not reducible to any historical form, including the church. No one can say: "There it is" or "There it was." No mere historical form, either political or ecclesiastical, can contain it, or totally reveal it. Neither nostalgia for, nor an actual return to, the "Good Old Days" will lead to the reign. It is never a return to some comfortable "womb" of the past, either institutional or individual. We do not get closer to the reign by returning to thirteenth-century Europe.

In the United States, where our culture extols rugged individualism, we need to be reminded that the reign is not individualistic. It is never *my* reign or *my* heaven. There are not a set number of individual roads to the reign. Either we "go" into the reign as a community, as a people, or we don't "go" there at all.

Nor is the reign merely in the future. It is simply not bound or defined by human clocks or calendars. People cannot shape or contain the reign by imposing their time-conditioned patterns upon it. The reign of God transcends time. Jesus said the reign "is like"; he did not say "it is."

The reign cannot be wrested from God by human power. It cannot be manipulated by human constructs, however sacralized. It cannot be commandeered by civil or ecclesiastical laws. It can't be "located" on earth by sacralizing an earthly person, shrine, or church through blessing, visions, or miracle.

Finally, the reign cannot be equated with the church. While Augustine (354–430) could distinguish between church and reign (e.g., in *The City of God*), nevertheless, he tended to equate the two: "It follows," he wrote, "that the church even now is the kingdom of Christ and the kingdom of heaven."[3] Pope Gregory the Great (540–604) continued to equate church and reign. Vatican II, however, definitely moved away from this kind of triumphalism and taught that the church is only a "seed" or "beginning" of the reign.

The identification of church and reign was a large factor in the militant crusades when Catholics killed thousands of Moslems "to the honor of God and pope." "If the church identifies itself with the kingdom," warns Thomas O'Meara, "the ministers may become domineering ascetics or powerful pontiffs who always claim to be the voice of God.... The scandals and missionary failures which come from identifying the church with the kingdom are visible in the ministry just as they are detected in every other aspect of the church's life."[4] The frail and human church tries (and often fails) to be a *sacrament* of the reign; but it will never *be* the reign.

Christ's command "Seek first the kingdom" applies especially to the church and its ministers. All historical forms of church have a humble, servant relationship to the much larger mystery of the reign. This relationship will have important implications when we deal with questions like: Can we offer our ministry in and to the reign apart from the church? Does the call of the reign or the call of the church define ministry? Or make it official? Do we define our own ministry in response to the Spirit's charism and then, on the strength of our own community's discernment, relate it to the reign? to the church? to both? more to one than the other?

Now that we have removed some of the obstacles to understanding reign, we may get a clearer, more positive view of the real reign insofar as that's possible under the dimmed light of our pilgrim journey. At the outset we must firmly cling to the truth that the reign is and will remain mystery. This means it is the continual, but partial, unveiling of the love and truth that is God. It is part of the dynamic of God's love, gently, yet insistently, inviting the believer into a loving communion with the divine mystery of the Holy One.

While by grace of revelation we can experience part of the reign, we need to own our pilgrim state and humbly admit that "now we see in a mirror dimly" (1 Cor 13:12). Those who offer themselves in ministry to the reign will themselves become part of the human mirror whereby the reign is dimly revealed. The reign, however, will always remain mystery. Those who offer themselves to ministry need to be open to be surprised by the continuous unveiling of the mystery of the reign through their own ministry. A pastoral visit to the prison or to the convalescent home often produces such amazing results that the ministers simply and humbly have to charge it to the power and mystery of the reign being revealed in their world, through their ministry. All ministry is open to, and leads to, the mystery of God. In fact, it can be called an act of praise and worship of the transcendent God. Paul did not hesitate to write: "The God I worship [Greek: *latreuō*] spiritually by preaching the Good News of his Son..." (Rom 1:9) In Romans 15:16 Paul again tells us that bringing the good news from God to the pagans is his priestly duty. For Paul the apostolic ministry is an act of worship offered to God.[5]

"Reign," like "faith," is best understood as a verb. It is God's active, dynamic reigning in the world, the same world God created and, in spite of sin, never abandoned. "Reign" is the human word that tries to describe the loving, active plan of God in and through history and our own limited and distorting appropriation of God's presence in our lives.[6] It is God reigning on God's terms, not ours. God's reigning activity cannot be manipulated or programmed by humans. We do not really *build* God's reign, even though many diocesan and parish council constitutions say so. God remains the master builder; we are only God's co-workers (1 Cor 3:9).

Since reign is *partly* an otherworldly reality, many human words have to stumble and stutter to express even the smallest part of that mystery. The New Testament uses *exousia* (power) and *dynamis* (power) to describe the inbreaking of the reign through the words and deeds of the historical Jesus. Healings and exorcisms are forms of the reign's power. When Jesus expels a demon from the man possessed by an unclean spirit (Mk 1:25), the people say: "Here is a teaching that is new . . . and with authority behind it." When Jesus cures the woman with a hemorrhage (Mk 5:30), he is immediately aware that "power has gone out from him."

The reign is not really described by, or bound to, any historical forms of government, be they ecclesiastic, hierarchic, oligarchic, monarchic, democratic, or theocratic. Therefore ministers are not necessarily serving the reign because they are working to establish a specific hierarchic or democratic form of government either in the church or in the political order. They are not necessarily ministering to the reign because they are "under" the hierarchy. The reign does not necessarily function more from "above" than from "below." We just cannot canonize or absolutize any historical form of government in the name of the reign. This does not mean that Christian ministers are negative toward, or absent from, the human process of government. It does mean that the reign is not reducible to a *specific* political or ecclesiastical system. Politics is the art of government in a finite world. And the reign is a world of no boundaries.

That said, we need to remember that the reign, as the liberation theologians remind us, does have its political component. Jesus did not preach a merely spiritual, otherworldly reign. He was crucified as a political criminal because his words and actions judged and confronted the religious and political establishments. Feeding the hungry, working for peace, and espousing the cause of the poor, as Jesus did, are always political acts. The reign, as it becomes part of the blood and sweat of this world's citizens, will always be, in some sense, political. Since reign shapes the ministry, it too, in greater or lesser degrees, will be political. The blood of Archbishop Oscar Romero, the four American women, and the six Jesuits murdered in El Salvador bears witness to the political dimension of all Christian ministry. Their blood, like the crucifix, helps us keep the reign and today's ministry in the real world.

To return to the reign of the New Testament — the growth parables unveil part of the mystery of the reign. "The sower went out to sow" (Mk 4:3). "The kingdom of God is like a grain of mustard seed" (Mk 4:30). "The kingdom of God is as if a man should scatter seed upon the ground" (Mk 4:26). For the Jews who heard these parables about the seed there was no proportion between the small seed planted in the spring and the great harvest of wheat in the fall. "The modern hearer of these parables immediately thinks of organic growth, but the idea of natural development was alien to people of the ancient world. Between seed and fruit they saw, not continuous development, but contrast, and recognized a divine miracle."[7]

In view of these growth parables, we can understand God's active reigning as an ongoing miracle. Ministering people are involved in the planting and the tilling of the reign, but they also rejoice in awe, wonder, and surprise as they see the miraculous results of their labor. This aspect of the reign has a message for those ministers who are influenced by the semi-pelagianism or the voluntarism of numerous self-help books, which in effect say: "*We* build the reign by our own hands. *We* can do it, if we really *will* it."

For those who believe in it, the reign becomes pervasive. It becomes a worldview. It has been described as an atmosphere, a horizon.[8] The reign inspires, energizes, and motivates the whole of Christian life. While it remains in the world, it is not of the world. While it exists in the present, it points to the future, to a horizon that can be seen only with the eyes of faith.[9]

Jesus proclaimed the reign (Mk 1:14) and then revealed its presence especially through the following actions: healing, teaching, exorcising, liberating, reconciling, showing compassion, and bringing the gift of God's peace. Finally, through his resurrection Jesus proclaimed the victory of the reign of God over the kingdom of satan, the mystery of evil. After the resurrection the reign breaks into the world through the words and actions of the risen Christ. It is not proclaimed primarily as an invitation to a state of life or to a caste of leaders; it is a call to the risen Christ's disciples to share in his continuing ministry of healing, teaching, reconciling, and liberating.

As seen from the human side, "The kingdom of God expresses man's utopian longing for liberation from everything that alienates him, factors such as anguish, pain, hunger, injustice and death, and not only man but all creation."[10] Through his power, his work, and his signs, the Jesus of the New Testament moves and acts in a ministry to the reign. Jesus brings freedom to those who are in bondage: "to the sick who are helpless in themselves and dominated by a stronger force; to the lepers who are cultically separated from the rest of society; to the Samaritan woman who is regarded as a schismatic."[11] He eats meals with public sinners, freeing them from their stigma. He meets those possessed by demons and by his power he frees them from Evil's bondage.

Jesus himself defined his ministry in terms of Isaiah: "He has sent me to proclaim release to the captives, . . . to set at liberty those who are oppressed" (Lk 4:18–19). The power (Greek: *exousia*) with which Jesus is empowered refers especially to God's freedom to act (Lk 12:5; Acts 1:7); it comprises both right and power. It is the very power of the Creator, bringing this world into existence by a Word.

The power (Greek: *dynamis*) of Christ reveals his victory over sin, death, and satan. In Christ the reign has removed the believers from the dominion of satan or other intermediary powers and placed them under the dominion of Christ. This power is expressed through the saving, liberating activity of Christ. That same power passes through the disciples who then continue to proclaim that same saving and liberating message. Every one who truly ministers is proclaiming saving news. All the ministers' actions make sense only in the context of the saving activity of Christ expressed through the reign now present in power and moving toward fulfillment through the words and actions of those who minister in Christ's name. So, to some extent, the ministering actions of Jesus have to shape and define today's Christian ministry. It is important, therefore, that today's ministers have both a theoretical and especially an experiential understanding of the ministering activities of the historical Jesus.

The Ministries of Jesus

The historical Jesus was a prophet, not a priest; he did not come from the Aaronic or Levitical line. Neither did he serve in the Temple with the priests. In fact, he suffered opposition from the priestly caste. He did not bother to reform or renew the old priesthood. So we have to be careful that we do not view the ministries of Jesus through the image of the Old Testament priesthood or even through that of today's priesthood.

The ministry of the historical Jesus can best be described as that of a prophet, or, better, that of *the* eschatological prophet. This does not mean he predicted the future, but that in his public ministry he stood in the prophetic line of Israel. "He is the great prophet, he is the one who fulfills the Old Testament prophetic movement by his own prophetic activity."[12] Like Amos, Jeremiah, and Isaiah, Jesus was first a messenger of God, proclaiming a divine revelation. He was conscious of a special call to proclaim what he had seen and heard. "Prophet," when applied to Jesus, is more correctly understood as a function, an earthly work.[13] It is not a title. Like the prophets of the Old Testament Jesus confronted the entrenched value systems of the religious establishment: "The Sabbath was made for man, not man for the Sabbath" (Mk 2:27). "Woe to you, scribes and Pharisees, hypocrites! For you are like whitewashed tombs" (Mt 23:27). If we are going to view the ministries of Jesus from any kind of angle, we would do best to see them from the prophetic, not the priestly, tradition.

Another frame of reference for understanding the ministries of Jesus is that of servant. Jesus is called servant five times; six times the New Testament cites the servant songs of Second Isaiah. In the Jewish culture a servant was one who worked for another or who belonged to another like a slave. He or she was committed to another for twenty-four hours a day in loyal allegiance. The ministry of the Servant of Yahweh was first of all to proclaim God's word of justice. His second function was to suffer and to offer his suffering as an intercession for the sins of the people. This suffering would bring about the healing of the people, free them from their sins and restore them to wholeness.[14]

With an eye on the unique role of the prophet and the servant of Yahweh, we may be better prepared to reflect on the ministries of Jesus. It's quite plain from the Scriptures that one of the first and most important ministries Jesus undertook was *healing* (Mt 4:23). The Greek word for healing is *therapeuō*, from which come our English words "therapy" and "therapeutic." This word was so common in New Testament times that it became one of the words used for ministry. In Jesus the reign breaks into the world to heal it of the traumatic effects of evil. In his healing ministry Jesus does not limit his care to the body. He is concerned for the whole person. Since the Jews did not divide the human person into a soul and a body, we must assume that all Jesus' healing ministry was directed toward human wholeness. More about Jesus' healing ministry in the next chapter.

A second ministry Jesus performed was *exorcism*. The reign breaks into the world through the anticipated power of the resurrection when Jesus casts out demons. In Jesus' time all kinds of illnesses were attributed to demons, or at least to demonic power. Since there were no enclosed mental hospitals, all the different forms of mental illness were very much in the public eye. Orientals saw the healing of these persons as a victory over the demons who had them in their power. Jesus' victories over the power of evil were signs of the dawn of the reign.

A quick review of the Gospels reminds us how often Jesus casts out devils. Through their resurrection faith, the first Christian communities came to believe that in Christ God had confronted evil and had come off victorious. The miracles of Jesus casting out demons are a powerful sign that the reign of God is stronger than the reign of evil. "But if it is by the kingdom of God that I cast out demons, then the kingdom of God has come upon you" (Mt 12:28).

Mark, especially, depicts Jesus' exorcisms as a battle with satan (Mk 1:23–28). And when Jesus sends out his disciples to proclaim the reign he gives them power over these same satanic powers of evil: "And he called to him the twelve, and began to send them out two by two, and gave them authority [Greek: *power*] over the unclean spirits" (Mk 6:7). The success of the disciples' missionary journey is announced in terms of victory over demonic power: "Even the demons are subject to us in your name. He [Jesus] said to them, 'I saw satan fall like lightning from heaven'" (Lk 10:17–18).

It may have been the constant awareness of evil in times of persecution or the strong influence of dualism, but the early Christians accepted much of the contemporary ideas about demons. Even after Christ's resurrection victory the mystery of evil persisted. If evil was going to persist even after the resurrection until the coming of the reign in fullness, then the early Christians also needed some way to symbolize this mystery of evil. Demons, as fallen angels, served well as symbols of the mystery of evil. But Christians also needed some signs to proclaim their faith that through his Spirit, the risen Christ continued to be victorious over evil, whatever its earthly form. "Where sin increased, grace abounded all the more" (Rom 5:20).

The church, having received the exorcising ministry of Jesus, continued to proclaim Christ's victory over evil in two ways: First, it incorporated exorcisms into its sacrament of baptism, which remain even to this day. The baptismal exorcisms assume that the persons being baptized are being freed from the power of satan to minister for the reign of God. The baptized persons will now be engaged in a battle with the reign of evil just as Jesus was. Empowered by the holiness of the risen Christ, they will now become exorcising forces or ministers with respect to the evil still present in the world "until he comes."

Second, the church went further and actually instituted the ministry of exorcists. For many centuries the church, through the ministry of its exorcists, publicly announced its faith that in Christ it had the power to confront the mystery of evil and, like Christ, free the demon-possessed from their bondage. The St. Peter who was martyred with Marcellinus during the Diocletian persecution (304) was an exorcist. His name appears in our modern Eucharistic Prayer I.

The Christian churches of today that try to be faithful to the ministry of Jesus need to have many ministers who proclaim Christ's victory over the mystery of evil. They need to proclaim to all the world: "Christ's holiness overcomes evil." They may not be called exorcists, but they will be "sacraments" of the very holiness of the risen Christ restoring the world to the holiness and wholeness of the original creation: "God saw how good it was" (Gn 1:18). Those addicted to drugs and alcohol are in bondage to their own inner demons. They need the help of some kind of exorcising ministry.

A third ministry Jesus performed was *teaching*. The word "teacher" appears over fifty times in the Gospels; of these, thirty are applied directly to Jesus.[15] That Jesus was in fact a teacher and was regarded as one by the Jews is plain from the New Testament. He gathered a group of disciples just as the teaching rabbis did. He is described as a teacher of the Law (Mt 22:16, Mk 12:14, Lk 20:21). He was, however, different from the rabbis in that he taught on his own personal authority. In expounding the Scriptures Jesus demonstrated that the reign had arrived and was being fulfilled in him. He taught his disciples how to pray; he taught the people in parables; he promised to send a paraclete who would continue to teach the disciples. In his teaching, Jesus reveals the reign and proposes a new Torah.

So *teaching*, modelled on Jesus, is one way in which the reign will become present and will be recognized in our own world. Thus the Christian churches of today that are faithful to the Jesus of the New Testament will do well to include teaching, in its multiple forms, in their list of ministries.

The fourth ministry through which Jesus announced the reign was his *reconciling* ministry. Paul summarizes the ministry of Jesus as follows: "All this is from God, who through Christ reconciled us to himself and gave us the ministry of reconciliation; that is, God was in Christ reconciling the world to himself..." (2 Cor 5:18–19). This ministry of reconciliation assumes that before Christ people were in a state of alienation and estrangement from God and from each other. Paul writes: "For if while we were enemies we were reconciled to God by the death of his Son, much more, now that we are reconciled, shall we be saved by his life" (Rom 5:10). "For in him all the fullness of God was pleased to dwell, and through him to reconcile to himself all things, whether on earth or in heaven, making peace by the blood of his cross" (Col 1:19–20).

Jesus' reconciling ministry reached out to heal two broken and wounded relationships, those of people with God and people with each other. He started with people's relationship with God, but included people's relationships as well: "So if you are offering your gift at the altar, and there remember that your brother has anything against you, leave your gift there before the altar and go; first be reconciled to your brother, and then come and offer your gift" (Mt 5:23–24).

For Jesus, forgiveness was the means to reconciliation. "For if you forgive men their trespasses, your heavenly Father also will forgive you" (Mt 6:14); "Forgive and you shall be forgiven" (Lk 6:37). It is hardly necessary to list the many times Jesus says: "Your sins are forgiven" (Mt 9:2, 5; Mk 2:5, 9; Lk 5:20, 23; 7:48). The parables of the prodigal son (Lk

15:11–32) and the shepherd rejoicing as he brings the lost sheep back home on his shoulders (Lk 15:4) are very clear signs of the reconciling ministry of Jesus.

In the New Testament the reconciling ministry of Jesus reveals the presence of the reign. It brings the lonely leper back into his community; reunites the adulterous woman with her family; invites Matthew, the "sinner," to sit down at table with him; accepts the tearful repentance of Peter, welcoming him back into "the twelve"; and brings the good thief into the banquet of paradise.

If the New Testament in Jesus does not reveal a compassionate, reconciling God, we are all doomed. Every Sunday, however, God's people cry out: "Lord have mercy," knowing in their hearts that a compassionate, forgiving God hears and answers their cry.

If there is a church today trying to continue the ministry of Jesus, it must have a long list of ministries for forgiveness, mercy, compassion, and reconciliation. These ministries may not be sacraments in the same sense as those defined by the Council of Trent. They will not be found only in the churches, but they will be sacraments or signs of the kingdom's presence and of its power mightily at work in our world. And insofar as a church is an effective "seed" and "beginning of that reign," these reconciling ministries will also be fruitful signs in the churches. "In her very nature the church is the great sacrament of reconciliation. To live this truth fully she must at all times be both a reconciled and reconciling community."[16]

A fifth ministry Jesus offered to the world was that of *peacemaker*. Jesus proclaimed from the mountain: "Blessed are the peacemakers" (Mt 5:9). And he lived the words he spoke. On the day of his birth in Bethlehem the heavenly host had announced: "Peace on earth" (Lk 2:14). When he rose from the dead he greeted his disciples: "Peace be with you" (Jn 20:21). No wonder the early Christians greeted each other with "Peace" and a "holy kiss" (Rom 16:16). They believed the Messiah was the prince of peace and that in his reign there would be peace without end.

Of course no single English word can convey the rich meaning of that wonderful word *shalom*, which Jesus actually used. To the Israelite it meant completeness and perfection, a condition in which nothing is lacking.[17] It was a gift of God. When one possessed *shalom* one was in perfect and assured communion with God. In the Old Testament *shalom* included: "rain, abundant harvests, no enemy to terrify, no wild beasts, the covenant with God and his presence in the midst of his people."[18]

In the New Testament "peace" includes harmony and good order in society and, in addition, the health and welfare of the individual. It is a gift that Jesus brings. We sing it on Sunday: "Peace I leave with you, my friends, peace the world cannot give."[19] Peace is not an earthly achievement; nor is it merely the fruit of human ingenuity. It is a blessing of the reign: "For the kingdom of God does not mean food and drink but righteousness and peace" (Rom 14:17).

But peace is not merely a passive state. It expresses and reveals the activity of a saving God: "Then the God of peace will soon crush Satan under your feet" (Rom 16:20). Here "Satan is to be understood as the personification of all disorder and dissension and scandal in the community. God who shapes man's ways in peace will do away with such dangers threatening the community."[20] The peace of God is not a passive submission to the spirit of the world but the action and victory that overcomes the world.

Since peace is not automatic and since the evil symbolized by satan is still very much alive, there need to be peace*makers*. In the church these peacemakers may be called ministers. They may have the gift of bringing about harmonious relations within the Christian community itself; or they may take their peacemaking ministry into the world to be the agents of God's restoration of the harmony that existed in his original creation (Gn 1:31). Their "world" may be that of labor, government, politics, oppressive systems, or family relations. Since peacemaking is an activity of the reign, it will not be confined to ecclesiastical boundaries. Those who wish to make peace will need to learn self-effacement and humility before the mystery of the reign. For peace is not merely the accomplishment of a human agenda, however noble. Peace, as God's gift, makes headway in this world on God's terms, not people's. That's why peacemakers are properly called ministers.

A sixth ministry through which Jesus announced the reign was his *liberating* ministry. Jesus himself announced this ministry in his hometown synagogue at Nazareth: "The Spirit of the Lord is upon me ... to set at liberty those who are oppressed [lit.: crushed]" (Lk 4:18 RSV). In the Old Testament God is already depicted as one who buys back for the people the freedom they have lost. God redeems them and frees them from bondage in Egypt; through the "ministry" of Cyrus, God brings them back from their captivity in Babylon (Is 48). Redemption means deliverance and liberation for God's people.

In the New Testament Paul particularly presents Christ as the one whose saving activity has brought about "the glorious freedom of the children of God" (Rom 8:21). He tells the Corinthians they have been "bought with a price" (1 Cor 7:23) and have become free in the Lord. For Paul Christ has won freedom from the Law, from sin, from death, and from self (Rom 5–8). "For [real] freedom Christ has set us free" (Gal 5:1). "Both his miracles and his forgiveness of sins are primarily signs of the arrival of the kingdom of God. They are signs of liberation."[21] It is clear, however, that this freedom Christ has won is not yet complete, for Christians still "await the redemption of the body"

(Rom 8:23). Thus full and final redemption is still in the future (Eph 4:30).

We are indebted to Thomas Aquinas (1225–74) for the helpful distinction between freedom *from* and freedom *for*. Christ's liberating ministry frees us *from* sin, selfishness, and injustice. We have to be liberated, at least to some extent, from such bondage before we can be free *for* someone or for some ministry. " 'Freedom for' states the purpose of the freedom acquired: freedom for love, for communion; the attainment of love and communion is the final stage in liberation. . . . In the final analysis, to set free is to give life — communion with God and with others."[22]

In view of Christ's ministry, it is clear that the churches that try to be a sign of the reign will need many liberating ministries. For freedom in this world is indeed incomplete, unfinished. The forms of bondage vary from age to age, from country to country and from institution to institution. Sometimes those in bondage have grown used to their chains. They have become numb under an oppressive system or desensitized by an institutional pathology. They no longer have the will or the courage to risk freedom. They forge their own chains. In spite of themselves, they continue to hanker for the security and confinement of the fleshpots of Egypt. They do not want the burdens and responsibility of freedom. So discernment of the forms of bondage must come from outside the institution, country, or people. Only then can the various forms of liberating ministries take shape. These ministries, especially, will be shaped in a prophetic tradition of faith responding to today's forms of bondage.

The purpose in outlining the foregoing ministries of the historical Jesus is not to reduce the ministries of Jesus to exactly six. For one thing, there is considerable overlapping among the ministries. Then, too, we could understand Jesus' ministries as one ministry with six aspects. Besides that, Jesus' ministry, which dealt with the injustices of his society, had considerable social and political implications. We could easily see that part of his work as a social justice ministry. Listing and naming Jesus' ministries does run the risk of reductionism.

Nevertheless, this review of some of the ministries of Jesus is meant to stimulate reflection and evaluation with respect to the continuing redefinition of today's ministries. These six ministries represent a good part of the work and mission of Jesus. As such, they challenge all those who commit themselves to live as disciples ministering in the name of the same Jesus.

Ministries to the Reign

Now that we have a clearer understanding of the reign as announced through the various ministries of Jesus, we can reflect on the relationship of reign to ministry. At the outset we have to state clearly that the reign of God, rather than the church, is the horizon of ministry:

> The kingdom of God is the source, the milieu, the goal of ministry. The presence of God in our complex world enables ministry, gives ministry its life and its freedom. The church, rather than being the dispenser of ministry, stands with ministry within the kingdom as something derivative, fragile, secondary, temporary. At the end of time, ministry and church will have been absorbed into our life in God.[23]

Ministry may be performed within the church, but it gets its charge, its "mandate" from Christ proclaiming the reign of God. The church, the community of believers, may have some role (to be discussed in chapter 5) in shaping the external form of the ministry, but since the reign is broader than the church, the ministries will need to remain open to that part of the reign which is not found in the church. Insofar as the church is a faithful servant to the reign, it can provide a fragile and temporary form for the ministry. It must do so, however, with a humble tentativeness, ever ready to adjust to the new and unforeseen demands of the reign.

The whole pilgrim church is a community of ministers to the reign. The church is not meant to be a minister to itself. For this reason the primary and basic orientation of ministry will always be toward the reign. For this reason, too, many ministries will not be *official* "church" ministries. Nor will they be performed in the church building. Since the reign is always larger than the church, there will be a great variety of ministers in the "world" who, in God's own mysterious ways, are also advancing the coming of the reign. And since the reign itself remains mystery, we look in vain for precise definitions of those ministries. We will not, in this life, find answers to many of our questions about ministry.

Since the ministry of Jesus was not confined to the soul or to the establishment of a merely spiritual reign, today's ministries to the reign will not be limited to the spiritual either. They will all be ordered somehow to the restoration of full humanity:

> The whole of this [Jesus'] ministry is the God of human beings, concerned for humanity, who wants to make us people of God, in turn, like God, concerned for other people. What is striking about Jesus is his liberating "humanization" of religion which nevertheless remains the service of God, faithful to death: service to God and humanity. Here there is no question of a choice between the two — God and humanity. Jesus' whole life was a celebration, a

doxological celebration, of the rule of God and at the same time an orthopraxis, action in keeping with this kingdom of God, i.e. of God who wants to come into his own in human history, for the happiness of human beings in a society in which *shalom* prevails.[24]

The purpose of ministry, therefore, is not primarily to save souls, but to bring about a world community of love, freedom, and justice.

Discipleship

From the very beginning the ministry of Jesus shapes and forms the ministry of those who follow him, the disciples. It is simply impossible to reflect on ministry in the New Testament without linking it to the meaning of discipleship. In the New Testament the call to discipleship antecedes and shapes the ministry. The pervasiveness of this New Testament reality is confirmed by the frequent use of the term "disciple," which is found 250 times in the New Testament. Luke sometimes mentions seventy disciples; other times he mentions "a great multitude" of disciples (14:25). From Acts 6:1 to 21:16 all the baptized are considered disciples. It's not surprising, then, that even today there is no Sunday liturgy that does not use the word "disciple" several times. It's also understandable that Avery Dulles, in his expanded edition of *Models of the Church*, could say that the church as community of disciples has potentialities as a basis for a comprehensive ecclesiology.[25] Like "body of Christ" and "people of God," discipleship could easily be a paradigm or model for understanding the mystery of the church.

Except during the prophetic period, discipleship was fairly rare in the Old Testament. That is, there was generally no master/disciple relationship. Under the influence of Greek philosophical schools, however, discipleship entered into Jewish life, especially through the rabbis who taught their pupils how to interpret the Law. Thus in New Testament times we see references to the schools of Hillel and Shammai. Discipleship, in the Greek and rabbinic schools, was primarily an intellectual relationship. The disciples were expected to work within the teaching tradition of the master. Their discipleship was transitory because they would soon equal the master or surpass him. Among the rabbis the best disciple was the one who preserved the teaching of the master, even to a word-for-word repetition. Women were excluded from being disciples since, in the Jewish tradition, they could not give themselves to teaching and learning.

In the New Testament, disciples (Greek: *mathētēs*) are learners, pupils. But, more importantly, they have a very personal relationship with the master — a relationship that shapes their whole life. There is no doubt about who has the formative power. It is always the master.

While Jesus follows the master/disciple tradition, he adds so many unique features that one must conclude that Gospel discipleship is really quite different from that of the rabbis and that of the Greek philosophical schools. With Jesus one becomes a disciple through a personal call, initiated by Jesus himself: "Come after me and I will make you fishers of men." To Levi Jesus simply says: "Follow me" (Mt 9:9–10). The response is immediate: "Levi got up and followed him." By the Sea of Galilee Jesus calls Simon and his brother, Andrew, to follow him: "They immediately abandoned their nets and became his followers" (Mt 4:20).

The call of Jesus cuts through all the castes, "clean" and "unclean"; male and female; zealots and tax collectors. He called Mary Magdalene "from whom seven demons had gone out, and Joanna," a member of the official household of Herod Antipas. The call to discipleship is the great leveler: "One among you is teacher, the rest are learners. . . . Avoid being called teachers" (Mt 23:8–10). Since there were so many disciples, it's quite possible that not all were called individually by Jesus.

With Jesus discipleship is permanent, not transitory. The disciples do not become equal to the master or surpass him. Discipleship is the fulfillment of their destiny. The disciples have a relationship to the person of Jesus. They are not simply people who hand on the body of Jesus' teaching. They never outgrow their need to follow Jesus because they are always in process of being formed by him. They become attached to Jesus to such an extent that they share his vision of life and ministry. They are called to suffer with Jesus and share in his ministry. With Jesus the disciple relationship even includes the spiritual life. The disciples ask Jesus for a distinct, identifying prayer. Jesus responds by teaching them the Lord's Prayer (Lk 11:1).

The New Testament is quite blunt about the ordinariness of the disciples. As one Scripture scholar expresses it: "One of the consistent features of the disciples was a chronic dullness."[26] Two were nicknamed "hotheads." Two others belonged to the zealot party. Some were ambitious: "Who was the most important among them?" They slept through the agony in the garden. One betrayed Jesus. And, of course, all the disciples, except the women and John, left him when things really got rough. Bronzed heroes they were not.

The ministry of the disciples was to continue and extend the ministry of Jesus. They were sent: to preach the Gospel (Mk 16:15); to heal the sick (Mk 6:13); to expel demons (Lk 10:17); to forgive sins (Jn 20:22). Implicitly at least they were commissioned to feed the hungry (Mk 8:6). Unlike the Gentiles, the disciples were commissioned to serve like their master who "came not to be served but to serve" (Mk 10:45). The disciples were to be ready to embrace suffering and even death as part of their ministry.

After the resurrection, Jesus is not the disciples' teacher, but their Lord. The call to be a disciple is not a call to imitate Jesus who ministered in a Jewish culture but to be a witness to the risen Christ in the Gentile world, even to the farthest parts of the earth. Now it is clear, especially in Luke and in Acts, that women too are called to be disciples. They are the first to proclaim the resurrection; they are present in the upper room on the day of Pentecost when the Holy Spirit comes upon the disciples; they are partners in Paul's ministry.

From this brief review of discipleship we can draw some conclusions that may help to define the ministries of the church. Discipleship antecedes ministry and forms it; there are many different types of discipleship, such as prophets, evangelizers, teachers, leaders. Discipleship is one thing; its outward form is quite another. But there is no Christian ministry apart from some form of discipleship.

Discipleship is permanent. We can be dispensed from a specific form of discipleship such as episcopacy, priesthood, sisterhood, or brotherhood. But, as long as we have faith in Jesus, we cannot be dispensed from discipleship itself. Discipleship is not achieved through initiation or ordination into a caste of disciples. We cannot lay hold of discipleship merely by entering a specific group or vowed community.

There are no hierarchic degrees of disciples. One Christian is not more disciple than another. Discipleship is a process of becoming. Ignatius of Antioch, on his way to martyrdom in Rome (c. 110), hopes he can become a disciple: "Now I am beginning to be a disciple.... Howbeit through their wrongdoings [of his guards] I become more completely a disciple.... Then shall I be truly a disciple of Jesus Christ, when the world shall not so much as see my body."[27]

Disciples are not superpeople, but ordinary folks who share in the ministry of Christ in their human frailty.

The call to discipleship is a call to witness to Jesus Christ, including the martyrdom of his suffering and death.

The forms of discipleship that existed in the New Testament do not easily transfer into our modern forms of ministry. "The discipleship model," observes Avery Dulles, "seems to make excessive demands on the average Christian. The vast majority of church members live in the world with careers, possessions, families, and civic responsibilities.... But ... every Christian is called ... to participate in the apostolate of the church."[28] Just as there have always been a variety of ministries, so there will always be a variety of forms of discipleship.

The vision of the reign of God, the ministry of the historical Jesus, and the various forms of discipleship provide the rich soil for the Christian ministry. Yet this soil, while it is very helpful in providing growth for the ministry, is not able to provide a specific shape and definition to the church's ministries. We also need to reflect on the various models and images of ministry that emerge in other parts of the Bible, especially in the New Testament and the Pauline letters. There we may find more seeds for sowing in the rich soil for the growth of new ministries for today's Christian churches.

CHAPTER TWO

From Jesus to Paul

"But the seed sown on rich soil is the one who hears the word and understands it, who indeed bears fruit and yields a hundred or sixty or thirtyfold" (Mt 13:23).

Most dioceses have an office of vocations or, at least, a vocation director. This director may be a priest, sister, brother, or layperson. These offices are set up to foster and encourage vocations. While more and more of the directors of these offices see their role as fostering vocations to all the ministries,[1] in actual practice many offices are still narrowly focused on vocations to the priesthood, brotherhood, or sisterhood. Most of the funds channeled through these offices go for the education of seminarians to the priesthood. Rarely do they offer financial aid, through loans or outright grants, to laypersons or religious women who want to study theology to prepare themselves for the ministries of director of religious education, pastoral coordinator, or director of liturgy. So far these offices are not designed to promote vocations to the various "lay" ministries in today's church.

The Paluch Missalette often includes a "Prayer for Vocations" on its back cover, which encourages Catholics to pray "for men and women who will freely commit themselves . . . as sisters and brothers, deacons and priests." So far, Catholics are not being asked to pray, at least with any regularity, "that all the baptized commit themselves to ministry, according to their individual gifts, given according to the measure of faith." Twenty-five years after Vatican II the church is still not praying publicly for vocations (i.e., response to the call) to the common priesthood of the faithful.[2]

As a result, most Catholics still link the word "vocation" to the priesthood or to the religious life. They have narrowed its meaning

25

to three or four ministries linked to ordination or to the vows of poverty, chastity, and obedience. Since celibacy, vowed virginity, or at least separation from the world are central to these vocations, it is still hard for married laity to see themselves as really having a vocation. Since most Christians are married and of necessity deeply involved in the world, the word "vocation" is often reduced to a narrow "churchism" applying only to a very small percentage of Catholics. The bishops of Vatican II, in a rich chapter entitled "The People of God," tried to recover a broader meaning of vocation: "Christ instituted this new covenant . . . by calling together a new people."[3] In that chapter, the call or vocation comes through baptism. It goes out to all the people; it is not limited to those who hope to be ordained to the priesthood or hope to take solemn vows. However, the pastoral practice of the church, in spite of Vatican II, still has a long way to go to reconnect vocation to baptism.

Vocation in the Hebrew Scriptures

In both the Old and the New Testaments, vocation had a very broad and very rich meaning. The people of God image, recovered by Vatican II, has a long history in the Hebrew Scriptures. In the history of Israel the people of God became a people because they were called or elected by God and because they responded to that call. The fact that God called *all* the people is very clear: "For you are a people sacred to the Lord, your God; he has chosen you from all the nations on the face of the earth to be a people peculiarly his own" (Dt 7:6).

This vocation of all the people of God is revealed even more clearly through Moses on Mount Sinai. Here the call becomes part of a covenant relationship: "Therefore, if you hearken to my voice and keep my covenant, you shall be my special possession, dearer to me than all the other people, though all the earth is mine. You shall be to me a kingdom of priests, a holy nation (Ex 19:5–6). The phrase "kingdom of priests" is especially significant, first because it indicates a vocation to the priestly service of mediation. Already in the Hebrew Scriptures priests were mediators between God and humankind, offering sacrifices for the sins of the people. Second, the phrase points toward some separation from the pagan practices of the Canaanite neighbors.

The election and call of the people of God in the Old Testament is so significant that we need to reflect on the theological meaning of that call. First, we note that the call comes from God's gracious initiative; it comes out of God's holy freedom and goodness. It is an awesome thought that God, "standing" before an infinite number of possibilities and under no kind of constraint, should decide to call a specific people to be God's very own. Even though this call is revealed to the Israelites in time, it rests on God's prior eternal choice. "The called" are the object of God's free choice from the timelessness of the eternal now.

The reason for election is not in the people themselves. God does not elect the people because they have proven themselves worthy of such a call, or because they were culturally more advanced than other peoples, or even because they were holy. The call comes from God's goodness and gracious mercy.

Second, the people are called, not for themselves, but to accomplish God's purpose (Rom 8:28). They are called for a mission. The call is never separated from that mission which actually defines the call. The call is a means to an end — Israel is to be a blessing to the Gentiles. It is called to keep alive on earth the good news that God is one, that God is a good, merciful, and loving God; that God cannot be reduced to carved idols; that God deserves a loving response; and finally, that God is faithful. That's the mission and the vocation of the people of God in Israel.

God first calls individuals such as Abraham and Moses. Abraham, for instance, serves as a model for vocation. He is chosen not for himself, but that in him "all the communities of the earth shall find blessing" (Gn 12:3). But soon vocation, as exemplified by Abraham, expands to include all of Israel (Ex 19:3–6).

Vocation does not mean that God's hand suddenly falls upon a specific individual like Abraham or Paul. God's call is already at work through all those natural processes whereby an individual develops those natural gifts and qualifications suited to God's purpose. God is at work from all eternity through the process of creation. God "does not simply find his instruments; he creates them: he has had them, in a true sense, in view, and has been preparing them from the foundation of things."[4] The word of Yahweh is addressed to Jeremiah: "Before I formed you in the womb I knew you, before you were born I dedicated you" (Jer 1:5). Later Paul will echo the same theme about his own vocation: "But the time came when he who had set me apart before I was born and called me by his favor..." (Gal 1:15).

Along with the good news of God's election, however, comes the bad news that Israel failed miserably in its response to God's call. Not all Israelites were true Israelites (Rom 9:6). It seems for awhile that God's plan has been frustrated. But then we see through the prophets like Isaiah that God has shaped a remnant. God has kept a kernel to accomplish God's purpose. Paul refers to this kernel to prove that "God's word has not failed" (Rom 9:6). It is a sobering lesson to recall that the church, the new people of God, can also fail miserably in its vocation. No doubt we can hope that in our own time God would preserve a remnant who would be faithful to their call. But the Hebrew Scriptures' teaching of the people's failure to respond to their vocation leaves no room for any triumphalism in the church.

Vocation in the New Testament

In the New Testament some new developments emerge concerning the idea of vocation. While in the Hebrew Scriptures election is primarily nationalistic, the New Testament emphasis is first on the personal, spiritual character of God's call. First comes the individual call to faith and to salvation; then the church is formed by these believers who have been called to faith in Christ. First we have individual disciples; then we have a community of disciples.

But one idea in the Hebrew Scriptures remains: the disciples are definitely called to service. They are to be light to the world (Mt 5:13–16); they are to be co-workers with God (1 Cor 3:9); they are called to show forth the glorious works of the One who called them (1 Pt 2:9); they are called to bring all things in the heavens and on the earth into one under Christ's headship (Eph 1:10). A vocation is still given for service to the mission, not for status or privilege.

In the New Testament, vocation is linked not to ordination or religious profession, but to baptism. Jesus himself begins his own public ministry with baptism (Mk 1:9). He refers to his coming passion, the culmination of his vocation, as a "baptism to be baptized with" (Lk 12:50). The early church interpreted the cure of the blind man (Jn 9:13–34) as a symbol of baptism. The blind man recognized his vocation to become a disciple of Jesus as soon as his blindness was removed (Jn 2:28).

The first part of 1 Peter's letter is devoted to the sacrament of baptism and its implications for the Christian life. Here "baptism is not viewed merely as a rite of initiation into the Christian community but as a source communicating to the believer the life-giving power of the glorified Christ."[5] It is on the occasion of their baptism that 1 Peter exhorts the new Christians on the implications of their vocation: "as he who called you is holy, be holy yourselves in all your conduct" (1:15). Baptism in 1 Peter is a celebration of the Christian's vocation to "be built into a spiritual house, to be a holy priesthood" (2:5).

Commenting on 1 Peter, Raymond Brown pointedly notes the problem created in the Roman Catholic tradition by an overemphasis on the ordained priesthood. "I believe," he writes, "we Roman Catholics need to recover for our people 1 Peter's sense of priestly dignity and spiritual sacrifices, precisely as a way of underlining the status conferred on all Christians. . . . Most Catholic laity are completely ignorant that the term priesthood is applicable to them."[6] "In my own church," Brown continues, "some would find surprising this almost elementary affirmation:

the day when a person is baptized is more important than the day when a person is ordained priest or bishop."[7]

Many theologians, reflecting on the deeper meaning of vocation, would probably agree with H. Richard Niebuhr that

> a call to ministry includes at least these four elements: (1) *the call to be a Christian*, which is variously described as the call to discipleship of Jesus Christ, to hearing and doing the Word of God, to repentance and faith, et cetera; (2) *the secret call*, namely, that inner persuasion or experience whereby a person feels himself directly summoned or invited by God to take up the work of the ministry; (3) *the providential call*, which is that invitation and command to assume the work of the ministry which comes through the equipment of a person with the talents necessary for the exercise of the office and through the divine guidance of his life by all its circumstances; (4) *the ecclesiastical call*, that is, the summons and invitation extended to a man by some community or institution of the Church to engage in the work of the ministry.[8]

Only during the fourth stage, the ecclesiastical call, does vocation begin to take on its "church" form through assignment to a specific task.

Recalling these four elements will reduce the danger of expecting the leaders of the church to be totally responsible for defining the Christian's vocation. Church communities, including parishes, may offer the gift of discernment in behalf of their members regarding the first three elements of the Christian vocation. But they must do so with a humble reverence for the mysterious ways in which God calls, secretly and providentially, before they impose an ecclesiastical form upon the Christian's vocation.

For the individual Christian, vocation is not necessarily a call to a recognizable church job. It is a process of becoming. Lynn Rhodes explains:

> The clergywomen acknowledged that they had a strong sense of call. They did not find, however, that their sense of call was to a particular job; it was, as one said, "becoming who you were meant to be." What people are called to, then, is not a specific job but a willingness to move ahead through their life with the sense that it has meaning and purpose. They are called not only *out of* who they are, but *to* who they are becoming. Some women talked about the spiritual dimension of this experience of call as being akin to an energy source that moves them forward.[9]

In view of this biblical theology of vocation, the officers of the church would do well to reconsider their pastoral practice with respect to vocation to ministry. With a humble reverence for God's Word that "my thoughts are not your thoughts, nor . . . your ways, my ways" (Is 55:8), the church may have to modify its expectations for vocations to the traditional priesthood, sisterhood, and brotherhood. The church may not "get" vocations until it does so. The whole church (including its officers) may need a real conversion, a change of heart, to experience itself as the "community of the called," or better, as "ready and waiting to be called," *on God's terms.* "God put Abraham to the test. He called to him, 'Abraham!' 'Ready!' he replied" (Gn 22:1). The church needs to ask itself if it is preparing all its members to be ready to respond to God's call.

A truly religious vocation requires a permanent attitude of readiness, rooted in baptism, to be called on God's terms to do God's work in God's place and in God's time. Such a religious vocation, of course, may have nothing to do with the traditional forms of ecclesiastical vocations. It would be better for the church to pray that all the baptized be ready, as true servants, to respond to God's call in God's "ways." We don't have to pray for God's call, because God does not fail to call. We proclaim this truth during our Sunday liturgies: "He (Jesus) called us to the glory that has made us a chosen race, a royal priesthood";[10] "You call them to be your people."[11]

So there is no shortage of vocations. God may, however, be calling the baptized to many new ministries and the church may be failing miserably in recognizing, discerning, and supporting those new vocations. It is possible that the "shortage" of vocations is, at least *partly*, a sign of the failure of the church's leaders, not the failure of the baptized. This failure may consist in a nonresponse to God's first and most basic call, the call to conversion, or change of heart, about how God calls.

The Holy Spirit

We cannot read the New Testament for long without being impressed and awed by the pervasive role of the Spirit in the creation of ministries. That role is evident in two ways: first, as the source and inspiration for all ministry and, second, as the master artist of the outward forms of ministry, especially through the charisms given to the baptized.

Basic to the understanding of the biblical theology of ministry is the recognition that all Christian service is grounded in the Spirit.[12] Paul confirms this truth when he writes: "we serve not under the old written law but in the new life of the Spirit" (Rom 7:6). It is this new life in the Spirit that gives birth to ministry. Beginning with baptism the Spirit empowers and, indeed, propels the new Christian to ministry:

Ministry results from the Spirit and its freedom gained in baptismal initiation. Not only freedom but action! Paul saw that the freedom of the Spirit is . . . a contact which flows into activity. The mission of the Spirit bears in it a drive toward activity, and this service — a being sent to serve — flows out of the freedom and community of the Christians.[13]

In the Catholic Church we have tended to link the Holy Spirit with the sacrament of confirmation. In the New Testament, on the other hand, the Holy Spirit is definitely linked with baptism. John the Baptist announces that Jesus "will baptize you with the Holy Spirit and with fire" (Lk 3:16). Paul reminds the Corinthians: "For by one Spirit we were all baptized into one body . . . and all were made to drink of one Spirit" (1 Cor 12:13). In Acts 1:5, Luke tells us that the power which the apostles will receive from the Spirit for their ministry flows from baptism: "For John baptized with water, but before many days you shall be baptized with the Holy Spirit." Moreover, Peter tells the Jews: "Repent and be baptized . . . and you shall receive the gift of the Holy Spirit" (Acts 2:38).

In the New Testament, Christians do not have to wait for another rite, like confirmation or ordination, to receive empowerment from the Spirit. It is true that there seems to be an exception to linking the Spirit to the reception of baptism in Acts 8:16–17. However, this exception is "undoubtedly . . . a Lucan device to insist that the gift of the Spirit comes through the Church, represented by the college of the Twelve in Jerusalem."[14] We shall see later that the early church, after the New Testament era, continued to believe that the Spirit, through baptism, empowered Christians for the ministry of presiding at the Eucharist. In the third century confessors who had "been in chains for the name of the Lord" did not need ordination to become presbyters. The church recognized the presence of the Spirit through their heroic actions.

The Ministries in Paul

In Paul's letters the Spirit is not only the source of ministry but also the architect of its external forms. Paul uses three words to describe the spiritual gifts that are revealed in the various outward forms of ministry. In 1 Corinthians 12 Paul uses "charisms" (*charismata*), "services" (*diakoniai*), and, finally, "energies" (*energēmata*). These three forms of spiritual gifts flow from a primal charism who is Jesus Christ the Lord (Rom 6:23). It is this primal charism that provides the source and foundation for the more specific activities of the Spirit. There are many kinds of spiritual gifts only because there is a charismatic wellspring from which all flow. In Peter's speech in Acts 2:17–18 we see "that charism as a basis for special ministry is not confined to an elite within the Christian community. Instead, since this is now 'the day of the Lord,' the promised Spirit of God is poured out on the entire people."[15]

In using these three words Paul is not trying to be a precise systematic theologian. He is simply telling the Corinthians that the life of the Christian community, including its ministries, is shaped by the explosive power of the Holy Spirit. "The horizon of the Spirit in baptized men and women is a life which is charismatic in terms of its source, but diaconal in terms of its goal. Spirit leads to ministry."[16] The value of these charisms is not in their possession, but in their exercise for the benefit of the community.[17] They are all *functions:* preaching, healing, teaching, giving aid, discerning, etc. They are not states of life.

When Paul uses the word "energies" (*energēmata*), he is emphasizing operations, workings, activities. The word comes from the Greek verb *energeō*, meaning "I am at work." In the passive tense this verb means "I am made operative (effective), *I am made to produce my appropriate result,* I am set in operation."[18] After Paul has used "operations" to describe the gifts, he uses the verb *energeo* to tell us that God is "operating" all the works in everyone (12:6). It is plain that the ministries Paul is about to list are God's "operations" or workings and they are flowing into all the baptized.

Since Paul is attributing these operations or workings to God, we can hardly miss the connection with the creation account in Genesis where God is also "working" for six days to create the world. For Paul, God's ministers are "God's fellow workers" (1 Cor 3:9), who are called to help rebuild creation, once "subjected to futility." "For creation awaits with eager longing for the revealing of the sons of God. . . . Creation itself will be set free from its bondage to decay and obtain the glorious liberty of the children of God" (Rom 8:19–21). For Paul, ministry does not turn inward into the church, but outward into the re-creation of the world. Tendencies to limit ministry to the church, the sanctuary, or "the spiritual" find no justification in Paul.

It may be helpful to have a panoramic view of all the charismatic ministries in Paul. We find four different lists in four epistles:

1 Cor 12:8–10	1 Cor 12:28	Rm 12:7–8	Eph 4:11
wisdom	apostles	serving	apostles
knowledge	prophets	teaching	prophets
faith	teachers	exhorting	evangelists
healing	miracles	contributing	pastors
miracles	healers	giving aid	teachers[19]
prophecy	helpers	acts of mercy	
discernment	administrators		
tongues	tongues		
interpretation	interpretation		

While we are reflecting on these ministries in Paul's epistles, we would do well to note, first of all, the tremendous variety and, second, the functional nature of all the ministries listed. All these ministries are for "upbuilding" — they are not ontological states. They do not require vows, celibacy, or even a lifetime commitment. As charisms, these ministries are all relative to the upbuilding of the community. That's why Paul could tell the speakers in tongues to "keep silence in church" (1 Cor 14:28). The charism is given primarily for the community, not for the individual. When the ministry's upbuilding function ceases, then the ministry ceases. There is no indication that Paul is opposed to a lifetime commitment to any of these ministries, but it is also clear that he does not require it.

Since the Spirit gives the gift of ministry, Paul respects the freedom of the Spirit to breathe when and where she wills in giving her gifts (1 Cor 12:11). Since all the gifts are given "according to the measure of " or "in proportion to" faith (Rom 12:3–6), we could expect the gifts of ministry to "flow" and move with the process of faith. We could expect them to be given "for term" — the term of faith and the term of upbuilding. When faith ceases, the ministry ceases. When its upbuilding function ceases, the ministry itself ceases.

There is no reason why the Spirit could not give one gift, such as that of teaching, for one part of life and another, such as administering, for the second or third "career" of life. The true disciples are always at the Spirit's disposal to minister on the Spirit's terms, not their own. We would expect ministries to be fluid, in transition, constantly in process of re-definition, as new needs emerge in rapidly changing conditions and as ministers themselves respond to the changing experiences in their own faith life. Setting aside one ministry, such as priesthood, and beginning another, such as teaching, could well be a truly faithful response to the Spirit's new gift. Change can be a form of fidelity. Since we are dealing with the Spirit's gifts, we must assume such changes are part of a spiritual discernment process.

In describing the various ministries Paul had no intention of drawing up a final or closed list. Today's Christian communities would indeed be faithful both to the Spirit and to Paul's teaching on ministry if they added other ministries to Paul's lists, such as pastoral coordinators, D.R.E.'s, parish secretaries, C.C.D./religious education teachers, ministers of service and jail ministers. In reading Paul we have more justification for believing that the Spirit, even today, is superabundant rather than stingy in allotting her gifts of ministry. Vatican II tells us that Christ "fills the church...with his divine gifts so that she may grow and reach all the fullness of God."[20]

Being faithful to Paul means that we view these gifts as ordinary, not extraordinary. We ought not to think of charisms as miraculous or as "supernatural" exceptions in the life of the Christian community. We need to be careful not to think that ordained ministry is ordinary and charismatic ministry is therefore extraordinary. Hans Küng explains: "We have seen that charisms are everyday rather than fundamentally exceptional phenomena, that they are various rather than uniform in kind, ... that they are phenomena not exclusive to the early church, but present and contemporary; and not peripheral phenomena, but central and essential elements in the church."[21]

Actually, the *absence* of a variety of charismatic ministries is extraordinary, unusual, an exception. In the absence of such ministries Christian communities could well ask if they have been faithful to Paul's command: "Do not quench the Spirit" (1 Thes 5:19). Of course charismatic ministries can be difficult to regulate, as Paul himself discovered. They can lead to confusion and disorder. After Paul's death the charismatic Corinthian church became embroiled in dissensions and disorder. The "younger hotheads," as we learn from Clement of Rome (d. c.,101), rose up "against their lawfully appointed presbyters" and threw them out of office.[22]

The church, nevertheless, is called to believe that the Spirit who gives her gifts will also give the gift of ordering and organizing this tremendous variety of gifts for the unity and upbuilding of the church. It is significant that Paul, after listing a variety of gifts (1 Cor 12), would include the gift of "governing," *kybernēsis*, toward the end of his list (v. 28). This Greek word literally means "steering," "piloting," or serving as the helmsman of the ship. In early Christianity the church is often described as a ship. Sometimes Christ is depicted as a pilot with his hand on the rudder. Cyprian of Carthage referred to the church as Noah's Ark.

Paul understood that no society can exist without some order or direction. The church that in 1 Corinthians 12 is blessed with an explosion of gifts can also count on someone being graced with the gift of governing all those gifts. No matter how many different gifts are on hand to sail the ship, someone or some group has to steer it. In 1 Corinthians 12 the gift of governing does not rank above any of the other gifts. Prophets and teachers continue to perform their own leadership function in proclaiming the Word. Later in the New Testament governing becomes the ministry of the presbyter who is called an overseer.

It is most important that the church respond in faith and humility to the mysterious energy and activity of the Spirit, even if the governing ministry becomes a difficult task. The "governor" needs to remember that the ministries are not the product of the institutional church but a visible sign of the charismatic life of the community present in structure, diversity, and unity.[23]

Before we leave Paul and his charismatic ministries let's summarize some of his principles: (1) charisms are not limited to a particular group; (2) they are given to all the baptized according to the measure of faith; (3) they are not given primarily for possession by an individual, but for the upbuilding of the community; (4) they are not necessarily permanent; (5) they cannot be separated from the body of the community; (6) within the body they are interdependent, i.e., the foot needs the hand, the speakers in tongues need the interpreters; (7) within the body the ministries give life to each other; (8) it is not the nature of the work, but the degree of love which inspires that work, that makes it ministry; (9) ministry is a function, not a state of life; (10) charismatic ministries are ordinary, not extraordinary; (11) charismatic ministry becomes useful and fruitful through the power of the Spirit, not through appointment, installation, or ordination.

The "Deacons" in Acts 6:1-6

The first reading in the liturgy of the ordination of deacons comes from Acts 6:1-6. Catholics often assume, when they hear this reading, that Acts here reports the first ordination of deacons. Traditionally this section was actually titled: "The Institution of the First Deacons."[24] However, the word "deacon" never appears in the text. The absence of this word is significant, since, if Luke had intended to describe the institution of deacons, he would certainly have used "deacons," the more technical term. In his Gospel Luke is very precise in describing the institution of the twelve, "whom he named apostles" (Lk 6:13).[25] The New American Bible, in its title above this section, calls the seven "assistants." The actual Greek text simply says: "seven men." It uses the verb *diakonein*, "to serve" or "to minister," to describe their function. The word here could mean "to wait at table" (it was often used to refer to the service of slaves who poured the wine for dinner guests.) Or it could mean "to supervise the meal." But it could also mean "to manage the money table" for exchanging currency.[26] It's at least possible that some widows, returning to Jerusalem from the Diaspora (Alexandria or Asia Minor), had Greek drachmas in their purses. Perhaps they needed Greek-speaking money-changers similar to today's bilingual managers of the *casas de cambio* (houses of exchange) along the Mexican border.

What is happening in this section of Acts? First, the Greek widows "murmur" (RSV) to express their need: "They are being neglected in the daily distribution." Second, in response to the murmuring, the twelve acknowledge the need for a new ministry. Third, the twelve ask the Greek-speaking faction to "pick out" from their own seven men full of the Spirit and of wisdom. Fourth, the twelve accept and confirm the

Greek community's choice. Finally, the twelve, perhaps along with the rest of the disciples, lay hands upon "the seven" selected by the community and "commission" them for the ministry. A careful reading of the Greek text makes room for the opinion of James Dunn that "it was the crowd of disciples and not 'the apostles' who laid their hands on the seven" (6:6).[27]

A little historical background may help us extract the meaning of this event for ministry. The Greek-speaking widows evidently were born in the Diaspora, perhaps Cyrene, Alexandria, or Asia Minor. Perhaps they came back to Jerusalem to be buried in the Holy City. In the Jewish tradition it was customary to provide some relief for the poor, especially the widows:

> Every Friday the local poor would be given by three relief officers, enough money for fourteen meals — money first collected in the "box," by two relief officers from the local residence; poor strangers, i.e. those whose presence was only transitory, received daily offerings of food and drink from the "tray," which had been filled by three officers going from house to house.[28]

It is at least possible, as noted above, that the difference in language caused a problem in making change for the Greek-speaking widows. At any rate, there was an inequality in the distribution of alms. Another possibility is that the seven had some connection with another ancient Jewish institution: "for in Jewish communities the local council usually consisted of seven men known as the 'Seven of the town' or 'Seven best of the town.'"[29]

It may be helpful to note that the number seven is probably symbolic, evoking totality or plenitude. It may recall Deuteronomy where the Jews are instructed to appoint judges and scribes in each of the towns and "these must administer an impartial judgment to the people." The number seven indicates some connection with the municipal council of one of our villages today.

What does this incident in Acts teach us regarding the shape and process of ministry? First, we note that the community expresses its dissatisfaction by murmuring. It is quite clear that the impetus for a new ministry comes from a need assertively expressed by the community. Second, we see a reliance on indigenous ministry. The new ministers, with their Greek names, quite clearly come from the Greek community. Third, we see that the twelve trust the community to select their own ministers. The twelve then confirm the community's choice and send the seven on their mission.

Fourth, we note that the twelve announce some qualifications for ministry, such as a good reputation and evidence of the Spirit and of wisdom in the candidate. A qualification not mentioned, but certainly assumed, is the need to speak Greek. Fifth, we note that ministry is given a very flexible interpretation. In the very next chapter Stephen, one of the seven new ministers, is stoned to death, not for waiting on table, but for preaching the Gospel. Philip too, very soon after his selection, is seen in Samaria, actively preaching the Gospel to "multitudes," exorcising "unclean spirits" and "healing the paralyzed." It is quite clear that these seven new ministers did not feel they were bound exclusively to the ministry of waiting on tables. Since neither man was upbraided by the twelve for his actions, we can assume that their missionary activities were within the scope of their new ministry. Sixth, the new ministry combines the material, waiting on table or changing money, with the spiritual: baptizing, preaching the Gospel, and expelling unclean spirits. Finally, this interaction between the twelve and the Greek community reveals a combination of a theology of "call" and a theology of "sending." The need — the inequality of the daily distribution — and the selection by the community "call" the ministers to a new service. The imposition of hands by the twelve (and the disciples?) "sends" the new ministers on their mission.

The following conclusions seem to flow from this event: a new ministry emerges in response to complaints from the community; need precedes the formation of ministry; the new ministers are indigenous to the community; this new ministry, even after the laying on of hands, remains very broad and flexible, including preaching the Word, exorcising demons, and serving at table; the church, already at this early stage, feels it can impose qualifications for ministry; and, finally, it is the community that elects and the twelve who accept and confirm the community's selection.

Other Ministries in Acts

A quick survey of the rest of Acts reveals many other ministries. First, we see the ministry of teaching: "The men whom you put in prison are standing in the temple and teaching the people" (5:25). Next, we find the ministry of preaching: "Now those who were scattered went about preaching the Word" (8:4). "And every day in the temple and at home they did not cease teaching and preaching Jesus as the Christ" (5:42). It is clear that the preaching ministry was not limited to the twelve. In Acts 11:20 we see that those who were scattered after the persecution of Stephen went to Antioch and began preaching the Gospel to the Greeks in that city.

Another ministry evident in Acts is healing. In 5:15 we see the multitudes bringing the sick into the streets so that Peter's shadow may fall upon them, "And they were all healed." Later in Acts, Luke reports that "many who were paralyzed or lame were healed" (8:7).

A fourth ministry still being performed in Acts is that of exorcism. "For unclean spirits came out of many who were possessed, crying with a loud voice" (8:7). No doubt, the early Christians believed that, in virtue of the Pentecost Spirit, they possessed the power of Jesus to expel demons, and they exercised it as the need arose.

A fifth ministry evident in Acts is the ministry of public prayer. "Peter and John prayed that they might receive the Holy Spirit" (8:15). Many such passages could be cited. Prophecy is another ministry that was still very active in the churches of Acts. "Now in these days prophets came down from Jerusalem to Antioch" (11:27). And Philip "had four unmarried daughters who prophesied" (21:9). No doubt some prophets presided (Greek: *leitourgountōn*) at the liturgy (possibly a communal prayer service) in the church of Antioch (13:1–2).

The ministry of presbyters is also very much in evidence throughout Acts: "And they [disciples] did so, sending it [the collection] to the presbyters by the hand of Barnabas and Saul" (11:30). The presbyters play an important role in the "Council of Jerusalem." They are part of the decision-making process that removes the yoke of the Jewish law from the neck of the Gentiles (15:10).

A final ministry very much in evidence in Acts is forgiveness. "Let it be known to you therefore, brethren, that through this man forgiveness of sins is proclaimed to you" (13:38).

We can conclude, therefore, from this brief survey of Acts, that the early church felt an obligation to continue the main ministries of Jesus. The church was convinced that, through the Pentecostal Spirit, it possessed the same power for ministry that Jesus had. But Acts 6 also shows us that the early church did not feel its ministry would be limited to a mere continuation of the ministries of Jesus. With the power of the same Pentecostal Spirit, the early Christians acted creatively in empowering and raising up new ministries in response to new needs.

Words for Ministry in the New Testament

Before we conclude this brief survey of ministry in the New Testament, it may be helpful to reflect for a moment on the meaning of the various Greek words used to describe the ministry of the early churches. We need to be careful, however, that we do not isolate words from their context. They retain their full meaning only in the culture and history in which they are used. This review of words may give us a deeper appreciation for the variety and fluidity of the ministries in the New Testament. It is the cumulative effect, however, rather than the individual words that will give us this added insight into the evolving ministries of the early church.

One word used for ministry in the New Testament is *hypēretēs*. This word is used nineteen times for ministry in the Synoptics, Acts, and Paul. It gets its meaning from the sea and the trireme, a Greek warship. It must have been quite a sight to see the trireme plowing through the waves of the Mediterranean Sea at thirty knots with 170 rowers in a synchronized rhythm. Before the coming of Christ these rowers were called *hypēretēs*. During New Testament times this word was applied to the assistant of the helmsman. He was learning his task, like an apprentice, and would from time to time take over and steer the ship himself.

Hypēretēs is used four times in Acts: "For David, after he had served [*hypēretēsas*] the council of God in his own generation" (13:36). "You yourselves know that these hands ministered (*hypēretēsan*) to my necessities and to those who were with me" (20:34). "Then he [Felix] gave orders to the Centurion that he [Paul] should be kept in custody but should have some liberty and that none of his friends should be prevented from attending [*hypēretein*] to his needs" (24:23). "When they arrived at Salamis, they proclaimed the word of God in the synagogues of the Jews. And they had John as their minister [*hypēretēn*]" (13:5). Significantly, Luke uses this same word to describe the proclamation of the Word: "Just as they were delivered to us by those who were eyewitnesses and ministers [*hypēretēs*] to the Word" (Lk 1:2).

A second word used for ministry is *doulos* (slave). The Greeks valued freedom and the slaves had no right of personal choice; they were subject to the will of another. In the Jewish culture of the New Testament the slaves were not despised as in the Greek world. Nevertheless, they were classed with goods and property. They themselves could not own property and their families belonged to their master.

Doulos is used twice in Philippians: "But [he] emptied himself, taking the form of a servant [*doulos*], being born in the likeness of men" (2:7); "Paul and Timothy, servants [*douloi*] of Jesus Christ to all the saints . . ." (1:1). This word is also used in that dramatic and very touching scene at the Last Supper when Jesus washes the feet of his disciples. "Truly, truly, I say to you, a servant [*doulos*] is not greater than his master nor is he greater than he who sent him" (Jn 13:16). Here the word indicates that ministry is opposed to the power and glory of the secular world. Footwashing was the duty of slaves. Jesus, by his example, is teaching his disciples his understanding of ministry. The use of *doulos* indicates that ministry is not modelled on any of this world's ranking systems.

A third word used for ministry is *therapeuō*, from which, as noted above, comes our English "therapy" and "therapeutic." It means "to care for," "attend," "serve," "treat," especially of a physician, hence, "to heal." This word is found at least twenty times in the New Testament. Since the Jews, unlike some of the Greeks, did not divide the person into body and soul, we must assume the word describes a wholistic healing of the total person. In Matthew especially, healing is a demonstration of the power of Jesus by which he plainly shows that in Jesus the reign is breaking into this world to heal the world that has been wounded by a long history of evil.

A few selected excerpts will show us how this word is used in the Synoptics. "In that hour he cured [*etherapeusen*] many of diseases and plagues and evil spirits" (Lk 7:21). "And he went about Galilee, teaching in their synagogues and preaching the Gospel of the kingdom and healing [*etherapeusen*] every kind of disease and every kind of infirmity among the people" (Mt 4:23). "And those who were troubled with unclean spirits were cured [*etherapeuonto*]" (Lk 6:18).

Significantly, healing is often accomplished by touch. Thus we see in Mark 1:41 that Jesus touches the leper and in Mark 1:31 that Jesus heals Peter's mother-in-law, taking her by the hand. Again in Mark 5:41 Jesus takes the little girl by the hand and says: "Little girl, I say to you, arise."

A fourth word used for ministry in the New Testament is *latreuō*, meaning "to serve," especially God, or "to worship." This word is used twenty-one times in the New Testament. It usually describes a ministry or worship offered to God. "For God is my witness, whom I serve [*latreuō*] with my spirit in the Gospel of his Son" (Rom 1:9). "For we are the true circumcision, who worship [*latreuō*] God in spirit" (Phil 3:3). For Paul proclaiming the Gospel is service (worship) to God; and the whole of Christian existence is worship offered to God.

A fifth word used for ministry is *diakoneō*, meaning "to serve," "to wait at table," with particular reference to a slave who pours out wine to the guests. It includes giving food and drink, extending shelter, providing clothes, and visiting the sick and imprisoned. It is definitely a secular, nonreligious word. It was used to refer to the wine steward, the barber, the cook, the maid, the assistant helmsman, the eunuch of the king, and the spearman who tortured the prisoners.

In the New Testament Jesus sees in *diakonia* the thing that makes a person a disciple. Thus in Luke 22:27 we read: "Who is the greater, he who sits at table or he who serves? I am among you as one who serves." "For the Son of Man also came not to be served but to serve" (Mk 10:45). In the same vein, Luke selects this word to describe the ministry of Timothy and Erastus: "And having sent into Macedonia two of his helpers, [*diakonoi*], Timothy and Erastus..." (Acts 19:22).

In that famous section on the charisms of the Spirit (1 Cor 12:4–11), Paul calls the gifts of the Spirit *diakoniai*. These gifts are all described by the general word *diakonia* or ministry. Paul takes a secular word and, in the power of the Spirit, fills it with Christian meaning. However, Paul does not restrict his use of the word to the sacred or the spiritual. Four times he calls the collection for the saints in Jerusalem a *diakonia*, or ministry (2 Cor 8:19; Rom 15:15; 10:30; 2 Cor 8:1–6.) Paul could use this word for the collection because he had a very functional understanding of the word and could see the collection as a ministry — feeding the starving Christians in Jerusalem.

In general, Christian *diakonia* refers to any service of genuine love. Early Christianity learned to regard as *diakonia* all significant activity for the upbuilding of the community, a distinction being made only according to the mode of operation. All Christians are responsible for the *diakonia* committed to them as gift of grace. All disciples are expected to offer their lives as ministry.

Before we conclude this section on words for ministry in the New Testament, it may be helpful to recall what words are *not* used: *archōn, timē, hiereus,* and *laikos. Archon* meant "ruler," "governor," "leader." He was a man with a prominent position such as a Roman or Jewish official. This word is used for Beelzebub, the prince of devils, and for the rulers over the Gentiles who "lorded over them . . . " (Mk 10:42).

A second word not used is *timē*, meaning "honor," "price," "respect," "compensation," and, perhaps, "office." Even though the English RSV version of 1 Timothy 3:1 translates "office of bishop," the word "office" does not appear in the Greek text. A third word not used is *hiereus*. The noun meant "priest." The verb, *hierateuō*, meant "to discharge a priestly office." Jesus never calls himself a priest and he never calls his disciples priests. When the word *hiereus* is used it refers to the Jewish priesthood of the Hebrew Scriptures (Mk 8:4).

A fourth word missing in the New Testament is *laikos*. In secular Greek the noun meant "layperson"; the adjective meant "common" or "profane," as opposed to consecrated. Surprisingly, neither the Gospels nor the Pauline letters ever refer to a baptized Christian as a layperson. Paul uses the word *hagioi* to refer to the baptized. This word meant "holy," "sacred." *Hagioi* described the Christians as the new people of God, taking the place of the Old Testament people of God.[30]

Five Models for Church in the New Testament

If we cannot isolate the words used for ministry in the New Testament, we certainly cannot separate ministry from the cultural and historical conditions of the local church. In the Corinthian church, for example, we see that the charismatic ministries are in charge. Corinth was a typical city-state, autonomous, "a self-contained unit of free citizens, having its own territory as a supporting hinterland and ruled over by a council of citizens, at the head of which was the chief, an elected official."[31] In view of this cultural background Paul was quite prepared to let the Corinthian church have considerable autonomy. He did not feel it was necessary to appoint a bishop or a presbyter to preside over the Corinthian church. Instead, the charismatics, acting as free citizens, governed their own church. We know from subsequent history that this Corinthian experiment in a purely charismatic church order was not completely successful.

A second model of church in the Pauline letters is located at Philippi, a Roman enclave in Macedonia. In the letter to the Philippians there is no evidence of the presence of charismatics in the city. In the opening of his letter Paul refers immediately to the "bishops and deacons" (Phil 1:1). No doubt these bishops were simply overseers, since neither the deaconate nor the episcopate had yet been established as offices in the church. We will do best to understand both words as functions. It is clear, nevertheless, that the Philippian church has a different organization for its ministries than that of Corinth.

The third model for church and ministry is Antioch. In Acts 13:1 we see that prophets and teachers are in charge of the community, probably founded by Barnabas. No doubt both prophets and teachers were presiding at the liturgy (*leitourgountōn*). These prophets and teachers, without asking for permission from the twelve, sent missionaries to Seleucia: "Then after fasting and praying they laid their hands on them and sent them off" (Acts 13:3).

The fourth model of church is that of Jerusalem with its college of presbyters, also known as elders. These presbyters play an important role in the decision-making process at the Apostolic Council recorded in Acts 15. "Luke plainly regards a board of elders as part of the normal equipment of a Christian congregation.... The system of elders is therefore probably of Judeo-Christian origin (using that term without any particular theological emphasis) just as bishops and deacons were at first at home only in Gentile Christian congregations."[32] On the other hand, evidence from the Dead Sea Scrolls indicates that the Essenes (a Jewish sectarian group) also had overseers, i.e., bishops.[33]

The presbyteral system also seems to have been adopted in the Johannine churches near Ephesus. These were the house churches that received the second and third epistles of John. "By the end of the first century in many areas there was developing a church structure in which groups of 'presbyters' were responsible for the administration and pastoral care of a church."[34] As in Jerusalem, the collegiate rather than the monarchic form of church organization was still the norm.

The pastoral letters (1 and 2 Timothy and Titus) present us with a fifth model of church. Timothy is in charge of the church at Ephesus; Titus is in charge at Crete. Both churches are being attacked by the conservative

Jewish Christians who continue to observe the Mosaic Law and expect new Gentile Christians to do the same. Consequently, the church and its ministry retreats into a defensive posture of rigidly defined ministries to protect itself. So these churches concentrate on the "official" ministries of bishops, presbyters, and deacons. We also see the development of rules and regulations, indicating a growing concern for discipline in the ministry. The "bishop" must be "of one wife, temperate, . . . no drunkard, an apt teacher, not quarrelsome, and no lover of money. He must manage his own household well" (1 Tm 3:2–3). Good family men are preferred as leaders in the church.

In response to the dual threat of the Gnostics and the conservative Jewish Christians the church of the pastoral letters retreats into a fortress with proper officers in charge. The prophets and charismatics of the Corinthian church are not found in Crete and Ephesus. There is every indication that the church leaders are concerned about retaining control through neatly defined, institutionalized ministries.

While the above five models do not exhaust the diversity of church forms,[35] nevertheless, they do give some indication of the flexibility and fluidity of ministry and church in the New Testament. While we cannot simply transfer these models into our own time, we can learn from them how to be creative in developing new models that respond both to our own culture and to the needs of our own people. Nigeria does not need a European model of church; the United States does not need a Nigerian model. And neither Nigeria nor the United States need a Roman model.

"Established" Forms of Ministry

Apart from the charismatic ministries mentioned by Paul in 1 Corinthians 12 there are some established forms of ministry that, nevertheless, are primarily functional. At the same time, they share in the charism of the Spirit and, therefore, could also be called charismatic. Sometimes the charismatic ministries actually overlap with these more stable forms. It may be helpful, before we leave this chapter, to make a brief survey of these more established forms of ministry.

The first of these ministries, described especially in Matthew and Luke, is the ministry of "the twelve." Scripture scholars agree that the number twelve, like many other numbers in the New Testament, is symbolic, representing the twelve tribes from which all Israelites were believed to be descended. It indicated that Jesus' teaching was meant first for the whole of Israel. Twelve is therefore meant to be a sacred number for the new people of God just as it was for Israel. That's why Matthias had to be selected to replace Judas (Acts 1:15–26). The sacred number had to be completed. While the number twelve was sacred in Jerusalem, it meant very little to the Gentiles who were not descendents from the twelve tribes. Interestingly, the place of the twelve at the center of things diminished rather quickly. "Apart from two or three obvious exceptions, they began to disappear wholly from view — presumably at least because their role was thought of more in relation to the resurrection and return of Christ."[36]

A second word frequently used to describe a fairly stable ministry is "apostle." The word in its Greek form probably is the same as the Hebrew *schaliach*, which means that the apostle is an authorized representative who has the same authority and standing as the person who sends him. "Apostles are (a) those who are witnesses of the risen Lord, to whom the crucified Lord has revealed himself as living; (b) those who have been commissioned by the Lord for missionary preaching."[37] "Apostle" is not restricted to the twelve. Some of Paul's co-workers were named apostles (Phil 2:25; 2 Cor 8:23; 1 Cor 15:5,7). In Romans 16:7 Paul, perhaps using "apostle" in a wide sense, tells us that Andronicus and Junias, his fellow prisoners, were "outstanding among the apostles." It's quite likely that Junias is a female name, which would mean that women were ranked among the apostles. At the time of Paul, "apostle" describes a function rather than a formal office.[38]

In the later parts of the New Testament we meet the presbyter-bishop. Again the bishop is still primarily a functional overseer. It is not always clear to what extent presbyter is distinguished from bishop. The numerous presbyters mentioned in the Acts of the Apostles may simply reflect an old Jewish tradition of elders serving as councilors managing the affairs of the village. No doubt, by the end of the New Testament period, especially in the pastoral letters, presbyters and bishops acquire some of the stability of office.

Another ministry, at least mentioned in the New Testament, is that of the deaconess. In Romans 16:1 Paul commends "our sister Phoebe, a deaconess of the church at Cenchreae." It is at least possible that Prisca, also mentioned in Romans, is a deaconess. She is a very active "fellow-worker" who instructs Apollos, an Alexandrian Jew, who becomes a leading figure in the life of the church of Corinth. It is not easy to know when "deaconess" is a function and when it is an office. However, "the description of Phoebe as the *diakonos* of the church at Cenchreae indicates the point where the original charisma is becoming an office."[39] It is at least possible that "the women" listed after the deacons in 1 Timothy 3:11 are deaconesses. At least they must have more or less the same qualifications as the deacons listed in 3:8.

No doubt *prophets*, along with prophetesses, played an important role in the early church. In Ephesians 2:20 we see that the church is built "upon the foundation of the apostles and prophets." We saw ear-

44

lier that the prophets along with the teachers were in charge of the church at Antioch. Prophets represent a different kind of ministry since they are appointed and empowered by God. They are not chosen or commissioned by the community, but called by the Spirit.[40]

Prophetesses too played some role in the church ministries of the New Testament. As noted above, Philip, one of the seven, had four unmarried daughters who prophesied (Acts 21:9). A fourteenth-century manuscript even mentions their names: Hermione, Charitina, Irais, and Eutychiana. Paul allows a woman to prophesy in the church, but she must keep her head covered (1 Cor 11:5). On Pentecost Day Peter announces to all the people that the Spirit will be poured out on all flesh " . . . and your daughters shall prophesy" (Acts 2:17).

Teachers, mentioned earlier, have an important place both in the Pauline letters and in the Acts of the Apostles (Acts 13:1; 1 Cor 12:28–29; Eph 4:11; Hb 5:12; 1 Tm 2:7; 2 Tm 1:11). It is clear that the teaching ministry was a separate and distinct ministry. It is not until the pastoral letters are written that presbyters become the official teachers. Before that time teachers were considered charismatic ministers needed to build up the church.

Finally, the New Testament lists the *widow* (1 Tm 5:5) who "continues in supplications and prayers night and day." We learn that a widow should be enrolled if "she is not less than sixty years of age, having been the wife of one husband" (1 Tm 5:9). Evidently the widows were expected to show hospitality, wash the feet of the "saints," and relieve the afflicted (5:10). Even though these widows were "enrolled" we do not know much about their ministry. "Of a ministry exercised by these widows, nothing is expressly said. . . . They do not . . . seem to have been invested with a specific function; but they seem, instead, to display only the effects of a living faith and spontaneous charity."[41] Their ministry of hospitality may have been fairly significant at that time since the Jewish tradition considered hospitality a sacred duty.

Before leaving the New Testament we note that Hebrews 13:7 and 17 uses "leaders" to describe the ministers who direct the church in Rome. Since there is no detailed description of this term we may assume these leaders are functional overseers of the church. While the title "leader" (*hēgoumenoi*) is not precise, the leader does announce the Word of God and watch over the faithful.[42]

Some Pastoral Reflections

What does the New Testament experience of ministry say to the ministry of our time? Since we are so many centuries removed from the New Testament, we cannot expect *complete* answers for our own expansion and redefinition of the ministry. Nevertheless, since the New Testament is always the primary *locus* for reflection on the church and its ministries, we can summarize our reflections by listing some very general and flexible principles that can serve as seeds for the growth of ministries in the Christian churches.

First and foremost, there can be no *Christian* ministry apart from Jesus Christ. Agnostic humanists may clothe the naked and give drink to the thirsty but their acts cannot be called Christian ministry. Their ministry may indeed be ministry to humanity and may even be called a general/universal ministry. However, their human ministry basically has nothing to do with the Christian religion.[43]

There is no ministry apart from the Holy Spirit and her creative activity continually empowering the minister.

Christian ministry is done to and for the reign of God. The church may be the place of ministry, but it is not the goal of ministry.

There is no ministry apart from some form of discipleship. The New Testament clearly shows us that discipleship antecedes ministry and shapes it.

There is no ministry apart from a call or a vocation. It is clear that all the baptized have a vocation to some kind of ministry. Vocation describes the *called* state of the whole church or, better, the state of readiness to be called, on God's terms.

There is no ministry apart from a Christian mission. Christian ministry as a caste or state, apart from this mission, does not exist in the New Testament.

There is no Christian ministry apart from some form of community. Paul's images of the body of Christ and the building of God show that ministry is for the upbuilding of the community. There is no "Lone Ranger" ministry; there is no charism apart from the body of the faithful.

There is also no ministry apart from needs. Need antecedes ministry and shapes and defines it. Since needs change constantly, the ministries of the churches change constantly.

There is no *Christian* ministry apart from accountability. For the minister is accountable to God, the giver of the gifts, and to the community that supports the ministry and discerns its usefulness for the upbuilding of the community.

The *external forms* of ministry cannot be defined in absolute, unchanging categories. For they are always dependent upon the changing needs and the new calls of the Spirit who calls when and how she wishes. The outward form of ministry cannot be bound permanently by ecclesiastical laws or by any historical form of church. While the inner foundation of ministry, Christ now and forever, remains the same, its outward forms are always at the disposal of the Spirit. Thus, religious communities often retain the original charism of their founder but, in prayerful discernment of the Spirit, continue to redefine the outward forms of their ministries.

The orientation for all Christian ministry is given by the Gospel and the Jesus/Lord event. Christian ministry must move the people in the direction of God's reign. Even though Christian ministry is a response to need, it is not the case that the customer is always right. Christian ministry is not necessarily happening because church members are getting what they want. Sometimes the minister must minister by saying no.[44]

Women may not be excluded from any ministry in the church on the basis of the New Testament. In the words of the Pope Paul VI's own Pontifical Biblical Commission: "Scriptural grounds alone are not enough to exclude the possibility of ordaining women."[45] Much of the New Testament ministry is described by the functional terms of "apostle," "prophet," and "teacher" — all terms that included women.

Ordination as a rite and ceremony that confers power or office does not exist in the New Testament. Ministry does not need to be empowered by mandate or delegation of a superior possessing power. The forms of "ordination" are subject to the dispositions of the churches in any given period of history. Priesthood, as a specific type of ministry, does not exist in the New Testament.

"Ministry," or *diakonia*, is a nonsacral word. The early church leaned heavily on this secular term to describe its main ministering activity.

Ministry in the New Testament is primarily functional. It is concerned with *doing*, like teaching, preaching, governing.

The historical Jesus was not a priest. Nowhere in the New Testament do we find that Jesus is called a priest except in the Epistle to the Hebrews. Here "priest" usually refers to the Old Testament priesthood defined by the Temple and its sacrifices. In terms of the established priesthood Jesus was a layperson; in terms of the Old and New Testaments, Jesus is more correctly described as a prophet of the reign of God.

Ministries flow from the call, the gifts, the needs, the faith, the discipleship, and the Holy Spirit. Ordering or structuring the ministries is an after-effect done by responsible ministers themselves and, perhaps, by whomever has the gift of administration (1 Cor 12:27). Such "ordering" structures for ministry may be hierarchic, collegial, participative, etc. As an effective sign of the body of Christ such structures need to witness to the mutuality, reciprocity, and interdependence of all the members of the body.

With the completion of this reflection on ministry in the New Testament, we have gained some preliminary insights into those principles that have some normative value for the Christian ministry for all time. It remains now to see how these principles were adapted in the subsequent history of these first New Testament churches. We need to feel with the church as it responds to new needs, new cultures, and new calls of the Spirit. We also need to be ready to admit in all humility that, due to the mystery of evil still at work in the baptized, the church sometimes fails, and fails miserably, to respond to the new calls of the Spirit. Sometimes, alas, the variety of seeds gets "squelched." Even before the New Testament ends, the Lord rebukes the Church of Ephesus: "I hold this against you, though: you have turned aside from your early love" (Rv 2:4).

The next two chapters, therefore, will follow the church and its ministers through the centuries as they try (and sometimes fail) to be true to Christ's call and at the same time respond to the needs of the people of God scattered around this spinning earth.

CHAPTER THREE

From Ignatius to Gregory VII

"For we are God's co-workers; you are God's field..." (1 Cor 3:9).

We have seen that in the New Testament diversity and fluidity characterized the ministries of the emerging churches. Furthermore, ministry was primarily functional. We saw too that the early churches came to believe that the Holy Spirit was the primary force in shaping the ministries. In Acts 6:1 we saw that new ministries were created to respond to new needs. The churches, responding to the Spirit's prompting, felt free to create ministries as needed.

As we review the history of ministry, we see the body of the church is shaped by a variety of forces. Its ministry is also affected by these same shaping forces as it is defined and redefined through the centuries. Sometimes it is shaped from inside of the church by saints, mystics, cured alcoholics, charismatic popes, ecumenical councils, the emergence of religious orders, the monastic movement, the prayerful discernment of the Spirit, or new ecclesiastical structures. At other times, again from inside of the church, the ministry is shaped by money in the right pockets (bribes and simony), by friends in high places (cronyism and nepotism), or by the politics of a papal election (Gregory VII and John Paul II).[1] Still other times, the ministry is formed by forces coming from outside of the church, such as culture, society, politics, revolutions, war, slavery, plagues, hunger, poverty, civil laws, or powerful kings and emperors.

As the curtain rises on this exciting drama of history, we need to pay specific attention to the secular culture and society, which often has a more powerful influence on the church and its ministry than the

49

proclaimed Gospel or the faith communities. For seventeen centuries Catholics listened to the Gospel on Sunday and then continued to sell slaves on Monday, just like their secular counterparts. Bishops heard the Word of God condemning racial discrimination and then continued to exclude blacks and Mexicans from their seminaries and the priesthood. The hierarchy heard the Gospel of equality but then continued to discriminate against women just like the patriarchies of secular culture. The history of ministry is a tale of glory and of frailty, of grace accepted and of grace rejected, of the Spirit received and of the Spirit "quenched" (1 Thes 5:19).

Ignatius of Antioch

In the Acts of the Apostles we saw that the city of Antioch played a large role in the missionary activity of the early churches. It is now in Antioch that we meet that intriguing and charismatic personality, Bishop Ignatius (c. 50–c. 110). On his way to martyrdom in Rome, he wrote seven letters, which reveal the shape of the church and its ministries early in the second century.

Antioch in the time of Ignatius was a large, thriving, cosmopolitan city, surpassed only by Rome and Alexandria. Situated on the beautiful Orontes river eighteen miles from the Mediterranean Sea, it was naturally air conditioned. With a population of five hundred thousand it was a grand melting pot for Cypriots, Syrians, Macedonians, Romans, Jews, and Greeks. It was a prosperous city, filled with mystery cults and statues to most of the deities from the then known world. "In addition, the Antiocheans had an unfavorable name for civic disorders; quarrels and rioting were frequent, and the passions of a hot-tempered, turbulent and excitable populace led to many acts of violence and bloodshed."[2]

It is in the midst of this turbulent populace that we find Ignatius, Bishop of Antioch. Although we do not know how he came to be bishop, it is quite clear from his seven letters that he is definitely the leader of the church of Antioch. Surrounded by civic unrest and disorder, Ignatius had to deal with complex and largely undefined "heresies." He reports in his letters, "Many specious wolves with baneful delights lead captive the runners in God's race."[3] Repeatedly he warns his flock "to shun division and wrong doctrines." He was apparently waging a battle with three kinds of "heresies." The first and quite serious doctrinal aberration was Docetism, which taught that "Christ's human body was a phantasm, that his sufferings and death were mere appearance: 'if he suffered, he was not God. If he was God, he did not suffer.'"[4]

The second "heresy" was a slippery dualistic teaching called Gnosticism. It was difficult to combat because it was hydra-headed and always changing.... The Gnostics had two central preoccupations: belief in a dual world of good and evil and belief in the existence of a secret code of truth, transmitted by word of mouth or by arcane writings. Gnosticism is a 'knowledge' religion — that is what the word means — which claims to have an inner explanation of life.[5]

It is important to remember that at this time there were no clearly defined dogmas. So it was especially difficult for the new converts to distinguish the false teaching of the Gnostics from the truths of their Christian faith.

The third "heresy" creating problems for Ignatius was a faction of conservative Jewish Christians. They probably came to Antioch in large numbers after Stephen was stoned to death during the persecution of the Christians in Jerusalem (Acts 7:58). We saw in the pastoral letters, written to Crete and Ephesus, that these conservative Christians had created many problems for those churches. Basically, these Jewish converts to Christianity had not yet disengaged their new faith from the Mosaic Law and all its requirements, including circumcision. With a large Jewish population in Antioch, it is easy to see why Ignatius would have a real pastoral problem in protecting his young church from their influence.

In the context of this threefold threat to the unity of his church, it is understandable that Ignatius would have to take a strong leadership role. Since his new Christians were not sophisticated in theological matters, he had to insist on obedience to maintain the unity of his flock. Thus Ignatius writes: "Give heed to the bishop ... do nothing without the bishop...."[6] No doubt most historians would agree that the Gnostic sects brought about a crisis that revealed the necessity of having a single man as the focus of unity.[7]

It is often assumed, with some justification, that Ignatius was the originator of the monarchic episcopate. Clearly Ignatius is the chief ruler of the church of Antioch, even though he refers frequently to his fellow presbyters in his letters. In fact, he sees obedience to the presbyters, and deacons as a means for achieving unity in his divided church. Also, while it seems clear that the Antiochene church had the three distinct ministries of bishops, presbyters, and deacons replacing apostles, prophets, and teachers, it has not been established that this threefold order had a hierarchic form. The seven letters reveal that for Ignatius discipleship is still the primary "ministry." He himself yearns to become "a more complete disciple" through his martyrdom in Rome.

Many historians conclude that with Ignatius the monarchic episcopate is firmly established in Antioch. However, there is not complete agreement on this matter. Walter Bauer, for example, concludes that Ignatius's letters bear witness to his fervent desire for a monarchic episcopate but not to existing reality.[8] It is at least possible that the gradual emergence of a strong, monarchic bishop in Antioch is, to some extent, a response to "Gnostic anti-bishops."

It is quite probable, on the other hand, that some kind of strong leadership would have developed in the church at this time even if there had been no "heresies" to threaten the church's unity. Joseph Martos, commenting on this Ignatian period, concludes:

> Christian communities were growing from a few families in each city to a few hundred and in some metropolitan areas to a few thousand. In order to maintain all the ministries, more organization was needed, but about the only organizational structure known in the ancient world was an authoritarian one. Families were patriarchies and governments were monarchies, and so as local churches became more organized it seemed natural to have one person at the top overseeing all of the community's affairs.[9]

A careful reading of Ignatius's letters reveals that he was a Syrian mystic and charismatic. His fervent desire to be with Christ caused him to live in a supernatural "world." Consequently, he believed that the bishop was a type of God the Father, the presbyter a type of the apostle, and the deacon a type of Jesus Christ. He probably combined his mystical and charismatic elements with Antioch's patriarchy to fashion a monarchic episcopate to safeguard his infant church.

Whatever the historical circumstances, Bishop Ignatius has shaped the episcopacy of the Roman Catholic Church even to our own time. Chapter 3 of Vatican II's Dogmatic Constitution on the Church contains thirteen references to the Ignatian letters in support of its teaching on episcopacy. Citing Ignatius, this chapter asks the faithful "to cling to their bishop" as the center of unity; presents the episcopal order as the focal point for the unity of the priesthood; teaches that the chief place among the various ministries belongs to the office of bishop; defines the bishop as the "teacher of doctrine, the priest of sacred worship and the officer of good order."[10] Even though the constitution does not use the word "monarchic," it retains much of the bishop's office as shaped by Ignatius of Antioch.

The Didache

Published in 1883, the *Didache* has been determined to be an authentic early Christian document from Syria dated not later than 160 C.E. and perhaps about 140 C.E. It is of interest to us primarily because it reveals the important role of the prophets in the churches of that time. In addition, this document shows that the people played an important role in the selection of their bishops.

The prophets of the *Didache* are in fact equal to apostles. The text provides a way of distinguishing false prophets from the true ones: "Not everyone, however, who speaks in a spirit is a prophet, unless he have the behavior of the Lord. By his behavior, then, the false prophet and the true prophet shall be known" (11, 8).[11]

There is a distinct possibility, if not probability, that the prophets, without benefit of ordination, presided at the Sunday liturgy. The text is speaking in the context of prophets when it commands: "On the Lord's Day gather together, break bread and give thanks, after confessing your transgressions so that your sacrifice may be pure" (14). At least one patristic scholar feels that the Greek word *eucharistēsate* (give thanks) could be translated "celebrate the Eucharist."[12]

We noted above (chap. 2) that in Acts 6:1 the people elected their own ministers. In the *Didache* that custom is retained: "Elect for yourselves, therefore, bishops and deacons worthy of the Lord, humble men and not lovers of money, truthful and proven; for they also serve you in the ministry of the prophets and teachers. Do not therefore despise them; for they are your honorable men, together with the prophets and teachers" (15, 1).

It seems that the *Didache* reflects a double hierarchy: "Bishops and deacons on the one hand, and apostles, prophets and teachers on the other."[13] It is also possible that apostles and teachers are more or less synonymous.[14]

The Apostolic Tradition of Hippolytus

In 215 Hippolytus of Rome collected the documents pertaining to the various church orders. His *Apostolic Tradition* gives us a fairly clear picture of the liturgy and the ministries of the church during his time. It is, in fact, the first written record of any formal ordination ceremonies. For our purpose, we wish to note first of all that the people still have a voice in the selection of their bishops:

> Let the bishop be ordained after he has been chosen by all the people. When someone pleasing to all has been named, let the people assemble on the Lord's Day with the presbyters and with such bishops as may be present. All giving assent, the bishops shall impose hands on him.[15]

It is interesting to note too that, according to the *Apostolic Tradition*, a presbyter does not always need ordination or the imposition of hands:

"If a confessor has been in chains for the name of the Lord, hands are not imposed on him for the diaconate or the presbyterate; for he has the honor of the presbyterate by the fact of his confession."[16] A "confessor" is a man who had been arrested, persecuted, and through all his trials "confessed" his faith, but was not killed. Through his "confession" he proved that he already had the power of the Spirit. He could, therefore, function as a presbyter (priest) and forgive sins without ordination.

These confessor-presbyters show us that ordination or imposition of hands does not yet confer any power possessed by the ordaining bishop. Instead, ordination recognizes and celebrates the power already conferred by the Spirit. The *Apostolic Tradition* seems to indicate:

> that the kind of elder status (presumably with proved virtue, prudence, fidelity, etc.) recognized by the presbyterial ordination would already have been sufficiently indicated by the individual's heroic behavior in the face of persecution. If so, this gives us an important element of understanding: ordination was seen as recognition of the action of the Spirit already present in the ordinand, rather than as simple human choice which the Spirit would ratify. Ordination would not then be expected to infuse the qualifications desired in bishop or presbyter.[17]

In the *Apostolic Tradition* the deacon appears to be a secretary to the bishop, but he ranks lower than the presbyter: "He has no part in the council of the clergy, but is to attend to his own duties and is to acquaint the bishop with such matters as are needful. He does not receive that Spirit which the presbytery possesses and in which the presbyters share."[18]

Besides the bishops, presbyters, and deacons, the *Apostolic Tradition* lists widows, lectors, and subdeacons as recognized, but unordained, ministries in the church. These ministries are "designated" or "appointed" by the bishop. There appears to be a fairly clear distinction at this time between the ordained and the nonordained ministries. But, as noted above, ordination is not yet an empowerment to the functions of office; it is primarily a public recognition of the presence of the Spirit in the one ordained. The frequent reference to the Holy Spirit in the liturgical text indicates that it is the Spirit received at baptism, not the ordaining bishop, who empowers the ordinand for ministry.

Cyprian of Carthage

In the year 258, Edward Benson reports, "A sailing vessel running before a fair wind from Ostia [Rome], could reach Carthage [modern Tunis] on the second day."[19] Situated on the Northern coast of Africa, Carthage was a second home for many Romans. Rebuilt on the ashes of a Punic city, "it was repeopled by Roman colonists, old soldiers, speculating farmers and hosts of slave labourers.... In population and wealth it was equal to Alexandria and second only to Rome."[20] The influx of Romans imposed the Roman culture and legal system on the native Punic traditions. As a result, Carthage, during Cyprian's time, was becoming a Roman city in Africa. Its *decurions* (senators), its theater, and the omnipresent militia were all thoroughly Roman. The city was full of lawyers, architects, and engineers. Of course, many lawyers were needed to make the frequent transfers of property legal and valid according to Roman law.

With their well-known genius for organization the Romans structured Carthage very precisely, subdividing it into counties, parishes, and boroughs. They excavated the harbor and built a seaport for 220 full-sized triremes. Shipbuilding and sea craft became the dominant industries. The city was governed by an *ordo*, or bench, of senators and commanders of Roman armies. The administration of law was precise and rigorous. The busy seaport brought in many cults and religions, which were noted for orgy, cruelty, and secrecy. Incense went up continually before the bust of the Roman Emperor.

It is in this bustling city that we find Cyprian (c. 200–258), a convert to the faith in 246, a presbyter in 247, and a bishop in 248. The admonition that a bishop "must not be a recent convert" (1 Tm 3:6) was evidently ignored. Before his conversion, Cyprian had acquired a reputation as a lawyer and as a master of forensic eloquence. No doubt he belonged to the wealthy, ruling class. Some biographers feel that Cyprian was more pragmatic than speculative or theological in his thinking. In his studies he concentrated on the Hebrew Scriptures and on the writings of Tertullian (d. 250), another lawyer. Biographers suspect that Cyprian was single since no reference to his wife is found in all his letters. On the other hand, the absence of any such reference would not be unusual, given the status of women throughout the Roman patriarchy.

The church of Carthage suffered from the Donatist and Novationist schisms and from the Decian persecution. The Donatists believed that church orders were subjective, that is, invalidated by the personal unworthiness of the minister. The Novationists, named after Novatian, the first anti-pope, denied the church's power to absolve those who had lapsed into idolatry. The Decian persecution forced Christians to obtain a certificate (*Libellus*) proving they had sacrificed to the official gods. During these schisms and persecutions countless Christians, especially the property owners, lapsed from the faith. Cyprian himself for a time administered his church from a hideout.

During his episcopate Cyprian was called the pope of Africa. He convoked numerous councils of Africa's ninety bishops. This helped create a monolithic episcopate, an ecclesiastical ruling class. Cyprian modelled his episcopacy on secular officialdom, on Roman law, and on the Old Testament view of sacrificial priesthood. For him the bishops were the church and the episcopacy was the God-given principle of unity.

In Cyprian's day, the term "bishop" did not yet have the same meaning it acquired during the Constantinian period. Nor were the bishops trained or instructed in theology. Moreover, some bishops engaged in agriculture and commerce; others engaged in usury and the slave trade of the Sahara. Many were too ignorant to prepare catechumens for baptism and included heretical phrases in their public prayers.[21]

During a good part of his rule Cyprian fought with Stephen, the bishop of Rome, on the question of the rebaptism of heretics. This controversy "reached white heat, with Stephen denouncing Cyprian as Antichrist."[22] Cyprian seems to have followed the pastoral principle: "Fight with the pope; work with your fellow bishops."

Cyprian was convinced that each bishop in his own diocese was accountable to God alone. "While the bond of concord remains," writes Cyprian, "and the indivisible sacrament of the Catholic church continues, each bishop disposes and directs his own work as one who must give an account of his administration to the Lord."[23] The Seventh Council of Carthage (256), with Cyprian presiding, proclaimed that "every bishop has his own free will to the unrestrained exercise of his liberty and power, so that neither can he be judged by another, nor is he himself able to judge another."[24]

Cyprian's insistence on the authority and independence of the local bishop has shaped the ministry of the bishop even to our own time. The Vatican Congregation for the Doctrine of the Faith in its working paper "The Theological and Juridical Status of Episcopal Conferences" (1988) defends the "psychological freedom" and the "proper autonomy of diocesan bishops" against the "superior or parallel government" of national bishops' conferences. This "autonomy" of the diocesan bishop begins with Cyprian; it continues in the new Code of Canon Law, which defends the "legislative, executive and judicial power" of the diocesan bishop in the "particular church committed to him" (canon 391).

With Cyprian we see the beginnings of the gradual sacralization or sacerdotalization of the ministry. Tertullian had already used the word *sacerdos* (priest) to refer to the bishop, and Cyprian routinely did the same. Leaning heavily on the image of the priesthood in the Hebrew Scriptures, Cyprian used the term *sacerdos* in a derivative, nonliteral sense. In this connection Edward Schillebeeckx observes: "For the early church, *sacerdos* (as an Old Testament name for the Jewish priest) was applied allegorically, and to begin with only to the bishop, who was then the figure with whom the city community really identified and in whom it found its unity."[25]

In the church of Carthage deacons could administer the sacrament of penance. "If a presbyter is not found," Cyprian writes, "and death begins to be imminent, even before a deacon they are permitted to make their confession of sin, so that a hand may be imposed upon them in penance."[26] Since deacons related primarily to bishops, who had wide-ranging authority, we can assume that they undertook a variety of ministries, especially during the emergencies created by persecution. During these times, there probably were many occasions when the deacons actually presided at the celebration of the Eucharist.[27] This practice was later forbidden by the Council of Nicaea (325).

It is noteworthy that during this period the people of Carthage still have a voice in the selection of their bishops. Indeed, election by the people is for Cyprian a matter of divine authority. Writing to the clergy and laity of Spain in 256, Cyprian lays down the following principle:

> This very thing, too, we note, stems from divine authority — that a priest (actually, bishop) be chosen in the presence of the people and under the eyes of all, and that he be approved as worthy and suitable by public judgment and testimony.... And the bishop should be chosen in the presence of the people, who are thoroughly familiar with the life of each one, and who have looked into the doings of each one in respect to his habitual conduct.[28]

In a letter to the bishop of Numidia Cyprian writes: "Cornelius was made bishop by the decision of God and of Christ, by the testimony of almost all the clergy, by the applause [*suffragio*, suffrage] of the people then present, by the college of venerable priests and good men."[29]

While Cyprian understood his role as the ruling bishop of Carthage, he nevertheless made it a habit to consult the presbyters: "From the beginning of my episcopate," he writes to his clergy, "I decided to do nothing of my own opinion privately without your advice and the consent of the people."[30] Frequently he used the collegial term *compresbyter*, "fellow-presbyter." In doing so, he bypassed Tertullian and used the Latin equivalent of the Greek word *sympresbyteros*, which Polycarp (c. 135) had used in greeting the church in Philippi: "Polycarp and those who are presbyters with him."

Cyprian modelled his church order of ministers on the civil order of the rulers of the city of Carthage. Throughout the Roman empire the senators, literally, wise old men, occupied the common bench from which they ruled the city. "Bench" in Carthage had almost the same meaning it has in the judicial system of our own time. Today's newspaper will headline: "Jurist, 36, joins U.S. bench.... Judge ＿＿＿ will *join the bench* in *a ceremony* at 1:15 p.m. . . . " (italics mine). Of course, in Cyprian's Carthage no women could occupy that ruling bench. Following the model of secular officialdom, Cyprian instituted an *ordo* of ruling bishops in the model of the common bench. This *ordo* of ruling clergy was clearly distinguished from the laity. In excluding women from this ruling bench, Cyprian was following both the Roman civil system and the advice of Tertullian, his mentor, who wrote: "A woman is not permitted to speak in the church, nor yet to teach, nor baptize, nor offer, nor yet claim to herself the right of any masculine function, much less of the sacerdotal office."[31]

Cyprian did not spend much time discussing the universal priesthood of all the baptized, but there is no doubt that he believed in it. We can assume he agreed with Tertullian that "where there is no Bench of ecclesiastical order you (a layman) offer (the sacrifice) and you baptize and are your own sole priest."[32] Pierre van Beneden, commenting on this passage of Tertullian, confirms the view that the word "offer" refers to the celebration of the Eucharist. Baptism and Eucharist are so important for the life of faith, explains Beneden, that the laity, sharing in the priesthood of the people of God, can celebrate these two sacraments when an ordained person is not available.[33] Cyprian adds a new note to Tertullian regarding the origin of the royal priesthood of the laity. According to him it is "an inheritance from the apostles and a succession to the Levitic Priesthood."[34]

In shaping the episcopal and presbyteral ministries Cyprian was responding, at least partly, in a very pragmatic way to the dual threat of schism and persecution. Paul Johnson concludes that Cyprian "had to face the practical problems of persecution, survival and defense against attack. His solution was to gather the developing threads of ecclesiastical order and authority and weave them into a tight system of absolute control."[35]

For this reason Cyprian asserted unambiguously that "the church is founded upon the bishops, and every act of the church is controlled by these same rulers."[36] For him there could be no church without bishops and there could be no salvation without the church: "If anyone outside the ark of Noah was able to escape, then perhaps so someone outside the pale of the church may escape."[37]

With Cyprian, we begin to see a clear distinction between the bishops who rule and the laity who are ruled. Obedience becomes the important virtue. "Do not let them [laity] imagine," writes Cyprian "that the way of life and of salvation is still open to them, if they have refused to obey the bishops and the priests."[38]

There can be no doubt that Cyprian was very influential in shaping the ministry of the Roman Catholic Church. Hans von Campenhausen (1953) concludes: "The image of Cyprian . . . controls . . . the ecclesiological thinking of Roman Catholicism to this day."[39] As if to confirm Von Campenhausen's opinion, Vatican II, in its Dogmatic Constitution on the Church cites Cyprian eight times to support its teaching on the episcopacy.

To summarize the ways in which Cyprian shapes the ministry of his time and, to some extent, our own time, we can state the following: he makes a clear distinction between the *ordo* of bishops and the laity; he sacralizes the priesthood according to the Old Testament model of sacrifice priesthood; he establishes a monolithic episcopate which is the same for all of Africa; he links ministry to sacrifice, again in the image of the Temple priesthood; he shapes the church as a clearly defined institution of salvation; he models the bishops in the image of Roman senators, thus excluding women; and finally he consolidates the ruling powers of bishops through numerous episcopal conclaves.

Paul Johnson, an English historian, also summarizes Cyprian's influence on the shape of the ministry in the Catholic Church:

> With Cyprian, then, the freedom preached by Paul and based on the power of Christian truth was removed from the ordinary members of the Church; it was retained only by the bishops, through whom the Holy Spirit still worked, who were collectively delegated to represent the totality of Church members. They were given wide powers of discretion, subject always to the traditional and attested truth of the church and the scriptures. They were rulers, operating and interpreting a law. With Bishop Cyprian, the analogy with secular government came to seem very close.[40]

Constantine

In the year 312 Constantine (c. 280–337), with inferior forces, gained a great victory over Maxentius, the Western emperor, at the Milvian bridge near Rome. On the day before the battle, so the legend goes, Constantine had a vision of a cross imposed on the sun with the words "By this sign you will conquer." Before the battle Constantine prayed to the God of the Christians and ordered the Christian emblem "Chi-Rho" to be inscribed on the soldiers' shields. After the defeat of Maxentius, with most of his troops drowning in the Tiber, the cry went up: "The God of the Christians gave us victory." With this victory began the rapid spread of Christianity under the benign protection of Constantine, the new "Christian" emperor. Not surprisingly, he remained a catechumen until his deathbed baptism. It was normal at that time to postpone baptism and its forgiveness of sins to the end of one's life, especially if official duty required the torture and execution of criminals.[41]

Constantine, while not yet a Christian, was very actively involved in the internal affairs of the church. He called the Council of Nicaea and presided over its first assembly. He instituted Sunday as a Day of the Sun both for Christians and for worshippers of the sun. Sunday then was set aside as a day of rest on which Christians gathered for worship. This also meant that for one day of the week the clergy were officially "in charge."

Constantine significantly shaped the ministry of the church, appointing bishops as civil magistrates throughout the realm. The bishops' miter, staff, and ring probably date back to this period. Bishops were appointed civil officials and wore these insignia in recognition of the role Constantine had assigned to them in the imperial hierarchy.

Whereas during the time of Cyprian the people had a voice in the selection of their bishops, now they are appointed by Constantine without any consultation of the people. With Constantine we begin to see a union of empire and priesthood with the bishops seen as both civil and ecclesiastical rulers. Constantine acknowledged the existence of a clerical caste and supported it. He began the "transfer of privileges to Christian clergy almost from the start, exempting them from compulsory public office (which was onerous and expensive) in the towns, and in non-urban areas from the payment of district taxes. This implied class status, with the secular underwriting the spiritual. Indeed Constantine was the first to use the words 'clerical' and 'clerics' in this sense."[42]

The clergy were recruited mostly from the uninfluential ranks. St. Jerome complained: "One who was yesterday a catechumen is today a bishop; another moves overnight from the amphitheater to the church; a man who spent the evening in the circus stands next morning at the altar, and another who was recently a patron of the stage is now the dedicator of virgins."[43]

After Constantine the church organized itself along the lines of the Roman regional districts called dioceses. Bishops became the sole legislators and administrators of church property. Constantine delegated to them the power of approving wills and arbitrating disputes as civil judges. When bishops were deposed by a regional synod, they were also exiled by civil authority.

When Constantine moved to Byzantium, the "new Rome," he left the bishop of Rome as the most important figure in the West. With Constantine, the church began a long process whereby the church and its ministry became ever more united to the state. Eventually, Pope Pius IX (1864) in his *Syllabus of Errors* would condemn the teaching that "the Church is to be separated from the State, and the State from the Church."

The Trend toward Mandatory Celibacy

Many historians feel the *legal* struggle for mandating celibacy in the Western church began with the Council of Elvira at Granada, Spain, in 305;[44] it ended with the Councils of Lateran I (1123) and Lateran II (1139). During the eight centuries in which the law of celibacy evolved, we find many heated debates between bishops, presbyters, and popes. The legislation that emerges from all these discussions comes out of a particular historical milieu and culture. The thought patterns of this period are very much influenced by certain cultural, theological, psychological, and historical factors. It is possible to identify at least six of these historical/cultural antecedents that influenced the church to pass laws and decrees requiring celibacy.

The first historical factor that prompted a movement toward celibacy was the church's acceptance of a dualist, Greek anthropology. The human person, in this view, was divided into body and soul. Growth toward perfection consisted in disciplining or repressing the body in order to obtain the release of the soul, especially its intellectual and spiritual powers. Perfection in this theory was measured in terms of intellect; it was achieved, not through the body but in spite of it, and especially in spite of its emotions. Perfection consisted not so much in achieving the integration of the person's physical, emotional, and spiritual faculties as in achieving the soul's dominion over the body. Representing this view was Gregory of Nyssa (c. 335–c. 394), who wrote:

> If anyone withdraws his attention for a moment from his body and, emerging from the slavery of his passions and his carelessness, looks at his own soul with honest and sincere reason, he will see clearly how its nature reveals God's love for us and His intention in creating us. . . . By this grace, the illusion beguiling man is dispelled, the dishonoring preoccupation with the flesh is extinguished, and, by the light of truth, the soul, which received the knowledge, makes its way to the divine and to its own salvation.[45]

The second influence on the development of an attitude in favor of celibacy was Stoicism. The influence of the Stoics was already evident in the New Testament. Paul's image of the body (1 Cor 12), according to many Scripture scholars, came from the philosophy of the Stoics. Their teaching also influenced Tertullian and the later Christian ascetic writings. "The main attraction of Stoicism was its ethical ideal of *apatheia*, passionlessness. A wise person could face any situation with complete self-control and equanimity because he or she was not attached to this life."[46] Founded by Zeno in 300 B.C.E., the Stoic philosophy was fairly well known to the early Christians through the writings of Epictetus

(50–130) and Marcus Aurelius (121–80). It came into the early church primarily through the writings of Origen, Ambrose, and Augustine. By emphasizing reason and logic it fostered a negative view of the human emotions, thus promoting an ascetic climate favorable to the repression of sexual activity through celibacy.

The third factor that moved the church toward celibacy was Manicheanism. Augustine (354–430), one of the most influential thinkers of Christian history, brought with him into the church at least the taint of this dualist heresy. "It was characterized by an intense pessimism about the potentialities of human nature and its inherent goodness."[47] Thirty years after Augustine, Julian of Eclanum claimed that Augustine's "twisted views on sex were the direct result of his Manichee training."[48] Manicheanism taught that all matter, especially the body and its sexual appetite, was evil. Augustine taught that sexual intercourse, even for married couples, was sinful if they had relations for pleasure rather than for the purpose of producing children or if they did it for the proper reason and enjoyed it.[49] Of course Augustine was engaged in a verbal battle with Pelagius, who rejected the idea of inherited sin. Augustine thus felt he had to affirm and reaffirm the reality of "inherited" evil. After Augustine, the church began to teach that sexual pleasures were evil and therefore needed a justifying cause, such as the procreation of children, to make them good. This Manichean taint persisted, with varying degrees of intensity, well into the late Middle Ages and even up to our own times.

A fourth factor that influenced the movement toward celibacy was Encratism, from the Greek *enkrateia*, meaning abstinence. The Encratists asked their followers to abstain from "women, wine, and the eating of meat." Even though Jerome and other church fathers opposed all forms of Encratism, "This does not do away with the fact that during the first centuries the church placed true Christian perfection in *enkrateia* or continence."[50] At the beginning of the Encratist influence, complete continence was linked not to ministry but to baptism. Not only presbyters, but all Christians were encouraged to follow the ideal of complete continence. In the third and fourth centuries the fathers of the church extolled the continence of celibacy, often to the detriment of marriage. "Marriage, at least when it involved sexual intercourse, . . . was often looked upon as a decent outlet for weaker Christians."[51]

The fifth factor supporting the movement toward celibacy was the rise of monasticism. Beginning in the East with St. Anthony and St. Pachomius in the fourth century, monasteries grew rapidly. By the ninth century one hundred thousand monks were living under the rule of St. Basil. In the West, Benedict of Nursia (d. 547) founded a monastery first at Subiaco, then at Monte Cassino. Benedict's Holy Rule, blessed by Gregory I, became the norm for monastic life in the West and is still fol-

lowed today. The monastic lifestyle provided a much
on the practice of poverty, chastity, and obedience. It also
importance of the liturgy and a contemplative way of life well
with the blood and sweat of cultivating the land. Through obe
and a highly organized life under one roof the monastic life achieved
the order so often lacking in the secular societies of that period.

One by-product of this flight from the world and family life, however,
was the implied, unspoken message that the world and involvement in
family and material things were evil. The three monastic vows, including
chastity, tended to become first the ideal, and then the norm for Christian life. Marriage was a concession to a weaker brand of Christianity.
Virginity was the "higher" way.

Another side effect of the growth of monasticism was the selection
of bishops from the ranks of the abbots of monasteries. Of course, these
bishops' monastic formation influenced the clerical discipline they imposed on the secular clergy. If it worked in the monastery, why not in
the diocesan church? It is easy to see that abbot/bishops, celibate by
monastic vow, would be favorably disposed to make a "holy rule" en-
joining monastic celibacy on all their clergy. What's good for the monks
is good for the diocesan clergy.

A sixth factor moving the church to legislate mandatory celibacy
was the almost exclusive emphasis, after Nicaea, on the divinity of Jesus
Christ. When Arius denied the divinity of Christ, the Council of Nicaea
(325) responded to the heresy by emphasizing the divinity of Christ.
This stress on the divinity of Christ gradually moved Christology from
faith in the sinlessness of Christ (Hb 4:15), to belief in his incapacity for
sinning. In an effort to protect his sinlessness Jesus is now presented as
sexless. To become holy from now on means to become holy as Christ
was holy, that is, sexless. When priests are seen as "other Christs," the
assumption again is that they too, like Christ, must live without sex.

The seventh factor which provided the soil for the growth of the laws
favoring celibacy was concern for cultic (worship) purity. Numerous laws
dealing with celibacy refer to the Old Testament priesthood and the
custom of the priest abstaining from sexual intercourse with his wife
before offering sacrifice in the Temple. The assumption is that if the
sacrifice of the Old Testament required abstinence from sex then this
requirement would be all the more binding for the priests offering the
holy sacrifice of the Mass in the New Testament. This abstinence from
sexual intercourse before offering the Holy Sacrifice became a rather
serious problem when married priests, following the monastic model,
began to celebrate Mass daily.

A final influence toward celibacy came from Origen (d. 253), a brilliant teacher and spiritual guide living in Alexandria. Influenced by
Plato's separation of soul and body, he believed Christians, through

celibacy, could achieve a greater freedom from the limitations of gender imposed by society. Not being bound to a married society, celibate Christians would be free to give themselves more intensely to others. At the same time, they would already in this life be moving toward an invisible, angelic world and union with Christ. This more intense spiritual intimacy and communion of spirits would mean that physical bonds such as marriage and paternity would become insignificant.[52]

Legislating Celibacy

In the first stages of the movement toward legislating celibacy the issue was *conjugal* celibacy. In fact, celibacy, as can be seen from the very first council, referred to the separation of a married priest or bishop from his wife.

On the Ides of March in 309 nineteen bishops and twenty-six presbyters assembled for the Council of Elvira in Granada, Spain. They came to deal with serious problems of the day — the flamines (non-Christian priests), idolatry, the lapsed, marriage, human sexuality, and clerical discipline. They enacted a total of eighty-one canons or decrees. On the matter of celibacy, canon 33 states: "It is determined that bishops, presbyters, and deacons, or all clerics stationed in the ministry, are to restrain themselves completely and are to keep themselves away from their wives and are not to beget children. Anyone who does beget children is to be expelled from the honor of the clerical state."[53]

It is plain from this canon of Elvira that the fathers of that council were not forbidding marriage but, out of concern for cultic purity, were forbidding sexual intercourse. The same council forbade bishops or other clerics from living with women who were not their sisters or virgins dedicated to God. Commentators on canon 33 point out that the canon is directed against the married clergy of Spain. It does not command celibacy; it prohibits sexual intercourse.

During the First Council of Nicaea (325) there was an attempt to impose the conjugal celibacy of the Latin church of the West on the Greek church of the East. During the debates, however, Phaphnutius, a renowned bishop from Egypt, rose up to defend the custom of the Greek church of not requiring the priests to separate from their wives at ordination. With a loud voice he declared: "That too heavy a yoke ought not to be laid upon the clergy; that marriage and married intercourse are of themselves honourable and undefiled; that the church ought not to be injured by an extreme severity, for all could not live in absolute continency."[54] The bishops of the council found Phaphnutius' argument so persuasive that they stopped all further discussion and allowed each cleric to decide the issue on his own. This report about Phaphnutius has been questioned by some historians. However, Bishop Hefele, a distinguished historian of the councils, defends its historical accuracy because, among other reasons, it is "in perfect harmony" with the practice of the Greek church regarding clerical marriages.

Soon after Nicaea Pope Siricius (c. 334–99) began to insist on conjugal celibacy for the Latin rite priest. He asked priests to abstain from sexual intercourse with their wives in order that they might be pure to offer up the holy sacrifice of the Mass:

> Why then had the priests in the year of their service to dwell far from their houses in the Temple? For this reason, that they might not even have the opportunity to cohabit with their wives so that with an untroubled conscience they might be able to offer up a sacrifice pleasing to God. . . . We bind all priests and Levites (deacons) through the imperishable law that from the day of our ordination we pledge our spirit and our body in the service of sobriety and chastity, if at least we wish to be pleasing to God in all respects in the sacrifices which we offer daily.[55]

After the Councils of Elvira and Nicaea, between 325 and 633, the Western church had problems with the *virgines subintroductae*. These "virgins with vows" considered themselves united to the priest in a spiritual marriage for mutual assistance in achieving high spirituality. At the same time, they lived with the celibate priest to care for his domestic needs. From the fifth century the term *subintroductae* was applied to any woman who lived as a domestic in the home of clerics. Sometimes these virgins assisted the priest in the celebration of the liturgy and presented the chalice to the communicants. This practice of course horrified the bishops who condemned it.

There are indications that priests living in these spiritual marriages castrated themselves in order to live in peace with their young partners.[56] These priests may have been influenced by a popular Christian writer of that time named Sextus who taught that "prayer and sexual intercourse are contradictory, and therefore even castration is to be recommended for the sake of contemplation."[57] We know from other sources that castration was prevalent among Christians during the third and fourth centuries.[58] These spiritual "marriages" were eventually condemned by the Councils of Nicaea, Orleans, and Bordeaux.

Another factor prompting legislation in favor of celibacy was concern for the retention of church property, which could be inherited by the deceased priest's wife and children. Pope Pelagius I (556–61) refused to consecrate a married bishop because the church property might go to his wife and children. After waiting a year and receiving assurance that no transfer of property would take place, he allowed the consecration.[59]

Some legislation was designed to protect the priest's celibate reputation. Thus the Third Synod of Toledo (589) decreed: "Whoever has strange women in his dwelling so as to excite suspicion, shall be punished, and those women shall be sold by the bishop. The proceeds of the sale belong to the poor" (canon 5).[60] The Third Synod of Orleans (538) decreed: "No cleric from a subdeacon upwards must have connubial intercourse with his wife, whom he formerly possessed" (canon 2).[61]

In an effort to further protect the celibacy of priests even from any suspicion, the Council of Canterbury (1030) decreed: "Women may not come to the altar while the priest offers Mass but should stay in their own place. . . . Women are to be mindful that they are the weaker sex. Therefore, they are to respect with trembling the sacred things of the ministry."[62]

By the time the eleventh century arrived Pope Gregory VII (c. 1020–85) was very much concerned about church reform. He faced four problems: (1) lay investiture, (2) simony, (3) celibate and married clergy, and (4) the relationship between church and state. Lay investiture was the term used to describe the practice of knights or lay lords, especially emperors like Henry IV, appointing bishops to dioceses on their own authority. Lay lords "invested" the bishop or priest with authority to govern the diocese or parish. In practice these lay lords, who were not particularly concerned about celibacy, invested married bishops or priests with second or third dioceses or parishes so they would receive sufficient income to support their wives and children. So it was mostly the married priests who were involved in the abuse known as lay investiture.

A second problem facing Pope Gregory VII was the widespread practice of simony. This was an abuse whereby popes bought the papacy, bishops bought dioceses, and priests bought pastorates. Many of the clergy, especially those who were married, were willing to pay high prices for lucrative pastorates since they needed additional income to support their families.

Gregory VII struggled with the problem of celibacy and the married clergy with the zeal and energy of a typical reformer. In his time, concubinage was widespread among the unmarried clergy. Influenced by his strict monastic experience, Gregory was disturbed both by the vices of the unmarried clergy who were not observing the law of celibacy and by the married clergy who were engaged in simony and lay investiture.

With the help of Cardinal Humbert, Gregory VII inaugurated his reform of the church. At first he held synods that passed laws forbidding simony and married priests. For instance, his Roman Synod of March 13, 1074, declared that married priests were living in "fornication" and that laity should not attend their services since the blessing of such priests turns into a curse and their prayer into sin.[63] He then asked the bishops throughout the empire to follow his example. When they did not do so, he gave them a warning. If they persisted in their ways, he excommunicated the worst offenders. In addition, he applied pressure on civil leaders, including Henry IV, to punish and remove married clergy and replace them with celibates.

Gregory's reform continued after his death and prepared the way for the First Council of the Lateran (1123). Canon 3 of this council decrees: "We absolutely forbid priests, deacons and subdeacons to associate with concubines and women, or to live with women other than such as the Nicene Council (canon 3) for reasons of necessity permitted, namely, the mother, the sister or aunt or any such person concerning whom no suspicion could arise."[64] The same council in canon 21 decrees: "We absolutely forbid priests, deacons and subdeacons and monks to have concubines or to contract marriage. We decree in accordance with the definitions of the sacred canons that marriages already contracted by such persons must be dissolved, and that the persons be condemned to do penance."[65]

The Second Lateran Council (1139) went further. In canon 6 clerics "living with women" in marriage or with concubines are deprived of their office and ecclesiastical benefice. They are forbidden "to indulge in marriage." Canon 7 decrees that clerics who "have dared to contract marriage, shall be separated. For a union of this kind which has been contracted in violation of the ecclesiastical law, we do not regard as matrimony."[66]

It is worth noting that two-thirds of those voting for the law of celibacy during the First Lateran Council were abbots of monasteries. Many of the three hundred voting bishops had been abbots before they became bishops. We can assume that in the brief interval of sixteen years between the two Lateran councils their membership remained basically the same. We can conclude, therefore, that it was largely the monastic influence, through abbot/bishops, that, in 1139, finally imposed the law of celibacy on the Western diocesan clergy.

It is worth noting too that during eight hundred years of legislation on celibacy, the Matthean reference to celibacy or "eunuchs for the sake of the kingdom" (Mt 19:12) is not mentioned once. It seems clear that the frequent modern papal references to "celibacy for the sake of the kingdom of God" are attempts to use Scripture to suggest motivation for obedience to an ancient ecclesiastical law whose origin is based on a completely different rationale.

Linking the law of celibacy to the kingdom could easily be detrimental to the vocation of marriage, which is also for the sake of the kingdom. If we understand "for the sake of "[67] as a price to be paid *for* the kingdom, then celibacy takes its place among all the other sacrifices married disciples also make for the kingdom. On the other hand, we could understand "for the sake of " in an eschatological sense as a sign of, or witness to, the kingdom. Then, assuming the kingdom is at least partly a restoration of God's holy creation with its "divine image of male and female," we could make the case that, in terms of sign value, marriage, rather than celibacy, is for the sake of the kingdom.

Without dealing with the modern debates about celibacy, it seems quite plain that the law of celibacy continues to be the main cause for the growing shortage of priests. In a 1985 college student survey of Catholic leaders, 70 percent of the young men surveyed said celibacy was a "very important" reason for deciding "against becoming a priest."[68] The law of celibacy, by disqualifying numerous otherwise qualified young men, continues to have a profound effect on the shape of the ministry in the church. The shortage of priests means that in France alone more than twenty-two thousand parishes are without priests. The priesthood is increasingly composed of older men who are forced into a repetitious ministry of the sacraments. But more about this in chapter 11.

Before we take a look at the storms that battered the church and its ministries in the sixteenth and nineteenth centuries, let's summarize the main forces which have shaped the ministry so far: Ignatius of Antioch gives us the monarchic episcopate; Cyprian of Carthage makes bishops members of a Roman *ordo* and separates them from the laity; Constantine takes away the people's voice in the selection of bishops and makes them civil magistrates; celibacy helps create a clerical caste that, among other factors, tends to keep women from the church's ministry.

Next we will look at other powerful forces that shape the ministries for the next nine centuries. "God's field," graced with the breath of the Spirit, continues to be fertile for the growth of ministries. But it is also full of thistles and ravaged by political and ecclesiastical storms.

CHAPTER FOUR

From Gregory VII to John Paul II

"And a great storm of wind arose, and the waves beat into the boat . . . "
(Mk 4:37).

During the funeral of Pope Alexander II in April 1073, the excitable people of Rome shouted: "Hildebrand is pope! St. Peter chooses the archdeacon Hildebrand!" Having imparted the last blessing over the body of his friend, Hildebrand was immediately carried to the church of St. Peter and enthroned as Pope Gregory VII. This tumultuous "election" was a great victory for the Hildebrandine party. It was also "an open violation of the electoral law of 1059," which was in all probability Hildebrand's own creation.[1] Gregory VII had indeed hoped to win the papacy so he could formulate his theory of papal sovereignty over all worldly powers. He had known how to wait, but now "he became imperious, dictatorial and insolent."[2] Thus began the reform that bears Gregory's name.

We have already discussed the influence of Gregory's papacy in bringing about the law of celibacy. It remains now to reflect on the other ways in which the reform he launched shaped the ministries of the church.

When Gregory VII became the bishop of Rome he was well aware that the church was badly in need of reform. Before he became pope Hildebrand had lived for a while in a monastery. He knew how authority worked — top down. Besides the problem of celibacy and the priesthood already noted in chapter 3, Gregory faced the problems of simony, lay investiture, and the relationship between the church and state. He tackled these problems with a reformer's zeal.

The Effects of the Gregorian Reform (1057–1123)

In true monastic style Gregory began immediately to centralize the authority of the papacy in Rome. He held synods that passed laws against simony, concubinage, and the marriage of priests. After signaling the main thrust of his reform through local synods in Rome, he extended the reform to the rest of the church, concentrating on Germany. That part of the reform which shaped the ministry of the church focused on the implementation of a threefold policy: the adoption of Roman law, the elimination of lay investiture, and the development of the "two ends" theory.

Gregory "canonized" the Roman legal system by asking his friends, Cardinals Atto and Deusdedit, to search the known archives of Italy and review the collections of laws approved by previous popes.[3] Approval by a pope or Roman synod meant that the law would stand. In this way Gregory eliminated the laws of the Frankish and Celtic churches as well as the English tradition of the common law system. These collections, of course, had not been approved by a previous pope. The approved Roman collection prepared the way for the first comprehensive synthesis of church laws, which was produced by Gratian, a Camaldolese monk at the University of Bologna in 1141. Naturally, adopting the Roman legal system and rejecting the laws of other countries was a key factor in centralizing church government in Rome. Thus Roman laws came to shape the ministries of the entire Western church.

Gregory's second policy that shaped the ministries of the church concerned lay investiture. This practice enabled a sovereign such as Henry IV to grant titles, possessions, and temporal rights to bishops, abbots, and other spiritual lords. Lay princes routinely appointed bishops to dioceses and, at other times, left the sees vacant. In 1075 Gregory VII forbade the practice of lay investiture and thereby incurred the wrath of the emperors of his day. In this way Gregory wrested the authority of episcopal appointment from the kings and nobles. This put an abrupt end to the centuries-old tradition of lay control and lay patronage.

To achieve the goals of his program Gregory needed a theory of reform. For this he relied heavily on Cardinal Humbert, who furnished a theology to justify Gregory's reforming activity. Humbert proposed the theory that a Christian society has two ends: one spiritual, the other material. He taught that in a Christian society the king ought to deal primarily with temporal and material matters and the pope should have governing responsibility for the spiritual affairs. In practice the spiritual end, because of its "higher" eternal purpose, had priority over the material and was superior to it. So it was reasonable to assume that the spiritual authority, the pope, could command obedience from the "material" authority, the emperor. The implementation of this policy led Gregory VII to excommunicate bishops who were in fact subjects of Henry IV. It also meant that the emperor, whose power was now limited to the material and temporal, was expected to obey the laws and decrees promulgated by the pope whose power was spiritual and eternal.

In terms of ministry this theory of Pope Gregory VII led to the assumption that bishops and priests were responsible for spiritual matters and civil rulers for the material. In this way the church retained control of the spiritual domain and the ministry was confined more and more to the arena of the sanctuary, removed from the temporal, "secular" world of politics. The net result was an almost exclusive spiritualization and sacramentalization of the ministry, which now was limited more and more to the ordained clergy, the sacred caste.

In summary, most of the modern papacy, with its model of "trickle-down" authority and centralized ecclesiology, begins with Gregory VII. He subjects bishops and their dioceses to the bishop of Rome. After Gregory, the bishop is completely dependent on the papacy. Except for his priesthood, he is an agent of the pope.[4] This is quite a departure from the church of the fourth century when the bishop is mystically married to his diocese and cannot be "divorced" from it by transfer to another diocese; he is selected, consecrated, and deposed by a local synod of bishops; at the numerous regional synods, he witnesses to the faith experience of his own diocesan church.

Finally, Gregory canonizes Roman law, which subsequently shapes the pastoral practice of the ordained ministers and removes the voice of the baptized faithful from the governing process of the church. With Cyprian, authority resided in the local church, Carthage; with Gregory, authority resides in the center of the church, Rome. As noted above, the Gregorian reform culminates in Lateran Council I (1123) and Lateran Council II (1138), which bless and institutionalize Gregory's reforms.

The Council of Trent (1545–1563)

On All Hallows Eve, 1517, Martin Luther, an Augustinian monk, posted his famous ninety-five theses "On the Power of Indulgences" on the door of the castle chapel in Wittenberg, Germany. Thus began the debates of the Protestant Reformation concerning many of the traditional teachings of the Roman Catholic Church. It was indeed a "great storm" that shook the barque of Peter as the religious and political waters of Catholic Europe churned violently. The expression of Christian faith and ministry in the Western church would never be the same again.

Although there were delays and complicated political considerations, Rome eventually responded to the Protestant teachings by convoking the Council of Trent. By the time it ended in 1563, 199 bishops, 7 abbots, and 7 superiors general of religious orders signed the conciliar decrees which would profoundly influence the ministry of the Roman Catholic Church for the next four hundred years. The Council of Trent never intended to formulate a complete doctrine on ministry. In its own words, it sought "to condemn and anathematize the chief errors of the heretics." For this reason, many of the council's decrees and canons were simply responses or counter-positions to the specific teachings of Luther, Calvin, or Zwingli. In this context, history is a witness that Trent accomplished its announced purpose rather well.

The council's response to the Protestant teaching was largely shaped by the language, philosophy, and theology of the scholastic period of the twelfth and thirteenth centuries. Thomas Aquinas (1225–74), leaning heavily on Aristotle's language and philosophy, had developed a system of theology that became the major resource in dealing with many of the Protestant positions. Since the Scotists, Thomists, and Augustinians disagreed about many of the doctrinal matters discussed during the council, some issues relating to ministry were simply left unresolved.

Trent's teaching on ministry is best understood in the context of specific Protestant objections. For this reason we must refer briefly to a few of those teachings. Regarding the ministry, Martin Luther taught :

> that we are all equally priests, that is to say, we have the same power in respect to the Word and the sacraments. However, no one may make use of this power except by the consent of the community or by the call of a superior. (For what is the common property of all, no individual may arrogate to himself, unless he be called.)[5]

Proclaiming the priesthood of all believers, the Protestant Reformers denied the sacramentality of Holy Orders. Furthermore, they taught that there was no divinely instituted hierarchy and that the powers of the ministry were merely a delegation of powers possessed by all Christians. The Reformers criticized the Catholic Church for conferring an order upon someone who would never exercise it either because he was incapable of it or because the order no longer corresponded to a real function. Thus they taught that the minor orders, such as exorcist and porter, were vestiges of a bygone era and should be eliminated. The Reformers adopted a functional, less ontological, approach to the ministries. At the same time, they focused upon the ministry of the Word. Thus Calvin required that every administration of a sacrament should be accompanied by some kind of preaching so that the faithful would better understand the mysteries being celebrated.[6]

Reacting against these Protestant teachings, the Council of Trent reshaped the ministry of the Catholic Church in a variety of ways. First, the council finally joined sacrifice (sacrament) and priesthood. Canon 1 of the twenty-third session states:

> If anyone says that there is not in the New Testament a visible and external priesthood, or that there is no power of consecrating and offering the true Body and Blood of the Lord and of forgiving and retaining sins, but only the office and ministry of preaching the Gospel, or that those who do not preach are not priests at all, let him be anathema.[7]

In linking the priesthood so closely to the power to consecrate the bread and wine, Trent is not introducing anything new into the theology of ministry. The specific identification of priesthood with the power of consecration goes back to St. Peter Damian, an eleventh-century reformer. Duns Scotus (c. 1266–1308) and William of Ockham (c. 1285–c. 1347), two Franciscan theologians, had also taught that the essential power of the priest was to change bread and wine into the body and blood of Christ.

Responding to the Protestant objections to the church's minor orders, the council taught that there are exactly seven orders, four minor and three major. The minor orders include porter, lector, exorcist, and acolyte; the major orders are subdeacon, deacon, and priest. The council described these orders "as steps by which advance is made to the priesthood."[8]

Following Peter Lombard and Thomas Aquinas, the council reaffirmed the existence of a priestly character, "a certain spiritual and indelible mark," which was understood to be imprinted upon the soul in virtue of ordination to the priesthood. Augustine (354–430), responding to the Donatists who rebaptized the Catholic converts to their faith, insisted with the fathers of the church that a seal or character was imprinted upon the soul during *baptism*. Thus baptism did not need to be repeated. He spoke of this character not as a theological notion, "but as an image or metaphor,"[9] comparing it to the branding of sheep or the insignia of a soldier. As the sheep's owner was identified by the owner's brand or seal, so the baptized, "signed" by the seal or character of baptism, was known to belong to Christ.

For seven hundred years after Augustine very little was written about this indelible character. Then Peter Lombard (c. 1100–c. 1160) in his *Four Books of Sentences* resurrected the Augustinian teaching about the character. Thomas Aquinas, extending the teaching of Peter Lombard, applied the indelible character of baptism to confirmation and holy orders since they too were unrepeatable. The character itself then became the source of power for priestly action in the sacramental ministry. The Council of Trent accepted part of the scholastic teaching. It relied on the "character" to teach that he who has once been a priest could not again become a layman.[10]

One result of Trent's teaching on the indelible character was the continuation of the medieval, ontologizing approach to the priestly ministry. It emphasized *being* in the state of priesthood, rather than *doing* the ministry. This widened the gap between the ordained clergy and the nonordained laity. After Trent theologians continued to point to this indelible character as the source of the power that made the sacramental ministry efficacious even when the minister was unworthy. Some theologians taught that this indelible character remained imprinted on the priest's soul for all eternity.

Responding to Luther's denial of a divinely instituted hierarchy, the council taught that the hierarchy of bishops, priests, and deacons was a matter of divine ordinance. (The council deliberately replaced the word "institution" with "ordinance" in its final text.) Canon 6 of the twenty-third session declared: "If anyone says that in the Catholic Church there is not instituted a hierarchy by divine ordinance, which consists of bishops, priests and ministers, let him be anathema."[11]

During the same session the fathers of the council, moving toward disciplinary matters, decreed that no one should be ordained to the subdiaconate before the twenty-second year, to the diaconate before the twenty-third, and to the priesthood before the twenty-fifth. Those who have received tonsure, the council decreed, must wear the clerical garb.

In the context of substantialist scholastic theology, the council began to define ministry in terms of grades, degrees, and levels. The council spoke of ascending "through the minor to the major orders," under the assumption that the lower orders are steps to the higher orders; among "the ecclesiastical grades" the bishops are "superior to priests." It condemned Luther's teaching "that all Christians without distinction are priests of the New Testament, or that they are all endowed with an equal spiritual power." The language of levels, grades, and degrees remained part of the teaching of the church on ministry for the next four hundred years, including that of Vatican II.

To keep the Protestant word ministries at a greater distance, the Council of Trent moved the priestly ministry more and more toward sacrifice and sacraments. Also, the episcopacy was "defined" as superior to the priesthood because the bishop, in virtue of the law, could ordain priests and administer the sacrament of confirmation (canon 7). The practice of ordaining men without appointment to a specific local church was again condemned as it was by the Council of Chalcedon.

In response to Luther, the council eliminated the call of the community from the process of ordination: "The consent, call or authority, whether of the people or any civil power or magistrate is not required in such wise that without this the ordination is invalid."[12] With this decree the priestly ministry moved further away from the control of a particular church community and became an extension of the ordaining bishop. Vatican II retained this theology of dependence with its teaching that "priests are the aids and instruments" of the episcopal order.[13]

Finally, the council set up seminaries to train young men for the priesthood. The stated purpose for establishing these seminaries was to keep the youths destined for the priesthood from following after "the pleasures of the world" and to educate them from their tender years, "before the habits of vice take possession." These seminaries were placed under the control of the diocesan bishop who oversaw the course of studies and the ecclesiastical discipline. The seminarians, the council decreed,

> shall study grammar, singing, ecclesiastical computation and other useful arts; [they] shall be instructed in Sacred Scripture, ecclesiastical books, the homilies of the saints, the manner of administering the sacraments, especially those things that seem adapted to the hearing of confessions and the rites and ceremonies.... The disobedient and incorrigible and the disseminators of depraved morals shall be punished severely, even with expulsion if necessary.[14]

After Trent, with the hierarchic arrangement of ministry by "divine ordinance," we see the continuation of a theology of plenitude of ministry. Thomas O'Meara explains what this meant in the pastoral practice of the church:

> The theology of fullness of ministry residing in the bishop (and then in the priest) flourished under Platonic and Aristotelian metaphysics. As one ministry had absorbed the plurality of ministries, it soon returned to redistribute parcels of ministry out of its own fullness.[15]

Trent's acceptance of a step-by-step approach to ministry meant that ordained ministers could climb the steps from the bottom to the top of the pyramid. On the other hand, popes and bishops, from their plenitude of power, could reward their favorite climbers who were especially loyal to them by distributing some of their power to them. The laity were never part of this process. Schillebeeckx describes how this step model of ministry worked in its downward and upward movement:

> Here the higher stage possesses to an eminent degree what the lower stage has only to a small degree and with limited power. The competence of ministry — of all the lower forms of service — is to be found in absolute fullness at the highest stage; from ancient

times this was historically the episcopate. Thus all power began to come 'from above,' in accordance with the authentic Neoplatonist view.... Moreover, this hierarchy focused on the top of the church, devalued the laity at the base of the pyramid, so that they became merely the object of priestly pastoral concern.[16]

With the conclusion of Trent the ministry of priests is ontologically distinct from the ministry of the baptized laity. It has become a separate caste, standing on its own. The priesthood of the faithful, emphasized by the Protestant churches, virtually vanishes from the theology of the Catholic Church. Now the Catholic Church relies completely on the ordained priests and bishops to carry out the council's far-reaching reforms. The sacramental ministry of the Catholic Church becomes defensive and apologetic against the Word ministries of the Protestant churches. The ordained ministry remains all male and patriarchal. It is institutionalized, spiritualized, and "sacramentalized." For the most part, the ministry of the church is narrowed to the administration of sacraments by male clergy and will remain that way until the Second Vatican Council.

Vatican I (1869–70)

When Pope Pius IX called the First Vatican Council in 1869, he was concerned about deism, atheism, rationalism, Gallicanism, nationalism, and indifferentism. He was also concerned about the threatened loss of his temporal power over the papal states. In his *Syllabus of Errors* (1864) he had condemned most of the "isms." He was still nervous, however, about Gallicanism, which posed a serious threat to his authority as pope. This teaching, propagated in France, denied that "St. Peter and his successors received any power from God extending to temporal and civil affairs, declared princes to be subject to no ecclesiastical power in temporal matters,... declared the supremacy of ecumenical councils over the pope,... [and declared] that the judgments of the pope need the consent of the Church."[17]

As the storms of these "isms" battered the church, Vatican I was convened primarily to deal with the issue of papal primacy. The council never finished its business because of the sudden eruption of the Franco-Prussian War. Vatican I influenced the ministry of the church, however, in three important ways. First, it officially linked jurisdiction with the ordained ministry, the clergy. The word "jurisdiction" is used seven times in a very brief decree. It means that jurisdiction is necessary for bishops to teach and govern their dioceses, for priests to rule as pastors and to exercise their ministries of preaching, witnessing marriages, and absolving sins. In practice, it means that no layperson will hold an ecclesiastical office in the government of the church at any level requiring the exercise of jurisdiction. Teaching, from now on, is not a gift or skill, as it was in the Pauline letters, but an act of jurisdiction conferred from above. This is not new in the church. Vatican I, however, canonized a practice that had been developing since the Gregorian Reform. The bishop and the pastor, possessing jurisdiction, now had final authority over the teaching mission of the church.

Vatican I also reinforced the concept of ministry "from above." Bishops conferred part of their power upon those whom they ordained and upon whom they conferred jurisdiction. The ecclesiastical pyramid now was firmly in place with an infallible pope at the top. The mission of the church, through the laws of jurisdiction, flowed from the top to the lowest levels.

It will be only a matter of sixty years until Pius XI, in his encyclical *Non Abbiamo Bisogno* (1931), will teach that "Catholic Action is the participation of the laity in the apostolate of the church's hierarchy." The laity then will share in the apostolate, not in virtue of their baptism or the gifts of the Spirit, but in virtue of a special mandate from their bishop who has jurisdiction over them. Lay participation will be permitted only by delegation "from above." This will produce much of the passivity still evident today among Catholic laity.

Another effect of Vatican I was the gradual extension of papal infallibility to include more and more of the teaching of the pope and hierarchy. During the council's discussions some German and French bishops had expressed the fear that papal infallibility would be extended beyond the definition of dogmas of the faith. What they feared came to pass. Infallibility became a wider and wider umbrella extending to secondary objects of the faith such as canonizations, disciplinary decrees, the approval of religious orders, and papal encyclicals. Bishops, it seemed, as extensions of the pope, could now share at least in some degree in his charism of infallibility. The bishops' threefold function of teaching, ruling, and sanctifying seemed to be an extension of the same infallibility. Now the hierarchy was the church. And this church, endowed with the divine charism of infallibility, became more and more "divinized."

One result of this process of "divinization" was that ordained ministers were not subject to review and evaluation "from below." The extension of infallibility through the governing hierarchy was partly responsible for the triumphalism that continued until Vatican II. This emphasis on the divine nature of the church prepared the church to accept the identification of the church with one divine image or model, the Mystical Body of Christ. Infallibility further isolated the Catholic Church from its Protestant neighbors and hindered ecumenical progress until the arrival of Pope John XXIII.

Vatican II (1962-65)

Pope John XXIII opened the windows both for the church and for its ministry. On January 25, 1959, after being pope a mere ninety days, he made the unexpected announcement that he planned to convoke the Twenty-First Ecumenical Council. After almost four years of preparation, he formally opened the Second Vatican Council on October 11, 1962. He prayed to the Holy Spirit for its success: "Renew thy wonders in this our day, as by a new Pentecost."

As a young priest, John XXIII had been a professor of church history at the seminary in Bergamo, Italy. He was well aware of the importance of ecumenical councils. Since many bishops and theologians of that time thought that papal infallibility would make a future council unnecessary, the announcement of Vatican II was indeed a surprise.

The open and trusting temperament of Pope John XXIII influenced both the preparation and the actual first sessions of the council. Since Vatican I had not completed its work due to the sudden outbreak of war, it was understandable that Vatican II would take up the unfinished agenda of the episcopacy. Naturally, discussion of the bishops' ministry would have serious implications for all the other ministries in the church.

Vatican II brought an end to the long narrowing process of the ministries of the church. It did so, first by recalling the rich, biblical teaching of *diakonia*. Returning to this New Testament teaching on ministry opened the door to new approaches to ministry. Second, inspired by the truly impressive speech of Cardinal Suenens of Belgium, the council recovered the Pauline teaching on charisms given by the Spirit to all the baptized. This return to baptism and the Spirit's gifts opened the way to recognize a wider spectrum of ministries emerging "from below." In addition, the bishops voted to place the chapter on the people of God before the chapter on hierarchy, thus emphasizing the baptismal mission all share in common.

The people of God theme developed in the Dogmatic Constitution on the Church, proclaimed that the laity, in virtue of their baptism, shared in the priestly, prophetic, and kingly mission of Jesus Christ. No longer did the baptized need a special mandate or charge from the hierarchy to share in the mission of the church. Baptism once again became the foundation for Christian vocation, discipleship, and ministry.

The recovery of the ministry of married deacons at least began to separate ministry from the Western law of celibacy. The institution of the permanent diaconate also moved the ordained ministry back into the "secular" world. These married deacons brought into the ministry a tremendous variety of life experiences that enriched the ministry and contributed to the acceptance of more diversity even within the ordained ministries. No doubt their life experience enriched the church's ministry to families with their wide range of pastoral needs.

With the conclusion of Vatican II the laity take on a more expanded role. "The baptized, by regeneration and the anointing of the Holy Spirit, are consecrated into a spiritual house and a holy priesthood."[18] Through their baptism they share once again in the threefold mission of Christ. Once they are anointed by the Holy Spirit, they are already consecrated ("ordained") to serve as ministers to the Word, to the Eucharist, to the sick, to the poor.

The chapter entitled "The Universal Call to Holiness" ends the long monopolization of spirituality by the vowed or ordained religious. Laity too are called to holiness in virtue of their baptism and therefore have a right to all those resources that help them fulfill their vocation to holiness, including spiritual direction, efficacious proclamation of the Word, etc.

Vatican II quite deliberately does not repeat the Council of Trent's statement that the hierarchy was "established by divine ordinance." It clearly corrects Trent first by substituting "ecclesiastical ministry" for the unbiblical "hierarchy."[19] Second, it applies the words "divinely established" only to the ecclesiastical ministry as such, not to its historically evolved hierarchic form. And finally, it adopts a more functional and historical approach to ministry when it states that this ecclesiastical ministry is not "established," but "exercised" on different levels by those who from antiquity have been called bishops, priests, and deacons.

A renewed emphasis on the role of the Holy Spirit in the church highlights the unique gifts of all the baptized. These gifts make the baptized "fit and ready to undertake the various tasks or offices advantageous for the renewal and upbuilding of the Church."[20]

An Evaluation of Vatican II's Teaching on Ministry

Vatican II's teaching on ministry, as is widely recognized today, has proved to be incomplete and deficient in several respects. Specifically, a review of the teaching on the priestly ministry found in section 28 of the third chapter of the Dogmatic Constitution on the Church reveals several inconsistencies with the theology contained elsewhere in the same document, especially that of chapter 2, entitled "The People of God."

First, the text continues the "levels" theology of the Council of Trent. Thus it tends to separate the ordained ministry from the people of God. Defining the ministry with "levels" terminology reflects the caste society from which this language was borrowed. It leads to understanding power quantitatively as "sacerdotal dignity" rather than as various forms of service. It reflects an ontological (being) rather than functional (doing) approach to ministry. It keeps the ordained clergy as a category of ministry. As long as the priesthood remains a category of ministry, the laity will continue to be "defined" *in contrast with* the clergy.

"Levels" language has been helpful in the past in retaining the distinct identity of the hierarchic priesthood. We could even appeal to the Pauline letters (1 Cor 12:28; Eph 4:11) to show that the Spirit, in giving her gifts, is not a "grand leveler." The "higher gifts" are those that contribute to the greater upbuilding of the church. However, the levels in the church ministry are a historical development, an ecclesiastical construct. As such, they are subject to evaluation and discernment as to their upbuilding function. The Spirit's "levels" may be entirely different from those of the church.

In the same section (28) of the constitution we discover an inconsistency between the more biblical approach to the ministry of the faithful as set forth in chapter 2 and the ordained ministry as presented in chapter 3. In the people of God chapter the common priesthood of the faithful and the priesthood of the hierarchy participate in the one priesthood of *Christ*. Yet in section 28 of chapter 3 the priests become the "aids and instruments" (Latin: *adiutorium et organum*[21]) not of Christ, but of the *episcopal order*. In the "local congregations" they represent, not Christ, but their bishop. In chapter 1 of Vatican II's Constitution on the Liturgy, Christ is present in the liturgy "in the person of" the priest. This phrase is repeated in the first part of section 28 of the third chapter of the Constitution on the Church. Yet, in the last part of the same section, it is the bishop, not Christ, who is present in the person of the priest. The priest now takes on, not the mission of Christ, but "the duties and concerns" of the bishop. This text, to a large degree, makes the priests and the mission of Christ dependent on the bishop. When the bishop dies, his "aids and instruments" "die" with him. Because of this theology of episcopal dependency, the presbyteral council, the symbol of shared ministry, still dies with the bishop (canon 501, 2). Theoretically and symbolically, the hierarchic priesthood comes to a halt in the local church until a new bishop is appointed. The common priesthood of the faithful, not being dependent on the bishop, continues, alive and well, to carry on the mission of Christ.

In paternalistic language, written from a lofty height, the bishops become "fathers" and the priests become their "sons" (section 28). The priests, again in the same paternalistic language, are asked "to take care of the faithful," presumably from their "higher" level of ministry. Since jurisdiction is still linked to a specific level of priesthood, it cannot be shared by the common priesthood of the faithful except by a "downward" delegation to a lower level. Shared ministry, therefore, is not accomplished by a common participation in the priesthood of the baptized, but by sometimes arbitrary or canonically determined methods of passing on power from a higher level. Baptism is thus undervalued. Jurisdiction, still linked to levels of ordination, controls and shapes the ministries "from above."

Vatican II retains Trent's theology of plenitude: the bishop owns or embodies the wellspring of ministries. He distributes quantities of ministries, so to speak: a cup here, a thimble there, through various kinds of ordinations, delegations, appointments, commissionings. So long as this distribution is unequal or at different levels, true shared ministry will be difficult to achieve. Baptism will continue to be undervalued; the Spirit's gifts given "from below" will be shaped, or even quenched, "from above."

We have to ask if Vatican II, on the level of symbol, produced a schizoid Christ by teaching that the priesthood of the faithful is *essentially* different from the priesthood of the hierarchy. Will "two" priesthoods, *essentially* different, create difficulties in understanding the unity of Christ's priesthood? Since the one priesthood of Christ produces actions that are essentially different, one from the other, we could conclude that Christ's acts through the hierarchic priesthood are essentially different from the acts of Christ's priesthood through the baptized faithful. Are the acts of Christ essentially different when, in an extraordinary case, a laywoman baptizes and when a bishop baptizes? Is the validity of the baptism affected? Is the laywoman's baptism *essentially* defective? Must the bishop add the "missing" *essential* element to the laywoman's baptism by a supplementary ceremony of the hierarchic priesthood?

Finally, Vatican II's attempt to define the layperson falls short in many respects. In its sixteen documents Vatican II uses the word "layman" 206 times. Yet, it does not provide anything more than a descriptive definition of the laity: "A secular quality is proper and special to laymen." They are further described in functional terms as "engaging in temporal affairs and by ordering them according to the plan of God."[22] A careful reading of the "laity" texts leads us to conclude with Giovanni Magnani that: "The term 'layperson' is still weighed down not only with an historical and cultural linguistic usage expressing contrast, but also one expressing a relative identity that seems to be negative and that *Lumen Gentium* 31 was not able to avoid, although it reduced it to a minimum."[23]

Vatican II in its chapter on the people of God asserts the basic equality of all the baptized. "Equality is hence to be seen as a feature of the *basic identity* of every member of the Christian faithful, who share in the *same* word and the *same* sacraments within a *sole* community."[24] In spite of the emergence of numerous consultative bodies in the last twenty-five years, the church still does not have effective ministering structures that witness to this basic equality and identity of all the baptized. In actual practice, the laity are still treated as a category and negatively contrasted with the clergy. Often consultation becomes a one-sided process in which a secular lay "caste" advises a spiritual clerical caste.

Vatican II does not really give us a theological definition of the laity when it teaches that "a secular character is proper and peculiar to the laity." Commentators on this text have observed that this statement is more sociological than theological. Pope John Paul II's Apostolic Exhortation on the Laity, released in January 1989, reports that the 1987 Synod of Bishops tried to move away from a sociological interpretation of "secular" and give it a more theological meaning. "The term *secular*," writes the pope, "must be understood in light of the act of God, the Creator and Redeemer, who has handed over the world to women and men so that they may participate in the work of creation, free creation from the influence of sin and sanctify themselves in marriage or celibate life, in a family, in a profession and in the various activities of society."[25] Despite this more spiritual approach to "secular," we still have to ask if the laity are not being defined *in contrast with* clergy who, it is somewhat gratuitously assumed, are not "secular."

While Vatican II attributes a "secular quality" to the laity, Paul calls the baptized "the holy ones" and "the temples of the living God" (2 Cor 6:16). According to 1 Peter the newly baptized are "a holy priesthood" and "a spiritual house." Acts 9:13 refers to the laity as "the saints," a clear reference to their baptismal consecration.[26] Unfortunately, the rich biblical themes of chapters 1 and 2 of the Dogmatic Constitution on the Church did not shape the theology of chapter 4 on the "Laity." As a result, the laity are still confined to the secular arena. They are defined by *place* rather than by baptism, vocation, ministry, or discipleship.

Theologians continue to address other unfinished business of Vatican II. Kenan Osborne lists the following unresolved ministry issues:

- Collegiality remains unfinished.... For example, in what way do the Eastern bishops share in the collegiality of the episcopacy?

- The relationship of the pope to the college of bishops has not been satisfactorily worked out....

- The celibacy of the ordained minister remains an unfinished question....

- The relationship between the ordained and unordained ministry needs to be further developed....

- A further need for development centers on the relationship between the mission and ministry which comes from baptism (the priesthood of all believers) and the specialized ecclesial ministry....

- ...the question arises as regards the significance of ordination....

- The political position of both bishop and priest must be further addressed.... Serious questions are involved in this issue and clearly require further study.[27]

Fortunately, there have been many positive developments toward the diversification of ministry in the pastoral experience of the post-conciliar church. History may conclude that it was a great blessing that Vatican II did not in fact define the diversity of the baptized ministries. By patiently allowing room for the creativity of the Spirit within the baptized community, the council encouraged the ministries to develop "from below" in the actual pastoral experience of the church without pressing them *a priori* into rigid categories imposed "from above." These new and encouraging developments will be considered in more detail in chapter 12, "In the Year 2000."

To summarize the main historical forces that shaped the ministry during the last nine centuries: the Gregorian Reform centralizes the church and its ministry and moves it into the arena of the spiritual; Trent gives the church an ontology of ministry with three levels and canonizes a theology of plenitude vested in the bishop; Vatican I, with its decree on papal infallibility, "divinizes" top-down ministry and finally links ministry to jurisdiction; Vatican II stops the long narrowing process of ministry and opens it up to married deacons and to the charisms of the baptized sharing the threefold ministry of Christ.

"Great storms" blowing sometimes from inside of the church and sometimes from outside, have defined and then redefined the church's ministries. The Holy Spirit, breathing where and when she wishes, sometimes through councils and sometimes through the ministers themselves, has also shaped the church's ministries. Since Vatican II the baptized people of God have become more aware that they are no longer passive objects waiting for their ministries to be shaped by ecclesial, historical, or cultural forces. While they learn from history, they know they are also called to make history.

CHAPTER FIVE

The Church and Its Ministries

"While everyone was asleep his enemy came and sowed weeds all through the wheat..." (Mt 13:25).

We have watched the drama of the history of ministry as it unfolded through the centuries. We gained the perspective of history as we saw the church and its ministries both shaping and being shaped by the needs and crises of the times.

Now in our own time, as we approach the third millennium, we move from the role of audience to that of actors on the stage. Now it is our turn to shape the ministries of our own time in response to the Gospel and the signs of the times. To accomplish our task, we need to reflect on the relationship of the ministries to the church.

Already in Acts 13:1 we see that the ministries do not stand alone. They are linked to some form of church: "Now in the church at Antioch there were prophets and teachers...." The church of Antioch sends Barnabas and Saul on their first missionary journey to Cyprus. In Paul's first letter to the Corinthians (12:12) we see again that the ministries are members of the body of Christ. The gifts of ministry are given for the upbuilding of the church (14:12). It is clear from 1 Corinthians 14 that the ministries are also accountable to the church. If the speakers in tongues do not build up the church, "let them keep silence."

Through most of the history of the church ministers have been attached to, or incardinated in, some form of church community. It is true that in the late Middle Ages there were wandering clerics who roamed the countryside at whim. This practice, however, was soon condemned.

All clerics were asked to belong either to a religious order or to a diocesan or parish church. Already in 451, during the fifteenth session of the Fourth Council of Chalcedon, the church had condemned the practice of ordaining a priest or deacon without appointment to a specific church or chapel (canon 6). During ordination ceremonies the candidate for orders was presented by a local church. His suitability and worthiness were subject to review and evaluation by the local church. Before the bishop proceeded with ordinations he asked the archdeacon of the local church: "Do you know him to be worthy?" Already in the early church the scrutinies (a series of questions to the candidate), still performed before baptism, were part of every ordination ceremony. It is clear that the local church felt it had the right to hold its ministers accountable to the truths of the apostolic faith.

While we can assume that in the church there is no "Lone Ranger" ministry, we need to reflect theologically on the nature of the baptized minister's relationship to the church. Who defines this relationship: the minister? the church? or both? Is this relationship defined by baptism, by some kind of ordination, or by both? What does ordination (or commissioning) add to, or subtract from, this relationship?

Naturally, relationships are not static; they are not frozen in some neat formulation or definition. As human beings are constantly in process of growth and movement so also are their relationships to each other and to their communities. As such, they are constantly in need of redefinition. Ministers need to be conscious of this whole process of redefinition, which often continues with or without their knowledge. As husband and wife grow old together and consequently redefine their relationship, so minister and church grow old together and, in the process, change and redefine their relationships.

The first dimension of the minister's relationship to the church is faith. Needless to add, faith is dynamic, constantly going through various phases in the intensity of its form and expression. Educators and psychologists, for instance, have noted at least four styles of faith: (1) experienced faith; (2) affiliative faith; (3) searching faith; and (4) owned faith.[1]

Experienced faith is that of children, learned passively by interacting with others, such as believing parents. Affiliative faith develops when believers are wanted, needed, and accepted by a believing community. The believers move into searching faith when doubt and critical judgments assert themselves. Now the believers may need to act against an understanding of faith acquired earlier in life. It is a time for experimentation and questioning, not necessarily of the faith itself, but of the believers' style or stage of faith at this particular point in life. Owned faith is a time of inner conversion when the believers are ready to stand up for what they believe even against the community that nurtured their childhood faith. A long lifetime process, this last style of faith becomes part of the ministers' identity and moves of necessity into the witness of external action.

As the ministers' faith goes through various phases and styles, their ministry will be affected as it interacts with the process of this faith relationship. We can assume therefore that the ministers' faith relationship to the church is constantly in process. Today it may be warm, close; tomorrow, cold and distant. The faith may even have its "atheistic" period. As the ministers are called into the "dark night" of a personal crisis, they may revert from "owned" faith to "searching" faith. Their relationship to the church will reflect the changed status of faith. It is not a question, necessarily, of losing the faith but of dying to an old style of faith and then integrating and internalizing it in a new way. Ministers may need to convert from the catechism faith of their childhood before they are ready to internalize the owned faith of their adulthood.

Second, the ministers' relationship to the church will be shaped by the degree of love of neighbor and of the community. This love too is constantly in process of purification and redefinition. It has its own life and history flowing from the ministers' relationship to Christ and from the ups and downs of their own personal journey. Since ministry is charged by an inner love for Christ and his people it will depend in large measure on the degree of self-sacrificing love inspired by Christ's death on the cross. All Christian ministry requires a dying to the self on behalf of the other. Such dying is more or less possible, depending on the degree of love the minister has for the crucified Christ. This degree of love, therefore, will shape the ministers' relationship to the church.

A third ingredient shaping the ministers' relationship to the church is their degree of response to the Spirit. As Christians we believe the Spirit breathes in the church. We know from 1 Thessalonians 5:19, however, that ministers can fail to respond to that Spirit. Naturally, there will be degrees of failure and success in every minister's response. Paul tells us that the Spirit is given to "each according to the measure of faith" (Rom 12:3). In proportion as the ministers are resisting or responding to the call of the Spirit, "the measure" of their relationship to the church will increase or decrease. Ministry will be effective insofar as the ministers are at the Spirit's disposal.

Fourth, already in the New Testament we see that the ministers' relationship to the church is one of accountability. "This is how one should regard us, as servants of Christ and stewards of the mysteries of God. Moreover, it is required of stewards that they be found trustworthy" (1 Cor 4:1–2). If ministers are truly servants to the church and to the reign then their service will always be shaped, to some extent, by their community's discernment of the needs of the people of God. As a result, this part of their relationship to the church will also be in process of continual discernment and redefinition in view of new needs. Account-ability is a relationship to God, to the self as gifted, and to the people of God with their changing needs.

A fifth aspect of the ministers' relationships to the church is their need to support the ministries of others and in turn be open to receive the support of the other ministers in the community. The ministries are gifts given, not only to the individual, but also to the church. These gifts are constantly in need of support as the flower is in need of the warmth of the sun and the nourishment of water. Support is a relationship of reciprocity, mutuality, and owned interdependence. The ministry that becomes isolated or estranged from the life-support system of the body of Christ will lose its direction and soon dry up and be useless.

Sixth, the ministers' relationships to the church will grow in the mix of weeds and wheat that is the church. They will never be clean and neat. The ministers may not like to relate to the weeds in the church, but they have to, because the church without weeds does not exist. The reign of God or harvest time has not arrived yet. Until it does, the weeds will continue to grow and get all tangled up with the ministers. Neat definitions can be found in textbooks. But they don't exist in the real church. So there's no sense in looking for them.

Finally, the ministers' relationship to the church, in spite of all the weeds, can still be called sacramental. Since the church has been defined as the sacrament of salvation, we can affirm that the ministries within it, ordained or not, are part of that living sacrament. Vatican II's Dog-matic Constitution on the Church tells us that "the church is a kind of sacrament or sign of intimate union with God and of the unity of all mankind."[2] In the same document the people of God are called a mes-sianic people, a seed of salvation for the whole human race. The church is called the "visible sacrament of saving unity." Karl Rahner describes the church as fundamental sacrament:

> If it is true to say that the Church, as the continuance of Christ's presence in the world, is the fundamental sacrament of the escha-tologically triumphant mercy of God, then salvation is offered and promised to the individual by his entering into a positive relation-ship to the Church. This positive relationship may possibly have different degrees and grades of intensity, but if the individual is to attain salvation, [it] can never be entirely lacking.[3]

In spite of its obvious human frailty, the baptismal ministers need to see the church primarily as a redeeming institution in and through its visible sacramental activity. "The Church in its entirety is not only a sav-ing institution; as such it is also a saving and sanctifying community."[4] The ministers' relationship to the sacrament that is the church is a partnership with a saving and sanctifying community both for the ministers and for those whom they serve. The ministers in their partnership with the church are a living sign of salvation both for the church and for the world. Of course, the church is not the only sign of salvation in the world. For God saves also those who acknowledge the Creator, among whom are the "Moslems . . . and those who in shadows and images seek the unknown God." Jesus Christ, the Savior, and the kingdom of God are always larger than the church. And "the reality of God is larger than the reality of Jesus."[5]

Toward a Definition of Ministry

Since the beginning of Christian ministry the church has assumed the right to define its own ministries. We have seen in our brief history of ministry that the church has done this both through councils and through laws, either local or universal. We may indeed question the methods and the end result of the church's actions in defining its ministries. For instance, we can question the historical exclusion of blacks, Mexicans, and women from the ordained ministry and also the imposition of celibacy in the Western church. Nevertheless, we can hardly question the church's *right* to determine the number and kind of its ministries. All societies, communities, and organizations assume the right to choose their leaders and to require certain qualifications for leadership.

Even though we see tremendous fluidity and diversity in the ministries of the New Testament, no church could long survive as an institution or organization if everyone, without any distinctions or qualifications, were considered a public minister. Since Vatican II there has been a tendency to assume that all good acts are Christian ministry. The word "ministry" has become so diluted as to lose all meaning. If everything is Christian ministry, what happens to discipleship and the uniqueness of Christ? If Christ is unique and unsurpassable, then *Christian* ministry, in his name, must also have a unique quality about it, at least in its inner motivation. We cannot support a theology in which every good deed, every human project, is considered ministry. Making pizzas, selling insurance, and planting corn may be important, but neither pizzas nor insurance proclaim the Gospel of Christ directly or publicly.[6] By themselves these good actions do not witness to a unique and unsurpassable Christ. They are not automatically Christian. They can be performed by agnostics who hate Christ. It will be up to the churches with the help of their baptismal ministers to reclaim the full meaning of Christian ministry.

While attempts to arrive at a commonly accepted definition for all the emerging diverse ministries have not been successful, nevertheless, attempts at defining the ministries will continue. Such definitions will not always come out of books, but out of the pastoral experience of the new ministers themselves, laboring in the vineyards of different countries and cultures. Definitions begin with practice, with a specific need and a faith response. Richard McBrien admits frankly that "clear-cut definitions of ministry are indeed hard to find."[7] Edward Schillebeeckx, while not giving us a formal definition, tells us that ministry is a function, not a state. We become ministers to *do* ministry.

In arriving at a definition it has been customary to distinguish between the ordained and nonordained ministry. The Lima Document (1982) issued by the Faith and Order Commission of the World Council of Churches tells us that the word "ministry" in its broadest sense "denotes the service to which the whole people of God is called, whether as individuals, as a total community, or as the universal church."[8] The same document tell us that the *ordained* ministry "refers to persons who have received a charism and whom the church appoints for service by ordination through the invocation of the Spirit and the laying on of hands."[9] Appointment by the church and the laying on of hands were the key elements that distinguished the ordained ministry from ministry used in its broadest sense as applied to all the baptized.

As we move toward a definition of ministry, we may find it helpful, at least for the time being, to abandon the distinction between the ordained and the nonordained ministry. Following Yves Congar, McBrien offers other, more useful distinctions among the various forms of ministry:

1. General/universal ministry is any service rendered to another person or group of people who happen to be in need of that service. The call to ministry in this first sense is rooted in our common humanity. In other words, every human being is called to general/universal ministry....

2. General/specific ministry is any special service rendered by people specifically called to serve others in the so-called helping professions and other service occupations such as nursing, social work, and legal aid....

3. Christian/universal ministry is any general service rendered to others in Christ and because of Christ. The call to ministry in this third sense is rooted in our baptism and confirmation....

4. Christian/specific ministry is any general service rendered to others in Christ and because of Christ *in the name of the Church and for the sake of helping the Church fulfill its mission*. The call to ministry in this fourth and most specific sense is rooted in some form or act of *designation* by the Church itself. Thus it is sometimes called *designated ministry*....[10]

When we discuss the pastoral ministry of the baptized (or baptismal ministries) we are dealing with Christian universal and with Christian specific ministries. Many people, such as humanists or altruists, do good deeds (general/universal ministry) that remain good deeds and are not less so just because they are not *Christian* ministry. Saving grace can be mightily at work through the good deeds and general/universal ministry of unbelievers. Cyrus the Persian did not believe in the God of Israel, yet he freed the Jews from their Babylonian captivity. Isaiah (45:1) called him "the anointed of Yahweh," a title normally reserved to kings and priests.

Among the various definitions for ministry proposed so far, that of Thomas O'Meara will serve best for the rest of this chapter: *"Christian ministry is the public activity of a baptized follower of Jesus Christ flowing from the Spirit's charism and an individual personality on behalf of a Christian community to witness to, serve and realize the kingdom of God."*[11] This definition includes the traditional "ordained" ministry but is not limited to it. It includes the Christian universal and the Christian specific ministries but clearly excludes the general/universal ministry.

To clarify this definition we need to note, with O'Meara, that ministry has six characteristics: "(1) doing something; (2) for the advent of the kingdom; (3) in public; (4) on behalf of a Christian community; (5) which is a gift received in faith, baptism and ordination; and which is (6) an activity with its own limits and identity within a diversity of ministerial actions."[12]

We need to note here that Christian ministry is not limited to the ordained ministries of deacon, presbyter, and bishop. We have to state emphatically that a theology of Christian ministry in behalf of the community has to begin with baptism.[13] It is noteworthy that ministry, as defined above, is a *public* action. It is never separated from Christ's command to witness openly to the Gospel in the world. While inner piety may motivate and inspire ministry, it is not ministry in and of itself. The definition concludes by orienting all Christian ministry to the kingdom of God as its ultimate goal.

Functional or Ontological?

At this point in our reflections on our definition for ministry it may be helpful to recall the distinction between the functional and ontological approaches to ministry. We recall from chapter 2 that ministry in the New Testament was primarily functional. It meant *doing* something, such as teaching, preaching, healing, or prophesying. In the history of ministry outlined in chapters 3 and 4 we saw that ministry, during the scholastic period, gradually became primarily ontological. Being, state, caste, and, eventually, indelible character were emphasized to the detriment of *functions*.

Ontology is a philosophical science that constructs static categories of being for the purpose of study. Thus there are angelic beings, human beings, animal beings, and inanimate being. Applying these ontological categories to daily life we can say there are beings who are mothers (ontology) even when they are not "mothering" (function). Plumbers can be fathers (ontology) and at the same time do the "ministry" of plumbing (function).

Christianity will always need to cling to some ontological language. Consciously *being* a Christian, for instance, is more important than merely *doing* Christian acts. Holiness is first a way of being and then a way of doing. Union with God first brings about a new way of being. Contemplatives in the monastery witness to a way of being, a way of life. They are contemplative beings (ontology). They do not minister until they start doing things for each other, such as serving, preaching, and counselling. When ministry becomes a state of life, a way of being, it has become an ontological category.

The emphasis, before Trent, on the ontological aspect of ministry created a ladder of ecclesiastical orders; it created the possibility of "slicing" ministry into various degrees and categories before any functions were attached to these levels. Thus deacons were at a lower level than priests even if they preached better than priests. Ministry, like grace, became quantified in substantialist terminology. With the acceptance of a theology of *ex opere operato* (from the work done), qualifications to actually *do* the functions of ministry were deemphasized. The ministry was considered efficacious despite the lack of qualifications in the ordained minister. For this reason, since the Council of Trent, the church has often ordained ministers who, in practice (function), could not preach or teach or minister to the sick or reconcile with pastoral skill.

Because of this emphasis on ontology priests were ordained even if they were soon going to die. Bishops remained bishops and heads of dioceses even though they were confirmed alcoholics, poor preachers, or incompetent administrators. Like priests, bishops were assumed to have all the necessary qualifications in view of their "ontological" ordination. It was almost sacrilegious to suggest that a bishop could be bishop for a ten-year term or until he could no longer function properly as a bishop. It was the belief that those ordained belonged to a separate caste or category that led to the widespread adoption of distinctive clerical dress and lifestyle. Resignations from the ordained ministry simply could not happen because the qualifications and responsibilities inherent in an "ontological" ordination lasted until death. So long as the ordained minister could still pronounce the efficacious words over the bread and the wine, he was expected to persevere in his state. Naturally, ontological ministry would never be subject to evaluation; nor, presumably, would such ministry require any updating or the development of new pastoral skills.

Along with this ontological approach to ministry, we saw the gradual acceptance of absolute ordinations, the consecration of a minister who had no connection with a particular community. Even though, as noted above, the Fourth Council of Chalcedon (451) condemned any form of absolute ordinations, this custom grew in the church and is still practiced to this day. (Auxiliary or titular bishops, for example, have no jurisdiction in an actual diocesan church.) This practice gave rise to the wandering clergy of the Middle Ages. It also meant that the people gradually had no voice in the selection of those who were to be ordained. In fact, the Council of Trent, as noted in chapter 4, made it clear that the "call of the people" was not necessary for ordination.

"Ontological" ordinations were often understood to be simply a "handing on" of some of the power possessed by the ordaining prelate who had his power directly from Christ through the chain of apostolic succession. Naturally, if the ordained minister was not connected with a particular community, he could not be subject to accountability or evaluation for his ministry. He might be accountable, on the vertical line, to his ordaining prelate. However, basically he had become a metaphysical entity standing by himself.

We have a new manifestation of this ontological approach to ministry today when a diocesan or religious priest comes to a parish from outside on Sunday morning to preside over the community liturgy. He is often called the sacramental minister. He presides over the liturgy even though a pastoral coordinator presides over the community. It is true that he has some connection with the community through his participation in planning the celebration of the sacraments. But he is not the leader of the community.

The pastoral coordinators, who are the actual leaders of the community, often feel they are "renting" a "Mass priest" who, in virtue of his ontological ordination, can pronounce the sacred words they are not allowed to say. This practice is a rather serious departure from the ancient and sacred rule: The one who presides over the community also presides over its liturgical celebrations. The presider from outside, who is not organically united to the daily life of the faith community, distorts the communitarian sign of the sacrament. At the same time, he proclaims the message that there is no one in the community who is capable of presiding over the liturgical celebrations. By his presence, he teaches implicitly that the Spirit, in distributing her gifts, has neglected this particular community. As a "rented" presider, his gift is not part of the community and not accountable to it.

The people of the parish often sense that something is wrong when the pastoral coordinator does not preside over the Eucharist. A 1987 task force established by the diocese of Richmond, Virginia, to study the issues and questions facing the future of ministry concluded:

> When the central leader is not a priest there is a sense of incompleteness and sometimes frustration on the part of the parish which leads them to an openness or even a positive desire to ordain the pastoral coordinator so that the eucharist could be celebrated by that leader.[14]

As we recover the New Testament understanding of ministry, we will surely define the ministries of the future in more functional, less ontological terms. Our culture and society expect and, indeed, demand functional competence in preaching, teaching, leading, and "pastoring." In a democracy there is little tolerance for those who claim rank or leadership on the basis of membership in an ontological caste. Educated people expect leaders to earn their leadership positions by proving they have the skills and qualities admired and respected in society. In an age of growing specialization in all the professions, the people of God expect their religious specialists to be competent and skilled in their areas of specialization. Besides, all professions are required to adapt, to learn new skills, and to remain current in their field of expertise. Nor is it realistic for ministers to expect recognition merely because they present themselves as extensions of a higher authority such as the bishop. Today, all public servants, from the bus driver to the U.S. senator, are subject to evaluation regarding their performance. The people of God have a right to similar functional competence.

While we move toward a more functional understanding of ministry we need to be careful that we do not lose the values contained in an ontological understanding of ministry. "Being" antecedes and shapes the function. "So every sound tree bears good fruit, but the bad tree bears evil fruit" (Mt 7:17). Even though being holy is not ministry as such, it shapes, empowers, and sanctifies the ministry. In an activist, pragmatic culture it is especially important that ministry does not become mere *functionalism*. Ministry, to be authentic, must flow from an inner ontology, a state of communion with the transcendent God. Only then will the ministers' blessing truly be the blessing of God.

In terms of function we can, on the one hand, view the ministries as creating the church. On the other hand, we can view the church as shaping and forming its ministries. To understand this interaction and dynamic interrelationship between the church and its ministries we need to see the church as being constantly in process of being created anew. The church, not unlike other human communities, depends for its life on free, human decisions. The church of the New Testament was born "of a decision of the apostles under the impulse of the Spirit.[15] The rebirth and the re-creation of the church in our own time will also be the subject of human decisions responding to the call of the Spirit. Leonardo Boff explains:

> If the church itself sprang from a decision, it will continue to live if Christians and men and women of faith in the risen Christ and his Spirit permanently renew this decision, and incarnate, enflesh the church in the new situations with which they are confronted, be it in the Greek and medieval culture of yesterday or in the popular culture of today in Latin America.[16]

Without denying the importance of the universal church, it is helpful, when shaping the ministry, to concentrate on the particular church, to see the church "from below" rather than "from above." The church's ministers will "enflesh" the church from their own "base" or congregational church. Vatican II, in its Dogmatic Constitution on the Church, did not always limit the particular church to the diocese. In chapter 3 we read:

> This church of Christ is truly present in all legitimate local congregations of the faithful . . . united with their pastors, are themselves called churches in the New Testament. . . . In them the faithful are gathered together by the preaching of the gospel of Christ, and the mystery of the Lord's Supper is celebrated, "that by the flesh and blood of the Lord's body the whole brotherhood may be joined together." . . . In these communities, though frequently small and poor, or living far from any other, Christ is present. By virtue of Him the one, holy, catholic, and apostolic Church gathers together.[17]

The church is constantly in the process of becoming, at the local level, the level of the parish or the base community. That is where ministers will nourish or hinder that process of becoming. The incarnation of the church cannot remain an abstraction but must become visible as sacrament in concrete form in the actual life of the believer in community. It is here where the minister will haul the bricks and the mortar to build the church. It is here where Paul's phrase "for the upbuilding of the church" begins to have meaning. Ministers who are really hauling the building bricks will change in the process. Their ministry and their relationship to the church will change. For this reason, on the experiential and existential levels, there can never be a final, categorical definition of ministry.

Ordination/Certification/Commissioning

In earlier chapters we noted that baptism is the foundation for all the ministries. We need to recall here that the rite of baptism, even in its truncated form, celebrates the candidates' call or vocation to discipleship. The candidates renounce the reign of satan and publicly choose to take their stand with the reign of Christ. (In the ancient rite the candidates, in a moment of high drama, turned to the East, toward the rising sun, symbol of the risen Christ.) The candidates are then anointed with oil, which since the Old Testament period has been used to anoint priests and kings, making them charismatic officers to carry out a mission under the impulse of the Spirit. The baptismal anointing makes the candidates sharers in Christ, the priest and king (1 Pt 2:4–9). Toward the end of the rite, the newly baptized are anointed with the same chrism used for consecrating bishops, chalices, and churches.

Baptism also includes the imposition of hands, a symbolic rite that already in Acts 19:6 indicates the conferral of the Spirit who, with her charismatic gifts, empowers the candidates for ministry. With the New Rite of Christian Initiation of Adults (1972) the rich symbols of baptism have recovered their power to teach the people that this sacrament is already a seed and beginning of ordination.

Why, then, in view of our baptismal "ordination," do we need additional ordinations, commissionings, or installations? What can these paraliturgical ceremonies possibly add to baptism? Do we need a clerical empowerment when the Spirit has already empowered us? What mission or charge can a cleric confer upon us that has not already been given to us through baptism?

In recent years many Catholics have questioned the necessity of ordination. They have also debated the usefulness of certification, installation, and commissioning. Some feel that such ceremonies are another form of the clericalization of the ministry. To them it seems that the installing cleric is passing on his power "from above" to the new lay minister. The ceremony is not seen as the celebration of a more intense baptismal commitment or the recognition of a gift given by the Spirit. Others will complain that these ceremonies narrow the number of ministries to a set number of "official" ministries. The assumption here is that ministry becomes official only through some kind of recognized church ceremony conducted by a priest or bishop. Still others feel that such commissioning and installation ceremonies run the risk of blessing control by clerical power "from above."

David Power, writing about the ministries of reader, acolyte, and the special ministers of the Eucharist, explains that the installations of these ministries are seen "as a commissioning to special functions by the bishop." Then he asks: "If such ministry is a way of exercising the call received at baptism, what can justify this commissioning? Why is it necessary to commission laypersons, and even to set up special canonical offices, for services that are normally theirs in virtue of their membership in the Christian community?"[18]

Those who favor commissioning ceremonies make the case that ministry by its nature is public not private. Therefore, it is fitting to have some public ceremony to witness to the public nature of ministry. Those in favor of a public ceremony say that such ceremonies obviate the danger of individualism in the ministry. There is a constant danger in the still sinful human community that some will see ministry as an ego trip and seek power for themselves. The public ceremony highlights the community dimension of all ministry, requiring support, qualifications, and accountability.

Those who support some kind of ceremony believe that every gift of the Spirit deserves a public celebration. The ceremony is the time for the community to clap its hands and sing "Alleluia!" in gratitude for the Spirit's gift freely and graciously given, not only to the individual, but also to the community. Others favor a public ceremony to initiate a relationship of support and accountability. Those who say "Amen" to the commissioning ceremony are expressing their intention to support the ministers and, at the same time, letting them know that they will hold them accountable for their service to the community.

A Variety of Ordinations

Throughout history organized societies and communities have found some way of recognizing the persons who perform specific services or leadership roles in the community. Thus even the smallest city will have some brief ceremony to install its new mayor. Most fraternal organizations officially hand over the gavel to the new president as a symbol of the transfer of leadership. Whatever the symbol or ritual, it is meant to convey the message that a particular person is recognized by the community as performing a specific leadership service. Not everyone in the community is commissioned, "licensed," or certified to perform this particular public service. Not everyone in the community has the same leadership function.

We need to be aware that the word "ordination" historically is not limited to the sacrament of holy orders of the Council of Trent. As noted in chapter 3, there have been many kinds of ordinations throughout history. Before we begin to redefine "ordination," however, we need to get beyond the Tridentine "ordination," which still predominates in our own time. Yves Congar points out:

In antiquity ... ordination encompassed at the same time election as its starting point and consecration as its term. But instead of signifying, as happened from the beginning of the twelfth century, the ceremony in which an individual received a *power* henceforth possessed in such a way that it could never be lost, the words *ordinare, ordinari, ordinatio* signified the fact of being designated and consecrated to take up a certain place, or better a certain *function, ordo,* in the community and at its service. Does not all that hang together with a vision of things whose point of entry is community rather than the hierarchical priesthood defined at the outset for itself and seen as efficient cause? Does it not cohere with a conception of the laity and ministries not defined in isolation ... but seen organically within the communitarian reality?[19]

In view of this practice of the early church, we need to ask if it is still possible, at the pastoral level, to have a variety of nonclerical ordinations that have a sacramental character but that are not the sacrament of holy orders? Before Trent, as we saw in chapter 3, the church recognized numerous ordinations apart from the deaconate, priesthood, and episcopate. These ordinations did not consist in a transfer of power, but in a call by the community, an invocation (*epiklēsis*) of the Holy Spirit and a celebration of her gifts. There is no theological reason why we cannot, as Congar suggests, return to this earlier understanding of ordinations. These ordinations could easily be distinguished one from the other by the distinct functions mentioned by name in the ordination ceremony, such as teaching, reading, caring for the sick. The distinction between these ordained baptismal ministries and the other ordained ministries in the sense of Trent will not always be clean and clear-cut in terms of pastoral functions. At the parish level both priests and ordained "laity" will perform the ministries of teaching and bringing communion to the sick. Such occasional overlapping of function has not caused any confusion in the past and need not do so in the future. If ministering functions have no rank attached to them, they will not cause an identity crisis.

The foundation for all these ordinations will not be a transfer of power but will continue to be baptism, which, as noted above, is already an anointing to a share in the priesthood of Christ. Since the church is a celebrating and sacramental community, many kinds of admissions and ordinations to ministry must be developed. While we are still in the body, we need to bring the invisible Spirit to visibility through signs and symbols. The New Testament uses fire, wind, and doves. We too need visible symbols both to support our faith and to own our humanness, which needs to see, to hear, to smell, to feel, and to be touched. Sacramental symbols, in the rich Catholic tradition, are the pastoral part of theology. They reveal and celebrate the invisible in visible forms recognizable by earth-bound believers.

Besides, the candidates for these ordinations have arrived at a new place in their lives since their baptism. They have received new gifts from the Spirit, bringing new responsibilities for ministry. These gifts confirm the Spirit's continuing presence first celebrated at baptism. Just as we celebrate graduations, promotions, and weddings at different points in our lives, so we celebrate different ordinations to new functions and responsibilities. Far from demeaning baptism, these ordinations extend it and bring it to new visibility through the various stages of an adult life of service.

These ordination ceremonies do not create the ministry. But they confirm and celebrate that a Christian has been prepared and approved for public ministry in the church.[20] The forms of these ordinations need to be subject to discernment and review by the local community. The liturgical minister, no matter how imaginative or creative, does not construct ordination sacramentals apart from the sacrament of the celebrating community. On the other hand, the sacrament of the church can sacramentalize itself in many different ways.

Once ordination is separated from the scholastic ontology of the Council of Trent, it can be redefined for our own time. It cannot be understood primarily in terms of *what it gives* to the one ordained. It cannot be objectified so that it becomes some*thing* possessed. It cannot be, through instrumental causality, the transmission of "objectified" power passing through the hands of the ordaining prelate to the ordinand.

As the church in its pastoral practice opens up more and more to the diverse baptismal ministries, it cannot simply repeat ordination formulas of the past. John Coleman explains:

> The church retains a certain freedom to experiment, to learn from practical experience and renovate the forms of ordination which will guarantee the authentic teaching, ruling, sanctifying and pastoral tasks of the Church. . . . The purpose of ordination is to guarantee the requisite *order* in the church against chaos, instability or the threatened loss of essential pastoral functions. . . . The churches are free, within very broad limits set by the gospel and tradition, to devise that form of polity and ordered ministry which perpetuates for new generations the apostolic witness in preaching, teaching, charity and ways of sanctifying life. God wills that the churches be entitled to devise constitutional solutions for real pastoral problems. He wills the continuance of Christ's ministry in appropriate forms for each new age and culture.[21]

New forms of ordination for our generation depend on a new understanding of the church as relational and as continually reconstituted by the Spirit. While no order is absolute, the church never exists apart from *some* kind of order. This means that all the baptized exist at all times in some kind of relationship that can be called an order. The church simply does not exist as some kind of anarchy. The question is not, will there be an order or not, but what *kind* of order will there be? Paul's image of the body already reveals an order in the church. The hand does not do what the foot does. No matter how many charisms there may be, not everybody does everything. Further, church order itself is a manifestation of the Spirit. "For God is not the God of confusion but of peace" (1 Cor 14:33).

On the other hand, the opposite of anarchy is not necessarily hierarchy. Order can come about through democracy, through the responsible cooperation of all the ministers, through prayerful discernment, through "little councils," and through participative management. Such "orders" can also be the manifestation of the Spirit. Since Vatican II, hierarchy is no longer regarded as being of "divine ordinance." We have no evidence that the Spirit has made a permanent covenant with any one historical form of order. With the emergence of new ministries, we ought to expect an emergence of new forms of order. If we cling pathologically to a historical form of hierarchy, we run the risk of quenching the new ministries or of not ordering them at all. In that case, there will indeed be confusion, chaos and anarchy.

We can also assume, as noted in chapter 2, that the Holy Spirit will continue to bless the churches with the gift of governing (1 Cor 12:28). That gift may take the form of hierarchy in one century, and collegiality, consensus, discernment, or participative management in another. But all gifts, ministries, and ordinations need to relate, in one way or another, to some kind of governing ministry. The process of relating and ordering the ministries begins with baptism:

> To redefine ordination we have to recover the full meaning of baptism: In the first place, it must be stated emphatically, that there is no such thing as "non-ordained" persons in the church. Baptism and especially confirmation (or chrismation) as an inseparable aspect of the mystery of Christian initiation involves a "laying on of hands." ... The theological significance of this lies in the fact that *it reveals the nature of baptism and confirmation as being essentially an ordination.* ... The theological implication of all this is that ordination, i.e. *assignment to a particular "order" in the community,* appears to be paradoxically enough not something that *follows* a pre-existing community but an act *constitutive* of the community.[22]

Creating new forms for ordination will require sensitivity both to the tradition of the church and its orders and to the actual pastoral situation. New ordination ceremonies could include at least the following: (1) The *call* of the faith community through fasting and prayerful discernment of needs and qualifications. In large parishes this could be done through representative bodies such as parish councils; (2) *scrutinies* similar to the baptism questions, inquiring about intention and adherence to the apostolic faith; (3) *proclamation* of the Word announcing the presence of the Spirit in the ordaining community; (4) *invocation* (*epiklesis*) of the Holy Spirit; (5) the *laying on of hands* by the community presider and other leaders of the community; (6) *ordering* a specific ministry, such as teaching or reading, to a specific community; (7) *praise and thanksgiving* for the gift given to the community; (8) *sending,* perhaps through a community blessing or conferral of symbol of ministry; (9) the *Amen* of the people, confirming and supporting the ordination; and (10) some visible *communion* with the larger church.

These ordinations will be part of the ordering process that builds up and unifies the church. New ministers will be ordained (ordered) to an *order* of lectors, of teachers, of eucharistic ministers, of health care ministers, etc. They will also be ordered to a specific ministry and to a specific community.

Perhaps during an interim phase in the church, many of these ordinations could be seen primarily as "blessings" conferred by whomever is the recognized leader or governor of the community. The blessing ceremony could first bless God, as often happens in the Scriptures, and then bless the prospective minister, even with a laying on of hands. The ceremony needs to indicate clearly that the blessing is primarily a public recognition of the gifts of the Spirit already received.[23] These gifts of the Spirit are, of course, associated with baptism. The ceremony of blessing could also indicate that the process of discernment of ministry is being brought to a close. The community could by prayer and song offer its thanksgiving for this action, and then pray for the abiding grace of the Spirit.[24] No doubt many of today's pastors, harried by a deluge of directions from central offices, would shout a hearty "Amen" to David Power's comment: "There is no need for canonical formulations, or officially designated prayers, to guide this process. A good knowledge of the prayer tradition, a good discernment of spirits, and wise leadership are sufficient."[25]

As the church begins to emphasize the role of the baptized in the selection and support of its ministries, it needs to recover the people's role in whatever ceremony it adopts. Already in the sixth century the ordaining bishop, using the Missal of the Franks, asked for the people's public consent before he proceeded with ordination. He addressed the people in the following words: "We know that it will be more acceptable to God, if through the Holy Spirit there is unanimous consent; and therefore you ought to express your choice aloud and in public."[26] Then the bishop would pause and the people would cry out: *"Dignus est"* (He is worthy.) The Latin *dignus* can also mean "suitable."

Such prayerful consultation of the Spirit in the baptized is not the same as political democratic elections. These have caused considerable disorder in the church's history. In the church of Carthage, during Augustine's time, for instance, the people "clamored for the election of a Roman senator, Pinianus, in the hope that he would give his wealth to the Church. When Augustine refused, the trouble-makers threatened to have Pinianus ordained by some other bishop."[27] Because of abuses of this kind, popular, political elections were forbidden by the Council of Laodicea in 364.

The emerging baptismal ministries challenge us to creatively develop forms of discernment, training programs, ordination ceremonies, support systems, spiritual formation programs, methods of evaluation, and lines of accountability. These programs and structures will all be experimental. Some will fail. We are learning to adapt to a totally new situation. We are a church of frail human beings. There are "weeds all through the wheat." But we have the promise of the Spirit to sustain us as we journey, and sometimes stumble, on our way to the reign of God.

CHAPTER SIX

Ministering in a Sinful Church

"Let both grow together until the harvest; and at harvest time I will tell the reapers, gather the weeds first and bind them in bundles to be burned, but gather the wheat into my barn" (Mt 13:30).

During its third session (1964), the Second Vatican Council approved the Decree on Ecumenism. In it the council declared: "Christ summons the Church as she goes her pilgrim way, to that continual reformation of which she always has need insofar as she is an institution of men here on earth."[1] "During its pilgrimage on earth," the decree continued, "this People [i.e., the church] though still in its members liable to sin. . . ."[2] The phrase "in its members" was one of the nineteen last-minute changes requested by Pope Paul VI. He wanted to make sure that the final text would not say that the church *itself* was sinful. Thus he aligned himself with those theologians who say "that the subject of sin can only be an individual person, and that even if each individual member of the Church were a sinner, the Church as such could not be called sinful, since as a supra-individual and transcendent personality it is more than the sum of Christian individuals."[3] Charles Journet expresses the same thought, but with memorable brevity: "The Church, which is not without sinners, is nevertheless without sin."[4]

Other Catholic theologians are coming closer to the view held by many Protestant theologians that the church can be at the same time just or holy and sinful. Thus Hans Urs von Balthasar has produced numerous testimonies "from the Patristic period and the Middle Ages which show that at these periods the Church (as a concrete community of sinful believers) was widely regarded as holy and sinful at the same time."[5]

103

Soon after the close of Vatican II Karl Rahner wrote with refreshing honesty about the sinful church:

> Accordingly, in patristic times and in the Middle Ages one spoke without hesitation of the sinful Church ... and this *not only* in the sense that the mercy of God has turned sinful humanity into the holy Church, that is, of the sinful Church in so far as she is regarded in her origins, but also of the Church in so far as she *is* sinful *now*, of her sinfulness as a moral *condition*.[6]

We can conclude, therefore, with Francis Sullivan that if the church is the people of God, meaning real people who are both holy and sinful, then the church too must be both holy and sinful.[7]

A "Sinful" Church

Because of the long history of the notion of a "sinless" church it is still difficult for the pope, the bishops, and some people to really believe that the church itself is sinful. The Catharist temptation lurks in our inner psyche — we want to be a church of "the pure." Part of us is like the slaves of the Gospel who wanted to go and pull up all those nasty weeds (Mt 13:28). We still need the Master's reminder to let both the wheat and the weeds "grow together until the harvest."

It is quite important that church ministers realize, intellectually and *emotionally*, that their church in its concrete reality is indeed a community, not of angels, but of sinners. It is not for nothing that as we gather as a Christian community on Sunday, each of us immediately confesses "that I have sinned through my own fault ... in what I have done and in what I have failed to do." It is a weekly reminder that we ourselves are the weeds and wheat in the church.

Apart from our psychological resistance to being identified with a community of sinners, there are theological reasons that make it difficult for ministers, especially official ones, to publicly own the sinfulness of their church. The pre–Vatican II model of the church as the Mystical Body of Christ overidentified the church with the sinless Christ. With no other images to correct it, the single image of Mystical Body "divinized" the church. This meant that the church was seen as an incarnation of the sinless Christ. This image made it difficult to affirm the sinfulness of the church without at the same time imputing sinfulness to Christ.

At the same time, priests and bishops, the principal rulers of the church, were supposed to be "other Christs." This too made it difficult to see these other Christs as frail, sinful members of the common human pilgrimage. Then too, papal infallibility, defined by Vatican I (1870), added its own aura of a divine prerogative to the top of the hierarchical pyramid. Many Christians interpreted infallibility as sinlessness. Further, when ministry was defined by place, i.e., the holy sanctuary, it was easy to assume that the ministering priest or bishop shared in the holiness of the sanctuary, to assume that he was sinless.

Finally, most Catholics, during their catechism days, memorized the four marks of the church as one, *holy*, catholic, and apostolic. The overemphasis on the *holy* mark conveyed the impression of an "ideal Church floating above the human world."[8] Romantic descriptions of the nature of the church have not always been truthful. They have not shown the real church as ministers experience it day to day in its actual form, in its concrete, sinful reality.

Tendencies to "overdivinize" and over-spiritualize the church are as old as the church itself. Hans Küng speaks directly to this issue:

> To avoid compromising the Church, there have often been attempts to draw a distinction between the members who are sinful and the Church itself which nonetheless remains sinless. But it is an unreal distinction.... There is no such thing as a Church without members.... It is human beings, not God, not the Lord, not the Spirit, who make up the Church.... We must accept the realities of the case: the Church is a church of sinners.... Their sinfulness sullies the body of Christ, shakes the spiritual building itself, wounds the people of God itself.[9]

Ministers who are still uncomfortable in referring to their church as sinful might choose to follow Leonardo Boff and speak about the "pathologies" of the church. He lists two manifestations: "The institution of the church is absolutized in such a way that it tends to substitute itself for Christ, or to understand itself as his equal, ... the pretension to unlimited infallibility, to unquestionability, to absolute certainty."[10] We could add other institutional pathologies, like patriarchy, the officeholders' fear of women in ministry, obsession with secrecy, the preoccupation with sex, the compulsive need to control (especially the selection of bishops), the fear of sharing real authority, and, of course, racial, sexual, and religious discrimination.

To get more specific about one of the church's sins — discrimination is embedded in the very fiber of the system. And discrimination hurts. It hurts every day. Morning, noon, and night. Especially at night. It darkens the light of the church; wounds the body of Christ; increases the pain of remaining in the church; betrays the Word on the tongue of its proclaimers; burns a scar on the face of the church; nourishes anger in the hearts of women; makes them voiceless and powerless in their own house; quenches budding vocations; empties the seminaries;

brings tears to the face of the ministers announcing joyful news. Discrimination, in short, is one of the church's greatest sins, one of its deepest pathologies.

Another pathology is evident in the tight control and secrecy in the hierarchic system that selects only ultra-safe men as bishops. William Bausch, pastor of St. Mary's in Colt's Neck, N.J., goes to the heart of this pathology:

> I suggest that most bishops are really victims, victims of a system that chooses safe men, usually from administration and with the right Roman credentials, some of whom know they're over their heads but "out of obedience" accept the mitre. Prophets are avoided like the plague.... I repeat my contention that no man (yes "man" in our present age) should ever be considered for bishop unless he has spent at least 10 years in the trenches.... Furthermore, a consensus should be sought from the people he's served about his competence and compassion.[11]

In spite of Vatican II's call for reform, these systemic pathologies will not be easily cured. Those who hold power either in the political or ecclesiastical systems do not willingly give it up. During an election in the 1950s the late Paddy Bauler, a beer-guzzling alderman, uttered the famous rallying cry: "Chicago ain't ready for reform." Neither is the church. "It seems to be a truism that no persons and no institutions contain the power or wisdom to correct themselves."[12] The church's institutional pathologies are too deeply imbedded in its body. It does not want to be cured, yet. Since these pathologies have become part of its identity, the church is afraid to let them go. It has nourished them so long that they are now very much at home in the church. They are very dear pets. Giving them up will require a wrenching, emotional death — a death to a warm and comfortable relationship. True reform will require a miracle of grace, an intervention by the Spirit, "like the rush of a mighty wind" coming from outside of the church.

Part of the ministers' spiritual life will include prayer for the conversion, the change of heart, of their sinful church. As the prayer is answered, the church will suffer a painful agony in the garden and an even more painful death before its ministers will see the birth of what Pope John XXIII called the new Pentecost. Ministers will pray and work for conversion but, like the prophets of old, they may not see it in their own lifetime.

In the meantime, new ministers need to be careful that they do not become infected or contaminated by the church's institutionalized pathologies. They need to have patience with and a large-hearted compassion for the church's wounded, pathological condition. Through prayer, spiritual direction, and the support of a community at least *somewhat* free from the church's pathology, they need to immunize themselves from the diseases of their church; otherwise, they will pass them on to future generations and to future forms of church in process of being born through their ministry. Of course, no minister will ever become totally immune. But, for their own health, the ministers need to practice a preventive maintenance lest they catch the church's institutional diseases.

Theologically it might be helpful to see the church's pathology as "sin" in the biblical sense of "missing the mark." Then we could more easily own the truth that the human church does indeed fall short of the mark in many ways. In fact, the church, like the rest of us, is so often falling short of the mark that it can indeed be called sinful.

Or, if we are sensitive enough, we could feel the pathology of the church's sin as Japanese novelist Shusako Endo "feels" it. Elizabeth Beverly comments on Endo's feeling for sin:

> "Sin... is not what it is usually thought to be; it is not to steal and tell lies. *Sin is for one man to walk brutally over the life of another and to be quite oblivious of the wounds he has left behind."*
> To be oblivious. To be mindless. For Endo, this is sin. Evil exists; it is produced by humans. But it happens only because people stop thinking. Distracted by pride, or even by humility, they forget. And such forgetfulness is the source of all human sorrow. Mindlessness creates the atmosphere in which evil thrives.[13]

In the real church new "lay" ministers will soon come in contact with leaders' abuse of power, with their "walking over the life of another," with death-dealing legalism, with manipulative control, with the arbitrary power of hierarchy, and with various forms of unfaithfulness to the Gospel of love, compassion, and forgiveness. They will experience in a new way the weaknesses of ministers who are, after all, only vessels of clay laboring under the crushing burden of evil. The mystery of evil is alive and well in the church until the coming of the victorious Lord in fullness at the end times. Sin, both personal and communal, continues to infect the body of the church.

Perhaps the most painful form of evil or pathology in the church is the sinfulness of its structures. John Paul II, in his encyclical *On Social Concerns* (1988), speaks of the "structures of sin." Speaking about obstacles to development in the economic and political world, he writes: "The structures of sin... are linked to the concrete acts of individuals who introduce these structures, consolidate them and make them difficult to remove. And thus they grow strong... and so influence people's behavior."[14] Since the church is sinful, we have to confess that these "structures of sin" exist not only in the political world, but also in the church.

"All structures," writes Michael Novak, "built by human beings for human beings are 'sinful' structures.... The idea that all human structures are sinful ... is at least as old as the Constitution."[15] The church's structures are gifts of the Spirit, but, at the same time, the fruit of sin (especially "mindlessness") is always present in the body of the church. Thus canon law contains the wisdom of Spirit, and, at the same time, the sinful pathologies of a very human church; it reflects the church's heavenly vision and, at the same time, its earthbound blindness. Councils, conclaves, synods, and bishops' conferences are signs of the Spirit and, at the same time, signs of sin still at work in all the members. Insofar as bishops do not turn from, or exorcise, these sinful structures, they will perpetuate them.

Church structures, such as parish and diocesan pastoral councils, are sinful first because they were produced, not by angels, but by sinful human beings. Second, they are presently composed of sinful ministers; for the structures never exist apart from the people who use them. All church structures, including "democratic" elections, group dynamics, and prayerful discernment, can be manipulated by those who seek power for themselves. They are frail, fallible, and potentially sinful.

As new ministers, especially women, experience the various forms of evil in the church, they might well take to heart the advice of Hugo Rahner:

> We must learn to endure the Church. Our relationship to the Church is often that of children who have become knowledgeable and who discover the weaknesses of their parents.... The Church as she actually lives, suffers, and in many of her parts rots, is and remains also for us a test of faith — a trying, discouraging, a burning anxiety. She can become a danger to faith, because we all are tempted to wish that she would become more spiritual, more attractive, more impressive.[16]

New ministers need to learn how to endure the church and how to suffer within it without allowing bitterness to poison the fruitfulness of their labor. After some years in the vineyard, they may identify with the comment of the Dominican Hugo Clerissac: "It is easy to suffer for the church; the difficult thing is to suffer at the hands of the church."

Love Heals

There is no need to continue here with a long litany of the church's sins to stir up painful memories or open the scars of unhealed wounds. More important for the minister is a deeper understanding of the theology of redemption and compassion available in the Christian church, in spite of its sins. It is central to our Catholic belief that God in Jesus Christ lovingly and unconditionally embraced the sinful people precisely as sinful. God did not wait until this people was totally purified and free from all defects before lavishing infinite, purifying, and healing love upon them. Insofar as the ministers minister in the name of this same Christ, they are called to witness to Christ's unconditional, healing love for the sinful human condition, especially as it exists in their church. This witness will not be a condescending love from on high, but a keen awareness of one wounded healer being a sacrament for another's healing.

To survive in a sinful church the ministers need to remember that the church that preaches redemption is itself in need of redemption; that the church that preaches forgiveness is in itself in need of forgiveness; that the church that offers the compassion of Christ to the world is itself constantly in need of that same compassion.

The ministers also need to remember that they are sacraments of forgiveness and compassion not only to the world, but also, and especially, to the ministering members within the church, including its office-holders. The ministers, with all their flaws and weaknesses, can still be effective vessels for Christ's compassion pouring out on the wounds of the Christian community. All ministers, including popes and bishops, are "wounded healers" who themselves need healing. "Mother" church deserves our love, not because she is beautiful but because she has warts on her face and, therefore, needs our love all the more.

It may be helpful for new ministers, with Karl Rahner, to see office itself as a charism given to the church. They can then distinguish the office itself from a sinful or incompetent person who happens to hold that office at a particular time. In this way, they may find it easier to show reverence and respect for the office, the Spirit's gift of order in the church, while offering Christ's compassion to the weak person who happens to hold that office. The incompetent pastor or bishop will die, eventually. The office, as gift of order, will remain. All ministers might learn a truth from St. Catherine of Siena (1347–80). She had the ability to discern between legitimate authority and the unworthy bearer of that authority. Always obedient to Christ, the teacher and master of truth, she did not hesitate to call Pope Gregory XI "to be obedient to God's will."

On the other hand, our relationship to a sinful church cannot be defined completely on the theological level. As human beings with a full range of human emotions, we need to define and redefine our relationship to the church also on the psychological level. Ministers will learn to deal with the emotional component of this human relationship to the church in their own way. Naturally the process of defining our relationship on the psychological level is very personal and subjective. It is not unusual for ministers, especially women, to suffer deep hurt and anger from the church's "mindlessness." The church that hurts does not always heal, at least not immediately. The church is, of course, called to be a healing community. But in a concrete situation, such as a particular parish or diocese, the church may be unfaithful to its vocation. For this reason an individual minister may need time and distance especially from the abrasive institutional part of a particular church so that the healing process may begin. Some ministers may need more time than others. But in general, space, time, prayer, distance, and a very supportive community may eventually heal the hurt and anger. The healed ministers may then return to their ministry to be a sacrament of healing for others and, perhaps, for the church.

The alcoholic priest, for instance, may have suffered deeply from his authoritarian and moralistic bishop. Or he may feel unjustly imprisoned in a solitary confinement by the church's law of celibacy. He may have to gain distance from the church's authority structure for awhile to find healing in the more "Christian" community of Alcoholics Anonymous. Then, with the healing grace of time, distance, prayer, and support, he may return to minister again to others who are suffering in similar situations.

For long-range preventive maintenance, ministers could avoid investing themselves too heavily in the institutional part of the church. An emotional overinvestment will lead to high expectations that can never be fulfilled. Ministers will do better to pause now and then to reflect prayerfully on their relationship both to the church and to the reign of God. Naturally, in view of everything explained in chapters 1 and 2, ministers will be healthier, spiritually and psychologically, if they invest themselves more in the reign of God than in the church. The two are not the same. The church may be one place for ministry, but it is only a humble and poor servant to the reign of God. In its present form, it is passing away. The reign of God, with its faith communities, will remain.

Theologically and psychologically the ministers' relationship to the church will never be simple or static. Most likely it will always remain a love/hate relationship. The capacity to love, forgive, and have mercy on the sinfulness of the church will vary considerably during the ministers' lifetime. The church's faithfulness and unfaithfulness to Gospel values also varies considerably throughout history. Many times the ministers, responding to an uncomfortable but persistent prophetic call, may, like Catherine of Siena, call even the prelates of the church to repentance and conversion. Thomas Aquinas asks, "Whether Fraternal Correction Is a Matter of Precept?" He answers in the affirmative. Then he asks: "Whether a Man is Bound to Correct His Prelate?" He answers that a "subject is competent . . . to administer to his prelate . . . the fraternal correction which is an act of charity."[17] In offering this "fraternal" correction the ministers, of course, need to be humbly aware of their own sinful condition in the same human pilgrimage.

New ministers have to own their need for human and spiritual support from some kind of praying community. At the same time, they have to allow time in their own ministry to offer support to others. Such support must be noncontrolling, nonpossessive, and nonmanipulative. Freedom is the Spirit's gift to the baptized. The ministers approach that gift with awe and reverence. They minister to the other minister's growth and freedom or they do not minister at all. If support becomes a relationship of control or dependence, then the freedom and health of the minister being supported will suffer. The supporting ministers will eventually die or move. They need to leave behind other ministers who can stand on their own feet in their own mature uniqueness.

Office in the Church

Already in the pastoral letters (c. 110) we see that a distinct office has developed in the church: "If anyone aspires to the office of bishop . . . " (1 Tm 3:1). Just as in civil society we have the offices of mayor and president so in the church we have the offices of pastor, bishop, etc. We know from history that a church without office or leaders in *official* positions will not long survive. Those who are opposed to office in the church often extol the virtues of the charismatic Corinthian church. While the Corinthian model may be a useful corrective to an overly institutionalized church, it can't be adopted uncritically.

In spite of the many disadvantages that come with office one can hardly agree with Protestant theologians, like Rudolph Sohm and Emil Brunner, that office and institution stand in antithesis to the essential nature of the church.[18] If we own the human and incarnational dimension of the church, it is possible to see office as a gift to the church. Even though it is a mixed blessing, it is still grace.

To reflect for a moment on the dangers of office — it is quite possible for office-holders to exploit their office for selfish purposes: They can use office as an authority crutch and so manipulate the people; they can take refuge in office and so try to escape personal accountability; they can endow office with an aura of mystery and infallibility to keep others away; they can make office into such a holy thing that any questions about it will seem irreverent and sacrilegious; they can act as if office was awarded to them as a personal possession; they can use office as power rather than as service; they can, finally, forget that office is in the service of the church, not of the office-holders. Offices in the church, like offices in secular society, can be abused.[19]

On the other hand, office can be a positive, upbuilding charism in the church. "Ecclesiastical office and ministry," writes Karl Rahner, "is charismatic in character, if we understand by charismatic, what is in contradistinction to what is purely institutional, administered by men, subject to calculation, expressible in laws and rules."[20] Office can, therefore, be a gift that delivers the church from the personal whims of the office-holders; it can also deliver the people of God from that cult of personality condemned in 1 Corinthians 3:4–9; it can prevent the privatizing of religion; it can even protect the people from doctrinal error. Finally, office, with its public responsibilities, can serve as a more or less objective standard for holding the ministers accountable to the people.[21]

Naturally office in the church is not static; nor is it an absolute. All offices in the church are the product of particular historical developments. As a result they are, like the church itself, always in need of reform and renewal. Recent experiments with team ministries are even now reforming the pastoral offices in the church. No doubt, as more lay men and women become "pastors" or pastoral coordinators these offices themselves will undergo change and reform. Sometimes office will enhance the ministry; at other times, it will hinder it. But it will always be closely linked with the credibility of the church. When the sign or image of the church as institution suffers, its offices and office-holders suffer with it. If office is to remain a true service (*diakonia*) to the church it will constantly need to be reevaluated and redefined as a service to the people of God. An office that serves the people in one century may not do so in the next.

Ministers Re-creating the Church

Since the Council of Trent and since Vatican I's definition of papal infallibility, many Catholics have assumed that the structure of the church was permanent and unalterable. The assumption was that the pyramid structure was of divine institution. Like the very dogmas of the church its external form, it seemed, was divinely revealed. Since many Catholics are not well versed in church history, they may not be aware of the long process of the historical and ambiguous development in the external structures of the church.

If, in this postconciliar period, we place more emphasis on the charismatic nature of the church and its baptismal ministries, then we can see the church always in process of being built up. In responding to the Spirit, each minister is, in effect, a partner in building the church anew.

The ministers are re-creating the church. Leonardo Boff sees base communities as "reinventing the church." Whether ministers reinvent or re-create the church they are, in Pauline fashion, always building up the body of Christ.

If we highlight the charismatic structure of the church, we realize "that each individual has his or her place in the community, a place that is determined by the individual's charism; *it also means that each one co-constitutes the church.*"[22] In other words, the church in its external form is not a divine given, but is subject to the ongoing decisions of its ministers. The ministers themselves, by investing their charism and energy in their part of the church, will in the process re-create and reshape the church in their own time and place.

Many ministers may feel that the pyramid structure of the church still weighs heavily upon their creativity. Each minister, however, is free to decide what part of the church is life-giving and what part is death-dealing. The ministers who conscientiously recreate the church will nurture and breathe life into those parts of the church that are coming to birth. Every minister is a spiritual "midwife" for new life in the church.

Many ministering women in the church have already decided not to invest their charisms in the patriarchy of the church. Thus they do not support this "death-dealing" part of the church. The missionaries in the third world do not invest their charisms in the perpetuation of a European or Roman model of church in Latin America. For them it is not a life-giving model. In the process they are deciding what parts of the church will live and what parts will be given reverent burial.

Reception in the Church

The actual nonreception of patriarchy by today's women ministers leads us to the ecclesiological principle of reception and nonreception in the church. We are familiar with the rejection of organ transplants in modern surgery, the process whereby the human body tends to reject bodies that are foreign to its life. The human body does not "receive" organisms that are not life-giving. The human body lives on the principle of reception and nonreception. It "senses" some organisms as life-giving and others as death-dealing.

Since the church is defined as the body of Christ, theologians like Cardinal Newman have applied the same principle of reception and nonreception to the body of the church. Yves Congar defines "reception" as "the process by means of which a church (body) truly takes over as its own a resolution that it did not originate in regard to itself and acknowledges the measure it promulgates as a rule applicable to its own life."[23] The principle of reception applies both to doctrine and to discipline and practice in the church. With respect to doctrine, the teachings of some ecumenical councils, like that of Nicaea, were "received" into the church only after many years of contention.

With respect to discipline, only fifty-nine of the seventy canons of the Fourth Lateran Council were received into the Code of Canon Law of 1917. The remaining canons were simply not received by the assembled bishops. After the definition of papal infallibility (1870), Pius IX anxiously awaited the promulgation of the dogma in the particular dioceses throughout the Catholic world. The actual proclamation of the dogma meant that it had been "received" into the church.

Just as the church can receive doctrines and laws into its faith and practice so also it can refuse, or not receive, other doctrines and laws. When this happens we have a case of nonreception. For example, the church today does not receive the pope's right to depose monarchs even though the church had in fact accepted that practice for many centuries. In 1563 the Council of Trent enacted the *Tametsi* decree. It was supposed to deal with the validity of clandestine marriages. But the decree was never received by wide areas of the church, including entire nations. The decree, especially in the manner of its promulgation, just had too many shortcomings.

In 1960 Pope John XXIII in his constitution *Veterum Sapientia* prescribed the use of Latin in instructing the seminarians throughout the Catholic world. His constitution, almost immediately, became a case of nonreception. At some future time, the church may conclude that Pope Paul VI's encyclical on birth control (1968) is another example of nonreception. Naturally, nonreception is much more serious in doctrine than in the laws of ecclesiastical discipline.

Reception or nonreception does not create truth. Only God or the Truth can do that. Reception of a truth into the faith-consciousness of the church merely confirms that what has been proclaimed is in fact true.[24] Thus reception or nonreception of Pope Paul VI's encyclical on birth control is an important sign indicating whether Paul VI was correct or not. We do not take an opinion poll to *find* the truth to be proclaimed. But we pay attention to the people's sense of faith to see if the truth proclaimed is, in fact, received as true.

If we emphasize obedience rather than faith, the church as society rather than as living body, then we could conclude that examples of nonreception are merely forms of disobedience or instances of pride and selfishness on the part of the sinful members of the church. But Vatican II encouraged us to see the church also as a body with a "supernatural sense of faith." The Dogmatic Constitution on the Church, recalling a favorite theme of Cardinal Newman, teaches that the body of the faithful cannot err in matters of belief. The people of God exercise this sense of faith (*sensum fidei*) when they manifest a universal consent in matters of faith and morals.[25]

If this sense of faith as an instinctive sensitivity and discrimination is valid for reception of doctrines and practices into the body of the church, then that same sense of faith is also valid for nonreception. As already noted, if we see the church in a societal or militaristic model, then we arrive at unanimity through obedience. But if we see the universal church as a communion of churches, then we can arrive at unanimity at least in part through reception or nonreception. "It is certain," writes Congar, "that this second conception [communion of churches] was the one that prevailed effectively during the first thousand years of Christianity whereas the other one [obedience] dominated in the West between the eleventh-century reformation and Vatican II."[26]

Since Vatican II the church has moved away from the image of church as society, or *acies ordinata* (an army drawn up in battle array), which often overemphasized obedience to the detriment of faith and charity. It has recovered other images such as the building of God, the body of Christ, a tract of land to be cultivated, and the people of God. Now the way is also open for the ministers of the church to recover the ecclesiological principle of reception and nonreception. In other words, the ministers will often find themselves in a situation in the church where the best faith response is simply nonreception. Of course, ministers need to invoke the principle of nonreception in a spirit of fasting, discernment, and prayer for the Spirit's guidance to deliver themselves from the ever-present dangers of pride and individualism.

In the history of the church it is often the case that what *appears* to be illegitimate eventually becomes legitimate:

> Against the background of the existing church order, then, new and sometimes urgently required alternative possibilities are often only to be seen through the medium of what is bound to be regarded as at least temporarily illegal. This is not a new phenomenon in the Church — it has always been the case. In the early and high Middle Ages, when scholasticism was still very free, ... this temporary illegality was even raised to the status of a theological principle in the theory of the *non acceptatio legis* or the rejection of the law from above by opposition at the base.[27]

New ministers who see themselves as re-creating the church are constantly involved in a process of reception and nonreception. They will invest their charisms and their energy in those parts of the church that they receive and not invest themselves in the parts they do not receive.

Reception and nonreception is an ongoing process in the pastoral practice of the church. For example, in 1950, during Pius XII's very unecumenical pontificate, an old pastor was widely known as an ecumenical priest. While the official church firmly prohibited ecumenical cooperation, this visionary pastor joined the local ministerial association and other Protestant organizations. He labored incessantly with fellow ministers for the good of his community. Much of what he was doing was considered illegal in the eyes of the Catholic Church. In his pastoral practice, however, this pastor simply did not receive the Roman prohibitions. With his ecumenical ministry he created a local ecumenical church in his city ten years before the Second Vatican Council. With Vatican II's Decree on Ecumenism his "illegal" activity suddenly became legal. In this way he reinvented and re-created the local church in his own city. He did it by quietly invoking the principle of nonreception.

Ministering in the Local Church

Many theologians in the last twenty years have come to the conclusion that Vatican II did not deal adequately with sex, ministry, authority, and the local church.[28] The tensions in these four areas in the last twenty-five years reveal that part of the council's agenda was left unfinished or that it did not respond theologically or pastorally to the signs of the times. Much of the turmoil in the church since Vatican II stems from the incompleteness of the council in these areas.

Recently, there have been many efforts to deal creatively with the council's "unfinished agenda" in regard to the local church. The urgency of developing a theology of the local church can be seen from the seriousness with which theologians address this topic today. In 1981 the Catholic Theological Society of America devoted an entire convention to the theme: "The Local Church." Other theologians have spent considerable time and energy developing a theology of the local church.[29]

We have seen that Vatican II's Dogmatic Constitution on the Church makes only a brief reference to the local church known as the parish. In chapter 3 it states:

This Church of Christ is truly present in all legitimate local congregations which, united with their pastors, are themselves called churches in the New Testament.... In any community existing around an altar, under the sacred ministry of the bishop, there is manifested a symbol of that charity and "unity of the Mystical Body, without which there can be no salvation." In these communities, though frequently small and poor, or living far from any other, Christ is present.[30]

But even as we quote Vatican II we need to own the historical fact that the council simply did not give us a precise definition of the local church. Joseph Komonchak summarizes Vatican II's inconsistency:

Vatican II was not consistent in its use of the terms "local" and "particular" church. "Particular church" appears more often and usually designates a diocese, although it is also used to refer to groupings of churches into "rites" (OE 2–4). "Local church" is used of dioceses (AG 19, 27) and of patriarchal churches (LG 23); but "local congregations" gathered for the Eucharist are also said to be "churches" (LG 26, 28). In one passage, "particular" and "local" are both used, apparently without distinction, to refer to dioceses in the Eastern rites (UR 14).[31]

Theologians continue to reflect on Vatican II's use of the words "local" and "particular." When all the discussion is finished, however, it seems that neither "local" nor "particular" refer either to the parish or to base communities.

In canon 515 of the new Code of Canon Law "particular church" refers to the diocese. This canon, in defining the parish, reveals a shift from the institutional to a more personalistic approach with a new emphasis on community: "A parish is a definite community of the Christian faithful established on a stable basis within a particular church; the pastoral care of the parish is entrusted to a pastor as its own shepherd under the authority of the diocesan bishop." Naturally, saying the parish is a "definite community" doesn't make it so.

For our purpose, then, we need to explore the ecclesiology of smaller church units such as the parish and the base communities. We need to find out how these smaller units will shape the ministries. However, before we can speak of a theology of parish or base community we need to reflect for a moment on the meaning of community as such. The word "community" is often used rather loosely and with different meanings. Like motherhood and apple pie, everybody is for it. But few know how to bring it about. Since, according to the new code, community is constitutive of the parish and therefore, presumably, of the "local" church, we need a more precise understanding of its meaning.

Community has one meaning in sociology and another in theology. These two meanings, far from contradicting each other, are very closely related. From the viewpoint of sociology it is important to distinguish community from society:

In modern sociology it has become commonplace to contrast two types of social relationship: a formally organized or structured society, and an informal or interpersonal community. The two types are

117

often referred to by their German names, *Gesellschaft* (society) and *Gemeinschaft* (community). *Gesellschaft*... is a human association characterized by formal organization, structures, and office, such as the secular state, the school, the hospital, the hotel. The organization is maintained by competent authority, which is normally institutionalized in the form of office. Such societies are governed by explicit rules, often written.[32]

Community, as *Gemeinschaft* and therefore as distinct from society, includes some of the qualities of "primary groups" such as: "face-to-face association; the unspecialized character of that association; relative permanence; the small number of persons involved; the relative intimacy among the participants."[33] While these qualities help us to get a better grasp on "community," they still do not provide a sufficient sociological base for local church.

As a primary group, such as a family, moves into community as a social form it is characterized by "a common orientation toward some significant aspect of life; some agreement about values; a commitment to common goals; opportunities for personal exchange; agreed-upon definitions of what is expected of membership in this group."[34]

Community, according to one sociologist, "is a social formation in which human beings are oriented by a sense of reciprocity and belonging."[35] It is important for all ministers to remember that community never exists in an ideal state; it is always mixed with other social formations including those of society. Even the best community will be imperfect in many ways. "The longing desire for the warm and understanding total community is the search for a good mother, which is bound to end in disappointment and heartbreak. There are no good mothers and fathers, there is only the divine mystery summoning and freeing us to grow up."[36]

Ministers need to learn to feel at home with ambiguity and contrary dynamics as they help build community, knowing full well that their task will never be finished:

Realistically, one can only struggle for a type of sociability in which love will be less difficult, and where power and participation will have better distribution. Community must be understood as a spirit to be created, as an inspiration to bend one's constant efforts to overcome barriers between persons and to generate a relationship of solidarity and reciprocity.... Human togetherness will always be charged with tensions between the "organizational impersonal" and the "intimate personal."[37]

In spite of frequent and overly romantic references to the parish as "family" or "parish community," we have to admit honestly that the modern parish is neither family nor community. For Joseph Fichter, sociologist, "The typical U.S. parish is a secondary association rather than a community. It is a relatively large social structure, in which impersonal, formal roles and relations have their place. The popular slogan may be that 'small is beautiful,' but the living reality is that 'large is functional.' "[38] Ironically, when parishes become small enough to begin building a real community, they are often closed or merged, due to insufficient financial support.

A noteworthy development since Vatican II with respect to local church is the grassroots or base community, spreading throughout Brazil and other parts of Latin America. The members of these communities come from the "base" of society, the poor lower classes, and from the "base" of the church, the laity. Leonardo Boff offers a descriptive definition:

> The base ecclesial community is generally made up of fifteen to twenty families. They get together once or twice a week to hear the word of God, to share their problems in common, and to solve those problems through the inspiration of the Gospel. They share their comments on the biblical passages, create their own prayers and decide as a group what their tasks should be.[39]

It is easy to understand that the base community becomes the fertile soil for the growth of many "lay" ministries.

These new forms of local "church" received the blessing of the bishops first during the Latin Bishops' conferences at Medellín (1968) and again at Puebla (1979). The rapid growth of base communities indicates that a creative response to the need for community is more likely to happen among the poorest of people. Their poverty produces the interdependence, solidarity, and reciprocity that build a sense of community. Since the movement toward this form of local church is so new and so conditioned by the Latin American culture, it would be risky for other countries to copy it without some modification. Presently, the base ecclesial community at best can be described as a hope-filled experiment.

The bishops at Puebla noted the following positive characteristics of base ecclesial communities:

> They contribute to a more personalized or familial style of evangelization, contrasted with the increasing coldness of modern society; they lead to a more profound understanding of the Word of God and participation in the Eucharist; they promote both self-examination as well as reflection on the social reality; and they

foster active commitment to the new commandment of love, to struggle for justice and to the construction of a new society. Also a great value... are their close links with the family, the world of workers, the neighborhood and the local community.... They have been successful in fostering vocations, have encouraged the emergence of new types of lay ministry and have developed a very effective style of catechesis for simple people, both young and adults.[40]

Observers of the development of base communities have also noted some dangers: Often the link with the authority of the larger church seems to be weak; there seems to be a tendency toward elitism or degeneration into self-sufficient sects; there is insufficient awareness that the church is also called into existence "from above" through the proclamation of the Gospel and from the initiative of the Lord. The bishops at Puebla felt it necessary to caution lay pastoral leaders against using their authority for partisan or ideological purposes.[41]

The base Christian communities, while promising, can hardly be seen as an answer to the problem of oversized parishes or to the priestless parishes in many parts of the world. Nor can they be seen as the final solution in terms of ecclesiology. However, they may very well be one of the three stages of an "emerging church." Lacking full eucharistic celebrations, they may be called "church" only by way of analogy. Tomas Gonzalez, who has worked with the base communities in the Philippines, concludes:

BCCs are best suited to environments where people are already living and working together as members of a community. While BCCs inspire and direct people's lives in these natural communities, BCCs alone cannot create such communities. Hence BCCs are more likely to flourish in small rural villages, but not in urban areas with no natural communities. Moreover, people in rural areas must solve their own problems, since government is far away.[42]

Perhaps the most significant contribution to the development of a theology of local church is found in the writings of Karl Rahner. From him we get the potential building blocks for a theology of a local, grassroots church. Using the parish as his point of departure, Rahner builds the local church around a two-part thesis. First, the parish is the local representative actualization of the church. To actualize itself, the parish needs to be in a place: "The Eucharist can be celebrated only by a community which is gathered in one and the same place.... All this means that the Church, in its innermost essence, is itself directed to a localized concretization."[43]

Second, the parish, according to Rahner, is the *primary* realization of the church as event. For Rahner the key elements of church are: (1) celebration of the full Eucharist, (2) parish as event, and (3) parish as place. Perhaps the most important element in Rahner's definition of parish is the word "event." This word highlights the Pauline notion that the community is always in process of becoming church. Naturally this process has a wide variety of stages of development. It is also subject to many diverse cultural and sociological forces. For this reason, following Vatican II's emphasis on baptism and the people of God, it makes more sense to view the church "from below." From this viewpoint we can apply to the local church principles that Rahner developed in his brilliant little book, *The Shape of the Church to Come*.

His first principle is that the church exists only by a consciously renewed free decision of faith on the part of individuals belonging to a particular congregation. His second principle states that "basic communities will emerge from below . . . through the call of the gospel and the message of the church coming out of the past."[44]

Rahner gets to the heart of his theology of a local church in the following definition:

A basic community has grown to more than a group of sympathizers, and more than a small association of a few Christians, and become a basic element of the church — a local church . . . only when it can really sustain the essential, basic functions of the church (organized proclamation of the Gospel, administration of the sacraments, Christian charity and so on) and can be taken for granted as the place of the constantly renewed Eucharistic celebration.[45]

To follow up and develop Rahner's principles, we may summarize the main ecclesial elements of a local church as follows: (1) the proclamation of the Gospel; (2) the baptized people's public response of "Amen"; (3) the people's faith or active believing; (4) the beginnings of community, in process of becoming more community; (5) the celebration of the sacraments; (6) Christian charity; (7) a constantly renewed eucharistic celebration; (8) ministers, including a eucharistic presider; (9) place; and finally (10) some visible communion, through faith, Word, and sacrament, with the diocesan and universal church.

If we understand "church" in a univocal sense, with one clear meaning, the assumption is that a particular Christian community must have all these basic ecclesial elements in place before it can truly be called church. A Christian community, for instance, that does not have a "constantly renewed eucharistic celebration" could not be called church. Since many parishes still have the ten elements noted above, they could be called "local church," even in a univocal sense. There are, however, other ways of understanding "church."

The evolution of a community to the point when it can truly be called a church can be a long and sometimes difficult process. Naturally such a process includes both sociological and theological dynamics working in a pluralist and rapidly changing culture. Rosemary Haughton has identified three stages of the "ecclesial evolution" of small groups that she calls: "the 'pre-church,' the 'emerging church' and the 'church in mission.' "[46] To qualify as "pre-church" a small group, however organized, must include prayer, study, and action. "A 'pre-church' becomes a 'church' at the moment at which it becomes consciously aware that its identity as a group finds its name, centre and meaning in Christ."[47] Between pre-church and church there may be a long period of "emerging church." During this period there has to be a development of a deep awareness of the church as necessarily in mission. For there can be no church apart from its mission. The forms of the local church's ministries will emerge more clearly when there is an awareness of this mission.

If an "emerging church" is to become a truly local church it must, according to Haughton, acquire at least the following four marks or characteristics: visibility, hospitality, inclusiveness, and attractiveness.[48] Through most of its history the Roman Catholic Church has insisted on its visible nature as opposed to an overly spiritualized, invisible church "of the soul." "Hospitality" simply recalls a virtue considered extremely important in the New Testament churches (1 Tm 3:2) and throughout the history of the monastic communities. "Inclusiveness" means that this church really believes in a Christ who offers salvation to *all* peoples. "Attractiveness" highlights the church as a sign and light among the nations. It recalls the ancient comment: "See how they love one another!"

If we understand "church" in an analogical, rather than an univocal sense, we can, with Leonardo Boff, accept different "ways of being church."[49] Church as analogy points toward significant similarities and resemblance in particulars while at the same time allowing room for significant differences. Analogy opens the way for base ecclesial communities, for "emerging church" and for other nonparish forms of church to be true local churches. T. Howland Sanks asks:

> How would an analogical imagination approach the theological issues raised by our experience of the *comunidades eclesiales de base*? First, if the prime analogate of being church is a community of disciples gathered in the name of Jesus — "Where two or three are gathered in my name, there I am also present" Mt 18:20 — then there would be no question of whether or not the base communities are truly "church." They clearly are, and they are analogues to other forms of church in historical experience.[50]

If we see the church as a living organism rather than as an organiza-tion, we should expect the church constantly to be in process of becoming and progressing through various forms. We should not be surprised, therefore, that the church is constantly in process of dying to some of its old forms so that new forms may come to life. In this context it is also not surprising that the base communities speak of the "reinvention of the church." Indeed, "the church is beginning to be born at the grassroots, beginning to be born at the heart of God's People."[51]

As new ministers invest their charisms in the upbuilding of the local church, they need to be sensitive to what is dying and what is being born or "reinvented." There's no sense in wasting precious time on the dying part of the church. Leonardo Boff gives us a good picture of that part of the church which he feels is passing away:

> The church, in the Latin West, has been thought of in terms of a Christ/church polarity, within a juridical vision. The relation-ships between Christ and the church are formulated on the model of the relationships of a society with its founder. Christ transmits all power to the Twelve, who transmit it to their successors, the bishops and the pope. The latter have been considered as the sole depositories of all responsibility, and have been seen as amass-ing for themselves all power in the church, in such wise that they are pictured as in confrontation with the community. Thus the ac-tual community is divided between ruler and governed, between celebrants and onlookers, between producers and consumers of sacraments. In a like systematization, the hierarchy constitutes the sole representative of the universal church and the particular church.[52]

Besides having a sense of what is dying, ministers need a new vision of what is being born. That vision begins with the inner conviction that the church was born not only from the death and resurrection of Christ, but also from the Holy Spirit on the day of Pentecost. In this new vision the reality of God's people is primary, the form of its organization and structure is secondary. This vision honors and reverences the presence of the risen Christ and the Holy Spirit within the baptized, priestly people. The hierarchy is serving "a reality it has not created but discovered, and within which it finds itself."[53] And the most real part of this "reality" is the awesome presence of the Spirit with her diverse gifts, always giving birth to new forms of church. The charism of those who preside over the local church does not consist in accumulating or absorbing these gifts but in integrating and coordinating them.

The shift in emphasis from the hierarchic pyramid to the grassroots people of God is clear enough in Vatican II's Dogmatic Constitution on the Church. It has become even clearer in the twenty-five years since the council. The universal church, however, still needs the praxis of the local church and perhaps of the base ecclesial communities to translate largely theoretical teaching into lived pastoral experience. For this reason the whole church needs a large number of baptismal ministers of all ages and sexes who will labor at the grassroots level to reinvent the local church. As was the case in the New Testament, there is no clear blueprint, no list of directions. But the building process must go forward with many risks, with many false and new starts. These ministers may not necessarily build base communities. But they may well learn from them. They may also learn from the ecclesial principles developed by theologians.

These ministering builders need to remain in contact, not only with the Spirit given to them at baptism, but also with the long tradition of the church that contains the "footprints" of the same Spirit. As old forms die, they leave a record of the believing people. Even though today's ministers cannot use those records as they are, they still breathe with the testimony of the faith of millions. North American Catholics especially need to be aware that the Spirit teaches us both through history and through new signs of the times. New ministers need to stand humbly before that history and receive its message so that it may indeed teach them how to prepare the way for the birth of a New Pentecost and a new church.

There will always be "weeds among the wheat" (Mt 13:30). But there are also many new sprouts of wheat that may grow into fruitful ministries. These need a healthy environment and careful cultivation. Then God will make them grow (1 Cor. 3:6).

CHAPTER SEVEN

The Sacrament of the Human

"Indeed, like clay in the hand of the potter, so are you in my hand, house of Israel" (Jer 18:6).

The long history of the Christian tradition remembers a whole series of dualist heresies. Even before the Christian era, Zoroastrianism, originating in Iran, the land of the Magi (in about 400 B.C.E.), had taught the dualist philosophy that there was a cosmic war between good and evil. It had a powerful influence on Judaism and later on Christianity, especially through its dualist teaching on demons and angels. The church was hardly launched in the second century when its ministers had to deal with Gnosticism. Believing in a dual world of good and evil, the Gnostics concluded that matter was so evil that Jesus could not possibly have become human. Two centuries later, during the time of Augustine, the church had to fight with the Manichees, who taught that there were two eternal principles: God, the cause of all good, and Matter, the cause of all evil. Their teaching was characterized by a profound pessimism about human nature. In the twelfth and thirteenth centuries the Catharists, with their Albigensian and Bogomil offshoots, spread throughout Italy and France. They too believed that the material world was created by an evil principle.

These dualist philosophies, which, in various degrees, infected the body of the church, attempted to explain the vexing problem of evil, a problem that had tested the faith of Job, Jeremiah, and the psalmist. These dualist "solutions" left little room for any goodness in the "merely" human.

THE SACRAMENT OF THE HUMAN

Parenthetically, we note that the dualist temptation continues to knock at our own door. We too try to simplify one of life's gnawing complexities — the problem of good and evil. We may say with the dualist: "The demon is out there; the angel is in here." In society and in the church we often fall victim to a dualist reduction: "Drugs are out there, in Colombia, not in here, in our own apartment; the vocation problem is out there, in those materialistic parents, not in here, in our own church laws and structures."

The church has rarely been free from the dualist tendencies that try to draw a sharp line between the spiritual and the material, between the sacred and the profane. To some extent the church is often influenced by dualist strains in secular society. Novelists like Hermann Hesse teach that most of life is a struggle between good and evil. The success of the cowboy tales of America's own West reflects the dualist theory that there is a clear distinction between the white hats, "the Good Guys" and the black hats, "the Bad Guys." Carl Jung writes about the shadow or dark side of the human personality, which is "as inevitably a part of us as Mr. Hyde was a part of Dr. Jekyll."[1] Thus both "Good Guys" and "Bad Guys" touch a nerve within all of us.

In mythology, in novels, and in movies there is a constant attempt to exploit the tensions between the good and the evil. For dramatic effect the boundaries between good and evil have to be clearly drawn. The drama "out there" reflects every person's inner struggle, which even Paul admits in his own life (Rom 7:14). Because of this continuing inner tension and the "outward drama" between good and evil, the church does not always succeed in keeping a unity between the spiritual and the material, the sacred and the secular. As a society, the church likes to keep neat boundaries in place, putting the clergy on the side of the sacred and the laity on the side of the secular.

Besides absorbing some of these dualist negations of the human, the church in the past was also infected by the intense pessimism of the Jansenists in the seventeenth century. Centered at Port-Royal in France, they taught that it was not possible for humans to keep some of the commandments and that human life, "if it can be called such," is totally bad. "From the moment of its origin," writes the founder, Bishop Jansen, "the human race bears the full burden of its condemnation. . . . From the womb does not the child lie in impenetrable darkness? . . . already guilty of a crime, and incapable of virtue. . . . Who can describe the yoke that weighs on the sons of Adam?"[2] The dualist and Jansenist heresies disvalue the human because they simply cannot really accept the "scandal" of the incarnation, that God became human.

The Sacred and the Secular

Over the centuries organized religions have tried to "locate" the holy in a particular place, such as a church or sanctuary, and in a particular slot of time, such as Sunday. Yet we know by our faith that the all-holy God transcends both place and time. It is impossible to reduce the Holy to an object and then isolate or circumscribe it in a specific place or time. The Holy One created the material as well as the spiritual. *Both* are finite reflections of an infinite holiness, the artwork of an all-holy Artist. God is simple, having no parts. The Holy One, therefore, is not split up into the holy and unholy. Neither is the handiwork of the Holy One's creation.

As earthbound bodily creatures, however, we need to symbolize the Holy in finite, visible, and concrete ways. Thus we need a holy place and a holy time. But neither the place nor the time ever succeeds in actually locating or capturing the holy. Churches, shrines, and flags can never do anything more than *symbolize* the sacred. They are poor, fragile, and time-conditioned symbols. Their holiness remains primarily in the faith of the beholder. Their meaning can become very ambiguous when culture or belief systems change. When these earthly symbols are endowed with objective holiness, they can imply that everything outside the symbol is *un*holy: Sunday is holy, Monday is not; church is holy, K-Mart is not; soul is holy, body is not; priest is holy, layperson is not. "Locating" the Holy runs the risk of constructing a worldview based on the dualism of sacred/secular, supernatural/natural, and spiritual/material.

This dualist distinction then begins to link ministry to the sanctuary of the sacred as opposed to the world of the secular; to the soul as opposed to the body; to the supernatural as opposed to the natural; to the spiritual as opposed to the human. It creates a schizoid spirituality and anthropology. The "merely" human, as opposed to the spiritual, is then associated with weakness and sinfulness. In the Christian tradition we have not been free from the Stoic tendency to downgrade the human in order to upgrade the spiritual. In short, Christian ministry in the minds of many has often been removed from the arena of the human, the natural, and the material. In practice this has led to an overspiritualization of the ministry and an implicit denial of the incarnation and the full humanity of Jesus.

As a result, ministry seems to flow from Christ's divinity, not from his humanity. It is not far removed from the ancient heresies of Docetism and Monophysitism. It is not unusual to hear Catholic laity say: "We take care of the material things so Father can take care of the spiritual." In Catholic parishes the people who distribute the Eucharist in the sanctuary are called ministers. The men of the St. Vincent de Paul Society who feed the hungry in the "secular" world are not called ministers. Lectors, who serve in the holy sanctuary, are called ministers, but the members of the

Legion of Mary are not. Jesus, on the other hand, ministered in the streets, not in the Temple. He served as lector once, but mostly he ministered in the "secular" world of lepers, lawyers, fishermen, Samaritans, outcasts, prostitutes, and tax collectors.

Original Sin

Since Augustine, the churches have taught the bad news of the stain of original sin and its harmful effects upon human nature. Already during preparation for first communion children learned that they had inherited the effects of Adam and Eve's sin. They learned that "human nature" was deeply flawed. Often they were more disposed to think of themselves as under the shadow of evil than under the bright light of grace.

Insofar as Catholics today have an instinct for ministry, they often feel its purpose is to rescue fallen human nature and restore it to the arena of the holy. Some parents still rush their newly-born baby to the waters of baptism to rescue the baby's soul from the grasp of the evil one.

Much of history is indeed a witness to bad news, to the footprints of evil. Diseases, plagues, murders, earthquakes, wars, and the horrors of Auschwitz have created a pessimism with respect to the human condition. Even today we humans often feel weak, helpless, and pessimistic before powerful evil forces like drugs, crime, alcoholism, terrorism, environmental pollution, and moral corruption in business and government. We can hardly watch the evening news and then call up our friends and say: "Human nature is basically good."

Surrounded by human failures, it's not easy for Christians to continue to believe that "where sin increased, grace abounded all the more" (Rom 5:20). Rampant evil in our own world can produce a pessimism and mistrust with regard to the "merely" human. The person at our door is either a crook or a sales agent. And nowadays we're not sure there's a difference. All this means that it's tough for the baptized to see the place of the human in their ministry. For many, moving toward the holy and toward ministry has to mean moving away from the merely human. It means a flight into the sanitized haven of the spiritual. In view of the incarnation, however, ministry could mean the exact opposite.

The Incarnation Applied to Ministry

In spite of the dualist tendencies noted above, we Catholics, paradoxically, are quite comfortable with material things such as bread, wine, water, and oil as signs of the holy. Quite correctly we call these material things "sacraments." We have no problem believing that the all-holy

God who created these materials in the first place uses them as vehicles for the holy. They are in fact holy, even before they are used in the sacraments. It is true that sometimes these material things, like human nature itself, may be flawed and defective. However, even if the water used at baptism is dirty, it is, nevertheless, a holy sacrament for holy grace.

Besides these material things that become holy sacraments, the Catholic tradition uses numerous sacramentals such as blessed ashes, candles, medals, statues, pictures, palm branches, rosaries, etc. Furthermore, the church does not hesitate to bless cars, houses, animals, stables, Easter eggs, and sausage. This custom highlights the instinct of faith that all material things can in fact be placed in the service of God's holy creation. Ministering in and through these material things helps us remember the holiness of God's original creation. It also helps us overcome the dualism between the sacred and the secular.

Christian ministry always has to witness to the incarnation, which teaches:

> The gulf between heaven and earth, between God and man, between the supernatural and the natural, between the sacred and the secular . . . has once and for all been overcome so that now we can glimpse heaven on earth, God in man, the supernatural in the natural, and the sacred amidst the secular. . . . In the light of the Incarnation it must also be said that there is nothing here on earth which is exclusively profane for those who have eyes to see.[3]

Once the churches "have eyes to see" and really *believe* in the incarnation there will be less tendency to define either clergy or laity in separate categories by *place*. The laity cannot be defined as a class belonging *in* the "unholy" world; the clergy cannot be defined as a class belonging *in* the "holy" sacred. If, in Christ, God has eliminated the distinction between the sacred and the secular, it makes no sense to define the ministries in terms of a distinction that no longer exists. The church, including all its ministers, interpenetrates the world or it does not exist. Both "clergy" and "laity" need to be defined on an individual basis in terms of their ministering *functions*. Their *place* as such, being neither more nor less sacred in the incarnate Christ, contributes nothing to their definition. To give but one example: thousands of priests teach every day in colleges and universities, which, of course, are very much in the secular "world." Thousands more of the laity teach in the same institutions. Both laity and priests define themselves by their functions as *teachers*. The layperson teaching mathematics will be evaluated as a teacher. The priest teaching history will also be evaluated as a teacher. The church, through its diverse ministries, however ordained, exists in the secular, workaday world or there is no church. Catholics do not believe in an invisible church of "the soul" or of "the sacred."

For this reason it makes no sense to speak about "lay" ministry or "clergy" ministry. Both terms reflect castes that, in Christ, no longer exist. These labels are remnants of the days when the church was viewed primarily through the model of a class society and a dualist worldview. Such labels, however, do not fit the Vatican II models such as building of God, people of God, or body of Christ. Once both "laity" and "clergy" live the incarnation and then internalize the new models of church and ministry, they will reverently archive these contrast labels in the treasury of tradition.

All Christian ministry is a living sign of the enfleshment of the Holy One and to the reconciliation of the sacred and the secular, of the spiritual and the material. Christ, who hallowed the material world by his partnership with it, now, through his ministers, continues to overcome the distinction between the spiritual and the material. Thus the minister who ministers in Christ's name is also called to hallow the material world by becoming a partner with it. Through the power of Christ, ministers cleanse or exorcise the world/church of the trauma and contamination it has suffered from evil and restore it to its original wholeness. Ministry happens not only in the church but especially along the wayside, *in the world*, where the human condition lies beaten and wounded by sin, rape, drugs, alcoholism, and terrorism.

As part of our faith in the incarnation we believe that in Jesus Christ the all-holy God unconditionally and lovingly embraced the human condition in its "flawed" state. "The reality of Jesus Christ is that God in person is actively present in the flesh. God in person is the Subject of a real human being and acting. And just because God is the Subject of it, this being and acting are real. They are a genuinely and truly human being and acting."[4]

It should be clear now that by incarnation we do not mean the birth of Jesus as celebrated at Christmas. Incarnation, as used here, includes the earthly ministry of Jesus, especially his suffering and death. As we see in Paul, reflection on the incarnation begins with the death and resurrection of Jesus, not with his birth. "The nativity as such," explains Gerald O'Collins, "neither saves us nor can it serve as the baseline for our further reflection. . . . Baptism draws believers into the crucifixion and gives them promise of resurrection (Rom 6, 3–5). We are not baptized 'into the incarnation.' "[5] The mystery of the incarnation is not a transient episode, but "is an on-going reality which is continually taking place in different degrees all around us if we have the eyes of Christian faith to recognize it."[6]

The God of the Christians is now victoriously present in human creation. The Holy One is bigger than the Temple or the church. There are no more sacred shrines that "locate" the holy. The enfleshment of God in Christ means that the "merely" human is holy again and in process of becoming more so. Whatever effects sin has upon the human, it cannot destroy what God originally created holy. It is indeed true that human nature is still wounded and burdened by the cross of evil. It still lies beaten along the wayside. The full recovery of the human condition, however, is assured because of the power of the resurrection and the promised coming of Christ in fullness. The Christian ministers believe this so strongly that their eyes are radiant with hope and optimism. Thus baptized ministers, while clinging to an earthy realism, overcome the world's pessimism and its simplistic dualism.

In relating ministry to the incarnation we need to ask whether ministry is an extension of Christ's divinity, of his humanity, or both. Because of the long history of the overemphasis on the divinity of Christ, it is difficult for many Catholics to really include the humanity of Christ in their definition of Christian ministry. To see humanity as truly sacramental we need first to see the humanity of Christ as sacramental and salvific. A Christology without duality sees God's presence in the whole man, Jesus Christ. His saving activity lies not in the fact that a divine nature bears a human nature, but in the human nature, and above all, in the human person himself.[7]

Because of Christ's continuing presence in the humanity of his baptized people, he can and does renew his holy creation through their human ministry. "Precisely because everything is his creation, he reveals himself not beside the world, not by interventions exclusive of his creatures, but through bringing this creation to fulfillment. . . . He makes himself known not exclusively or primarily in ways of religiosity, but in ways of humanity."[8]

To this day we still have a problem in bringing the divine and the human together into one because the human still tends to get lost in the divine. Ministers still need to internalize the truth that the divine presence that Jesus brought into the world "goes on forever in the hearts of his people through the Holy Spirit."[9] We know from Scripture that the historical Jesus had a deep love "for the sights and sounds, the flowers and fields, the actual natural setting which was his. . . . His sensitivity to nature as shown in allusions in his teaching, as illustrated in his parables, is deeply rooted in the material."[10]

Those who find it hard to accept the holiness of the human condition could well pray and reflect on the Song of Songs: "Now let your breasts be like clusters of the vine and the fragrance of your breath like apples, and your mouth like an excellent wine" (7:9–10). This Word of God is enthroned in the sanctuary of our churches next to the tabernacle. It is carried with great reverence in procession to begin the eucharistic celebration. This same Word contains the beautifully poetic and very sensual descriptions of human love. The Song of Songs will forever proclaim that God has blessed human loving as part of holy creation.

The ministers who honor the human, even as flawed, need to saturate themselves with the basic and very human biblical images:

> The images which convey much more adequately the heart of the biblical message are those of the lover and his beloved, the husband and wife, the father and his children, the shepherd who cares for his sheep, or the ruler whose concern is not just to impose his will on his subjects but to provide for them and their needs in such a way that they find happiness, peace, safety (*shalom* is the inclusive untranslatable Hebrew word) under his just and sovereign rule of love.[11]

With a renewed emphasis on the humanity of Jesus Christ it should be easier for ministers to see their ministry as flowing not merely from the divinity of Christ but from a unity, the harmony, of both the human and the divine in one person. It should be easier to avoid the dualism of the sacred and the secular. Especially, ministers would avoid relegating the baptized laity to the arena of the secular as is done in Vatican II's Dogmatic Constitution on the Church. Here the laity are defined by place as belonging to the secular world: "A secular quality is proper and special to laymen.... [They] seek the Kingdom of God by engaging in temporal affairs."[12] Paul did better. He called the baptized laity "the holy ones" and "temples of the Holy Spirit."

In view of the incarnation we need to state unambiguously that "the church mediates the divine in and through the human so that the more human the church is in the spirit of its founder Jesus Christ, the more obvious will its divine origin become."[13] For this reason, all Christian ministers, in their humanity, are called to be sacraments of the divine.

The Human Qualities for Ministry

In view of all the above, ministers could well see themselves as restoring God's holy creation or as being co-creators with God. This is the first and most fundamental Christian vocation. The creation story in Genesis provides a basic orientation to all ministry:

> The scripture writer wants us to know very dramatically in the Adam and Eve story that God created us to be at one with creation, to work as co-creators in harmony with God and nature.... The first creation is unfinished. Creation continues and is an on-going

process. Thus we accept our place as co-creators called to a continuing conversation with God and to announce God's love to the world.[14]

To create is to be an artist. The artist's qualities, since they are deeply human, can also serve as preparation for the ministry of co-creation. Ministers, like the artist, need to develop the power to wonder, to be amazed — the power to be open to the beyond.[15] They also need a deep reverence for God's creation. It is "holy ground." Moreover, they need to develop their capacity to stand still and allow creation to speak its message to them. Before they begin to restore creation, they need first to be in awe of its beauty, to feel its pulse and hear its song.

If ministers are to become part of God's creative word, they need to retain a capacity for astonishment. What is true of a good theologian is true of good ministers. Karl Barth explains:

A quite specific astonishment stands at the beginning of every theological perception, inquiry and thought, in fact at the root of every theological word. This astonishment is indispensable if theology is to exist and be perpetually renewed as a modest, free, critical, and happy science. If such astonishment is lacking, the whole enterprise of even the best theologian would canker at the roots.[16]

If ministers are going to maintain an attitude of astonishment, they have to be disposed to risk themselves and their preconceived ideas. They have to be willing to die to the dogmatism of the ready answer. To become a partner in the sacrament of co-creation is to become a brush in the hand of the Master Artist. It is to become a partner with the unveiling of Mystery.

To minister to creation requires a vulnerability to persons and things. It includes Martin Buber's I/Thou relationship. It allows the others to speak their truth openly. It requires a reverent engagement with the others at their highest level of becoming. In view of the superabundance of grace (Rom 5:20), the minister has high rather than low expectations of others.

Ministry, insofar as it is part of a truly human process, requires a constant disposition to true dialogue. It means that ministers are dialogical persons who are disposed to be changed by the thing or the person with whom they are in dialogue. To be truly dialogic means to die to our own opinions and judgments so that our person becomes a hospitable place, welcoming the strangers, including material creation, into our lives on their own terms.

The ministers who have a reverence for the holiness of the human will see reality not as something to be controlled or manipulated, but as a mystery to be under. Christian ministers never really know what effects their words, actions, or the sacrament of their presence will have. All relationships are mystery and ministry is par excellence a relationship of mystery.

Transitions in Ministry

It is hardly news that in the last twenty-five years many ministers in the church have been in transition. We have seen many sociological studies citing the data of men leaving the priesthood and sisters and brothers leaving religious life. This phenomenon is not exactly new in the church. Since Vatican II, however, we have experienced a rapid growth in the rate of the exodus.

The causes are very complex. They include constantly changing conditions both in the culture and in the church. In the West we live in a highly mobile society. Affluence is conducive to upward mobility. The result is frequent change of job and career. Today we are used to second, third, and even fourth careers.

Besides, the inventions of yesterday, requiring specialized expertise, are obsolete tomorrow. The blacksmith, iceman, and milkman have all moved into new careers. With the help of advances in medicine we enjoy longer lives. So our creativity may not be sufficiently challenged by one job or one career. The search for second and third careers is no longer a sign of insecurity or instability, but a quest for fulfillment through the development of all our God-given gifts.

Transitions to new ministries can be the result of passing through the various stages in life's journey. Roy Lewis speaks of "The Thirties Transition," "Mid-life Transition," and "Retirement." He notes that "retirement is a great career."[17] Transition has become the norm, not the exception.

Whatever the cause, the movement of priests and religious from one form of ministry to another prompts theological reflection regarding this relatively new phenomenon of transitions in ministry. What do the Scriptures and the experience of tradition have to say about this growing trend in the Christian churches?

As we know from the Holy Saturday baptismal service, the Old Testament theme of the Exodus was a powerful symbol that helped the Israelites interpret their relationship with God. Through their Exodus they arrived at the profound understanding that their God went with them on their journey through their many transitions. The God of the Hebrews was not confined to a place. God's presence during this exodus was symbolized by a pillar of cloud by day, and a pillar of fire by night. "And so it was for every stage of their journey" (Ex 40:38). Yahweh's presence through these symbols sustained the Israelites through their transitions during an otherwise painful and lonely pilgrimage. This experience was so powerful as a saving event that the prophets appealed to this Exodus event to recall Yahweh's people back to fidelity to the Covenant.

The transition from Egypt through the Red Sea and through the desert became a paradigm of death-to-life themes. The condition for new life was always death to an old life. Yahweh was not bound to the old, but was waiting with open arms on the other side, the side of the new. After being with the Israelites on their journey, Yahweh was there to welcome them on the other side of the sea and again on the other side of the desert.

Perhaps it is not out of place, parenthetically, to recall the Christian symbolism of the guardian angel. Certainly this symbol of God's presence, so powerful in its meaning, teaches us that God goes with us as we journey from one place to the next and from one ministry to the next. The all-provident God runs before us to prepare our way even as God parted the Red Sea before the Israelites.

Perhaps the most significant Old Testament example of transition comes to us with Abra(ha)m: "The Lord said to Abram: 'Go forth from the land of your kinsfolk and from your father's house to a land that I will show you. . . .' Abram was seventy-five years old when he left Haran. . . . Then Abram journeyed on by stages to the Negeb" (Gn 12: 1, 4, 9). Both the Exodus and Abram's departure from Haran are recalled by Stephen in his famous discourse to the Jews (Acts 7:2). It is quite plain that these events were significant in the catechesis of the early church. Abraham was blessed and became the father of many nations because he left his native place to go where Yahweh directed him. He had faith that God was not confined to his home in Haran but would go with him in his transition, even at seventy-five years of age.

The prophets are also examples of transition becoming an occasion of repentance, conversion, and salvation for whole peoples. Thus we see that Amos, the shepherd, is called from his native Tekoa to become a prophet and preach in the northern kingdom of Israel. His prophetic word was efficacious in the northern kingdom; but one wonders what would have happened if Amos had clung to his vocation as a shepherd in the wilderness of Tekoa.

Ezekiel was a priest during the Jews' captivity in Babylonia (597 B.C.E.). Far removed from the Temple in Jerusalem, he could no longer offer the sacrifices expected of priests. He had nothing to do in that foreign land. So Yahweh changed his vocation from priest to prophet and asked him to preach to his fellow Jews living at Telabib (Ez 1–3). Ezekiel was reluctant to begin a new career. Eventually, he made the transition and proclaimed Yahweh's words of comfort to the Jews who, exiled from their homeland, were on the edge of despair.

Jonah too received a message from the Lord: " 'Set out for the great city of Nineveh, and announce to it the message that I will tell you.' So Jonah made ready and went to Nineveh, according to the Lord's bidding" (Jon 3:2–3). We know from the rest of the story that Nineveh heard Jonah's message and repented. His prophetic word became salvation for the Ninevites because he, even if grudgingly, made the sacrifice of leaving his native land. The prophets seem to confirm that salvation becomes available to God's people on the condition that God's servant has the faith to risk an exodus from the familiar to the mysterious unknown.

The New Testament, especially Paul's first letter to the Corinthians, indicates that ministers' lives are not permanently tied to one charism. When a particular charism no longer builds up the church it may not be imposed upon the community (1 Cor 14:28). It is clear that the Spirit gives other gifts to be offered for the upbuilding of the church within the same lifetime. We cannot assume that a minister's gifts will fulfill their potential for the church in only one form of ministry. Those who believe in the miraculous explosion of the Spirit at Pentecost can hardly limit the Spirit's activity to one gift per person for life.

From all this it follows that a particular minister may feel compelled to move into a new ministry that responds to new needs and has a greater capacity to build up the church. The true minister, like a faithful servant, is always listening for the new calls or "vocations" coming from the Spirit. Jealous lover that she is, the Spirit may call in new ways as life's journey goes through its various forms of exodus.

Without a doubt the status of a neatly-defined church position can become a this-worldly security that is an obstacle to spiritual growth both for the ministers and for the church. It can become a comfortable Haran from which the ministers never want to depart. Modern Ninevehs may never hear the saving Word if ministers are too afraid to embark on an exodus from their ecclesial nests. New life in the ministry is possible only for the price of a continuous dying to the comforts of the old. Christian ministers lovingly embrace the various deaths along their journey, firmly believing there is new life on the road ahead. Thus they take the sting out of their final death because they have learned to freely and lovingly embrace the various deaths along the way.

Psychologists like Erik Erikson have taught us that the price of growth to maturity is the painful passage through the six stages from infancy to maturity. Each stage presents a crisis that we must negotiate successfully before being admitted to the next stage. "Crisis," writes Erikson, "is used here in a developmental sense to connote not a threat of catastrophe, but a turning point, a crucial period of increased vulnerability and heightened potential, and therefore, the ontogenetic source of generational strength and maladjustment."[18] There is no escape. Failure to negotiate an earlier stage with its own death means the door is closed to a later, more mature stage of life.

With the help of Gail Sheehy's two bestsellers, *Passages* and *Pathfinders*, we are becoming more aware of the adult stages of growth. Based on Daniel Levinson's classic work, *The Seasons of a Man's Life*, Sheehy's works have sensitized most of us to the old truth, that all of life, if it is to be real life, is transition. As noted earlier, moving and changing jobs are no longer considered signs of immaturity and an unstable temperament. Living as we do in the era of future shock, mobility is the norm, not the exception. In the Middle Ages it was normal that the son of the shoe cobbler would himself be a cobbler. The stability of European society depended on such continuity of skill and profession. Nowadays society does not depend on such father-son continuity for its stability. In fact, modern society expects the opposite. We are prepared to accept the obsolescence of the father's trade by the time the son reaches his vocational decision.

The process of transition to a new vocation and ministry has three stages: (1) endings, (2) neutral zone, and (3) beginnings.[19] Beginning, as we do, with endings, we might reflect with T. S. Eliot:

> What we call the beginning is often the end
> And to make an end is to make a beginning.
> The end is where we start from.[20]

Each of these three stages has its specific tasks. Endings require disengagement, disidentification, including the loss, momentarily at least, of our own self-definition, and a disenchantment or the realization that a significant part of our old reality was in our head and not "out there." Then we go through a phase of disorientation, a time of confusion and emptiness. Between the old something and the new something is a time of nothing. Naturally, this time of ending needs to be owned, perhaps through public celebration. Irish wakes, graduation, bachelor and retirement parties celebrate the emotional experience of endings.

The second stage, the neutral zone, requires surrender to the sense of emptiness. This emptiness is the gap between the old and the new and is very much part of the transition. In a sense it is a moment in hell, the soul's dark night. The old has lost all meaning; it has become a dry shell. The new is only a frightening possibility on a very distant and sometimes dark horizon.

The third stage is called beginnings. New beginnings start inside, like little seeds, and move outward only when they are ready; "it is out of the formlessness of the neutral zone that new forms emerge; it is out of the barrenness of the fallow time that new life springs."[21] Like the "deep sleep" of Adam, this fallow time can be a very fertile period for the birth of a new life. But it is also a demanding lesson in patience.

In view of the Christian teaching on the incarnation we believe that God is present in and through the various deaths the ministers suffer in all their transitions. We believe that there is a time for our own desert experience — a time for our own agony in the garden, before we rise again with Christ on Easter morning. We call this "living the Paschal Mystery." The Eucharist is always an invitation to death as the gateway to life. The ministers who *proclaim* this mystery have first of all a vocation to *live* that mystery in their own Christian journeys. Such dying and rising is not merely a theoretical proclamation but a daily, existential witness.

It is important during transitions that ministers be faithful, that their vocational commitment to minister remain real and "unto death." Fidelity characterized the God of the Hebrews; it should also characterize God's ministers. The question is, "To whom and to what will the ministers be faithful?" In view of everything stated in chapter 1, ministers are called to be faithful to God, to the Word, to the Jesus/Lord event, to discipleship, and to the various new calls or vocations as they come to them. They are called to be faithful to ministry, but not necessarily to its passing, external forms. They are called to be faithful to discipleship, but again, not necessarily to its external, time-conditioned forms.

Ministers are called, finally, to be faithful to that inner voice of the Spirit constantly calling them to offer their gifts in response to the changing needs of the kingdom and the world. True faithfulness may require a painful death to the old familiar forms of ministry and embarking on an exodus to new, as yet poorly defined, forms. True ministry consists not *primarily* in a commitment to its outward form, but in that inner disposition, that inner vocation, to follow the Spirit into whatever forms of ministry she calls. Ministry cannot exist apart from some external form, but the form itself always remains relative and, probably, transitional.

Burnout

It's been almost thirty years since Graham Greene published his popular novel *A Burnt-Out Case*. Set in a Congo leper-mission, it was the story of M. Querry, a world-famous architect who lost his Catholic faith, his belief in his vocation as an architect, and the ability to love or feel anything. Many of Greene's readers easily identified with Querry's "burnt-out" condition.

Since then we have seen considerable research published in books and journals regarding the phenomenon of burnout, especially as it occurs in the helping professions.[22] Moses may actually have been the first "helper" to experience the symptoms of burnout. After Moses had spent a long, hard day settling a long line of disagreements among his people, his father-in-law admonished him: "You are not acting wisely. . . . You will surely wear yourself out. . . . The task is too heavy for you; you cannot do it alone. . . . Look among all the people for able and God-fearing men" (Ex 18:18, 21).

While burnout has many variations and manifestations, the following definition seems to be a good general description of the condition: "Burn-out . . . refers to a progressive loss of idealism, energy, and purpose experienced by people in the helping professions as a result of the conditions of their work."[23] Burnout is very much a human phenomenon. For this reason, no minister can expect to be immune to its symptoms. Moreover, all ministers are vulnerable to the causes that produce it.

We can gain a deeper understanding of burnout by describing its main characteristics:

Tedium and burnout are states of physical, emotional, and mental exhaustion. They are characterized by physical depletion, by feelings of helplessness and hopelessness, by emotional drain, and by the development of negative self-concept and negative attitudes towards work, life, and other people. They are the sense of distress, discontent, and failure in the quest for ideals.[24]

Burnout, according to G. Lloyd Rediger, is a version of the depressive syndrome. The physical characteristics include an exhausted appearance, frequent headaches, gastric upset, and loss of sexual vigor. Emotionally, burnout is characterized by apathy, loss of creativity, constant irritability, and complaints of loneliness. Spiritually, burnout is revealed by an abandonment of the prayer and meditational disciplines, one-track preaching and teaching, listless and perfunctory performance of duties, and finally the loss of joy and celebration.[25]

Statistical data for the incidence of burnout are hard to find, mostly because the symptoms cannot easily be distinguished from other human disturbances. Nevertheless, one counselor of clerics in Wisconsin, checking his files over a ten-year period, found that 2 percent of his clergy clients were suffering from burnout.[26] While the percentage may seem low, it amounts to a significant loss of ministering talent.

With the growing shortage of Roman Catholic clergy, cases of burnout will probably increase. The American bishops in their recent report indicate an awareness of burnout tendencies among Catholic priests. In reflecting on the morale of the clergy, they describe the problem as encompassing loneliness, unrealistic role expectations, and the lack of affirmation. The bishops conclude: "Many feel they worked hard and long to implement or at least adjust to the practical consequences of Vatican II. They sense that much of that effort is now being blunted or even betrayed *and they elect to drop out.*"[27]

Ministry burnout is a condition that develops over a period of time. Jerry Edelwich in his book *Burnout* lists the five stages of the process as: "enthusiasm, stagnation, frustration, apathy and intervention."[28] Ministers often need outside feedback to diagnose their own place in the stages of burnout. Honest and compassionate friends may be a greater help than professional helpers.

If Christian ministers are going to succeed in avoiding the pitfalls of burnout they need to be sensitive to its causes. While there is considerable variation in the ways in which ministers fall into burnout, psychologists have identified some of the more common causes. Ministers, belonging as they do to the helping professions, are susceptible to burnout because they share three basic characteristics: "they perform emotionally taxing work; they share certain personality characteristics that made them choose human service as a career; and they share a 'client-centered' orientation. These three characteristics are the classic antecedents of burnout."[29] These factors are particularly relevant for teachers, ministers, and social workers. They choose a helping profession as a career because they are sensitive to human needs. Perhaps too they are more vulnerable to the pain of the human condition. Being client-centered brings with it the usual trap, namely, professionals give, clients receive. It's a real trap because the helpers find it difficult to shift gears and become vulnerable receivers when they need support.

Specialists in burnout have noted some of the frustrations that lead to burnout: "Powerlessness; too much paperwork; not enough money; too many hours; career dead-end; not appreciated by supervisor; not sufficiently trained for the job; system not responsive to clients' needs."[30]

What are the remedies for burnout? Many authors have emphasized the importance of support systems as a form of preventive maintenance. A monthly luncheon with fellow ministers or telephone calls when things are going badly can go a long way to keep ministers out of the burnout doldrums. Public recognition and appreciation as well as spiritual direction and shared prayer can also provide a supportive environment for health in the ministry.

Ministers who offer support to fellow ministers may find themselves performing some of the following basic functions: (1) active listening, without offering advice or judgments; (2) technical appreciation and proper acknowledgment for a fine piece of work in the Lord's vineyard; (3) technical challenge, so fellow ministers will not fall into stagnation and boredom; (4) emotional support and challenge, so fellow ministers will be encouraged to stretch themselves to overcome obstacles and accomplish their goals; (5) sharing social reality, to help fellow ministers get through a period of stress and confusion.[31]

Ministering through Leadership Skills

When the church leaned heavily on ministry as an ontology, it did not pay much attention to the development of the human leadership skills. It assumed that the "magic" grace of the sacrament of ordination would be efficacious with or without effective leadership skills. In fact, the people became accustomed to ministry that was not sensitive to all the human dynamics that make up good leadership. They were quite disposed to accept "automatic grace" with a large tolerance for human defects in the style of the ministry.

With a more educated people of God, today's ministers simply need to develop those leadership qualities expected in today's society of any person in a similar leadership position. They need to *earn* their leadership positions on a daily basis to be credible as leaders. People no longer give authority to leaders because they present themselves as representatives of a higher authority, as members of a ruling caste, or as vehicles of "automatic grace." For this reason the need to acquire and develop leadership skills is becoming an essential part of today's ministry.

Leadership, to be effective, will somehow have to relate to the people's real needs. This does not mean that the leaders are simply responding to all the people's *felt* needs. The people may not, in fact, feel they have a need to hear the Gospel of the cross or to be challenged prophetically to grow in holiness, or to repent and undergo a painful change of heart. The ministers need the gift of discernment to know when to question the people's needs and when to respond to them.

If, however, leaders are going to motivate their people, they need to be *aware* of the hierarchy of their needs, including their felt needs. Abraham Maslow has performed an invaluable service in outlining the various needs that spur people to act. First come the physical needs concerned with survival: food, shelter, etc. Second are the needs that concern security, namely, resting safe with what we need to live. Third are the social needs of belonging and fitting into life with others. Fourth, there are ego needs, looking for recognition and approval from others. Finally, there are the needs for self-fulfillment. In his research, Maslow discovered "that until more basic needs were met, the physical and security needs, a person was not motivated by the higher needs of social, ego or self-fulfillment. Victims of a hurricane, for instance, are not likely to want to attend a self-development workshop; they need to be fed and housed and to regain some security."[32]

With the emergence of parish councils, shared ministries, and numerous planning meetings, there is a much greater need for leaders of groups to be sensitive to the dynamics of group process and development. Groups, like humans, grow slowly. The first stage of "growing into group" has been called the polite stage. Members stick to safe, non-controversial topics: "Nice weather we're having." "Who is going to win the game tomorrow?" During the second stage things get a little more serious. Hidden agendas begin to surface. Cliques promoting a certain point of view begin to form. Members begin to test the group to find out who is on which side. The third stage has arrived when some members begin to compete for leadership. They try to influence the thinking of the group. They also hope they will be recognized as leaders. It is only in the fourth stage that members really begin to listen to each other and respect different points of view and value systems. Now the group becomes more productive, positively enlisting the different talents of the group. Finally, the group becomes a cohesive, working team. Bonds of friendship are formed and the members support each other in their diversity even beyond the official meetings. At this point, the group becomes very effective, but it becomes more difficult to add new members because then the whole process of "growing into group" has to start all over again.[33]

In the development of their leadership skills ministers need to be aware that there is not one sure-fire leadership style. Different groups, contexts, and situations require different styles of leadership. The experts on leadership have identified the five most typical leadership styles: (1) *Authoritative* — the leaders identify a problem, consider alternative solutions, choose one of them, and then tell their followers what they are to do. (2) *Persuasive* — the leaders, as before, make the decision without consulting their group. They try to persuade the group members to accept their decision. (3) *Evaluative* — the leaders identify a problem and propose a tentative solution. Before finalizing it, however, they get the reactions of those who will implement it. (4) *Participative* — the leaders give the group members a chance to influence the decision from the beginning. They present a problem with relevant background information and then ask the members for their ideas on how to solve it. (5) *Laissez-faire* — the leaders participate in the discussion as "just another member" and agree in advance to carry out whatever decision the group makes.[34]

Every group leader eventually will have to deal with conflict. It is part of the human condition in a free community where creative thinking is encouraged. If the church were composed only of mindless sycophants there would never be any conflict and there would be no church. Already in the New Testament we see conflicts between Peter and Paul (Gal 2:11) and between Barnabas and Paul (Acts 15:38–39). History records conflicts between St. Polycarp and Pope Anicetus; between St. Cyprian of Carthage and Pope Stephen. There have been many theological conflicts between the Thomists and the Franciscans, between the Dominicans and the Jesuits. The question is not whether Christians will have conflicts but how they will deal with them.

There is a wide variety of ways to deal with conflict, including flight, defusing the conflict, and reconciliation. The process of reconciliation requires the basic skills of diagnosis, initiation, listening, and problem solving.[35] The ministry of reconciliation is not confined to the "confessional." Nor does it come automatically with office or "magic" words. It is a ministry that needs to be learned. During times of change and tension conflict increases. So there is an ever greater need to learn how to use the reconciling ministry God has handed on to us (2 Cor. 5:18).

Growing in leadership skills is part of life-long learning. As noted earlier, leadership does not come with office, ordination, or appointment. People quickly see through the façade of leadership symbols that never succeed in masking the incompetent. The crown wears heavy on the child.

In summary, there are many human sacraments that empower the pastoral ministries of the baptized. If the incarnation is real, the human is the apt vehicle for the divine. It is a sacrament for ministry.

The challenge of preparing for and growing in these ministries may, at times, seem a little overwhelming. However, while our ministry is in and through the sacrament of the human, it is not merely a human enterprise. We may be clay in the hands of the potter, but the hands are the hands of God.

CHAPTER EIGHT

The Ministry of Women

"But when Priscilla and Aquila heard him, they took him aside and explained to him the Way of God more accurately" (Acts 18:26).

On February 11, 1989, in Boston, the Episcopal Church ordained Barbara Harris as the first female bishop in the Anglican Communion. The voices of the dissenters were overwhelmed by cheers from thousands of fellow Episcopalians: "Bishop Harris was greeted with a roar of approval from about 8,000 people when she walked down the aisle for her consecration."[1] When the Most Reverend Edmond Browning asked the congregation "if it was their will that Harris be ordained, they thundered out: 'That is our will.' "[2] *Newsweek* covered the event, providing in-depth background on the movement toward the ordination of women. Quoting theologians from various Christian churches, it summarized the arguments for and against the ordination of women. The media highlighted this ordination because of the growing interest in the role of women in ministry. Discussions about women's ordination have heated up as the women's movement tackles sexism in all areas of our society.

The number of women in ministry, ordained or not, is growing rapidly in the churches: "More and more women are moving into the ranks of clergy, according to a study recently released by the National Council of Churches. According to the report, 'Women Ministers in 1986 and 1987: A Ten Year View,' the percentage of women ordained to the 'full ministry' in the United States has nearly doubled in denominations that ordained women in 1977...."[3] Citing data from the Association of Theological Schools in the U.S. and Canada, *Newsweek* reported:

145

Eighty-four Christian denominations ordain women.

About 21,000 ordained women now serve as ministers.

Between 1977 and 1987 the number of women graduating with Master of Divinity Degrees increased 224% (to 1,496), while the number of male recipients rose only 4.6% (to 5,394).

In 1987, 27.4% of all seminary students were women; a sharp increase from 1972 when they accounted for only 10.2%.[4]

The ordination of Barbara Harris to the episcopacy was seen as a new plateau in the history of the ordination of women. However, she was probably not the first woman to be ordained bishop. In 1935 Archbishop Michael Kowalski was the leader of the Mariavites, a Polish sect in schism from the Roman Catholic Church. Since he had been consecrated bishop by a Dutch Old Catholic bishop, his ordination, no doubt, was valid. In the mid-1930s, in Plock, Poland, he ordained a number of women to the priesthood. Subsequently, at least one of these women priests seems to have been ordained bishop since she was renamed Bishop Dilecta.[5] In 1962 this Mariavite sect, originally modelled on the Rule of St. Francis, numbered twenty-five thousand members with twenty-five priests, three bishoprics, and forty-one parishes.

The ordination of women to the priesthood is a fairly recent development. In 1944, during the emergency of World War II, a Chinese woman in Hong Kong was ordained to the priesthood by an Anglican bishop. In 1958, the Swedish Lutheran Church decided to admit women to the ordained ministry; in 1971–73, the Anglican bishop of Hong Kong ordained three women to the priesthood; in 1974, in Philadelphia, the Episcopalians again ordained women to the priesthood.

In the Roman Catholic Church, as far as we know, there have been no actual ordinations of women to the priesthood or episcopate. Discussions on women as ordained ministers, however, have continued apace. In October 1975, the Canon Law Society of America's Committee on the Status of Women in the Church reported that the code of 1917 "fails to recognize the dignity of women as persons and limits their opportunity for service in the church.... Many canons place women in an inferior position and... demonstrate either protectiveness and paternalism or defense against possible sexual provocation on the part of women."[6] In November 1975, an ordination conference entitled "Women in Future Priesthood Now — A Call for Action" was held in Detroit. In 1976, the Leadership Conference of Women Religious published a document entitled *The Status and Roles of Women: Another Perspective*.

All these discussions eventually led to the Vatican's publication of the *Declaration on the Question of the Admission of Women to the Ministerial Priesthood*. Released by the Sacred Congregation for the Doctrine of the Faith on January 27, 1977, the declaration was the Vatican's answer to the

146

question of the ordination of women. The answer was no. The Vatican, no doubt, hoped that this declaration would end discussion and settle the whole question in the Roman Catholic Church once and for all. But it was not to be. The Catholic discussions continued. With the growing shortage of male clergy, the debate will probably continue to intensify in the years ahead. When the body of the church hurts, it cries out for help.

Today's ministers and theologians pose serious questions regarding the historical exclusion of women from the ordained ministries of the church. Is women's reduced role due to the nature of Christianity? Is it due to the predominance of male imagery? Is it due to the patriarchy of Jewish and Roman cultures? Is it due to a positive and deliberate exclusion of women by the historical Jesus? Or, finally, is it due, as some allege, to women being inferior to men?

The Influence of Patriarchy

The theological questions noted above cannot be intelligently discussed apart from the influence of patriarchy in shaping the church and its ministries. But, if we are going to ask the right questions, we need a more precise definition of patriarchy. The word has been used rather loosely in the church to describe all abuses of power by religious leaders who happen to be men. Many women who have recently come into the church's ministry have experienced oppressive use of power, which demeans their dignity as human beings and as women who offer their own unique gifts in service to the church. Since they are new in the "system," they are especially sensitive to abuse of power that, as it happens, often comes from male office-holders. They have sometimes labelled this oppressive use of power (perhaps too quickly) with the umbrella word "patriarchy."

Abuse of power is not limited to gender. If patriarchy means oppressive use of power, then Queens Elizabeth and Mary Tudor of England and numerous mothers superior provide ample proof that women can be as authoritarian as men. Both male and female ministers have suffered from the oppressive use of power by both genders for centuries. Perhaps for their own protection they have desensitized themselves so they no longer feel the pain. For many, this is the price they pay for survival in the system. The church may need the ministry of women, especially their sensitivity to abuses in the system, to bring about a new awareness of the various forms abuse of power can take. To move toward a clearer definition of patriarchy, therefore, we need to distinguish it from other abuses of power and authority. With allowance for different shades of meaning across different cultures, I find Gerda Lerner's definition accurate:

Patriarchy . . . means the manifestation and institutionalization of male dominance over women and children in the family and the extension of male dominance over women in society in general. It implies that men hold power in all the important institutions of society and that women are deprived of access to such power.[7]

With this definition in mind, we may be ready to trace the history of patriarchy in the dominant cultures that shaped the politics and structures of the church through history.

In pre-Christian Roman culture the military occupied the positions of power; the heroes were the generals who had achieved victory in war and extended the empire. The women of conquered lands were usually sold into slavery, which often meant prostitution. Through much of Roman history during this era, women's dignity and status were totally dependent on their relationship to men. Patriarchy deprived women of educational opportunities, denied them a knowledge of their own history, and prevented access to the economic resources available to men.

In the religious world, we see patriarchy already in the Book of Genesis. In the second creation account Adam names, and so has power over, the animals.[8] Eve is the temptress. Under the Mosaic Covenant, circumcision of the male sex organ becomes the symbol of God's special relationship with the chosen people. The Covenant itself is made with Abraham, not Sarah. The Old Testament patriarchs become the religious symbols of a *holy* patriarchy. The Temple priesthood is all male. Women, like the despised Gentiles, are confined to an outer court in the Temple.

Women in the New Testament

As noted above (chap. 1), the ministries of the New Testament were shaped to a large extent by the Greek, Roman, and Jewish cultures. The status of women in these three cultures conditioned the roles of women in the New Testament churches. Naturally, the patriarchy discussed above was one of the most important factors in shaping the ministries of women.

Beginning with Greek culture we see some of the same characteristics we noted in the history of the Roman patriarchy. From 500 to 323 B.C.E., women's status in Greek society was just a notch above the slaves:

The primary duty of women in ancient Athens was to marry and to bear legitimate children so that the family unit might continue. . . .

148

The homes had separate women's quarters. When their husbands entertained guests, women were not permitted to be present. . . . Attic literature of the period generally portrayed women as inferior and of dull and unpleasant character. It was thought that women should not be educated since that would make them more dangerous to men.[9]

In Book V of the *Republic,* Plato describes his vision of a utopian state where women are equal to men. Aristotle, however, bypasses Plato's ideas and limits women to traditional sex roles. He expected them to obey men and stay in the home. As it happened, Aristotle exercised the greater influence on the thought patterns of the Greek culture. He believed "that inequality between men and women was based upon the law of nature. Man is superior, woman inferior. Husbands and fathers should rule over their wives and daughters."[10] It is understandable in this context that the dominant philosophical schools like the Stoics would exclude women.

In the Roman empire during the New Testament period, women were under the control of the *pater familias,* the head of the extended family unit. "His power extended to life and death. A death penalty could be imposed upon a woman for adultery or drinking alcohol. . . . A woman could not legally transact business, make a contract or a will or manumit a slave without the approval of her guardian."[11]

In Roman society infanticide, especially of female babies, was practiced with the blessing of the father who had all the power. Daughters were not given individual names; instead they were called by the feminine form of the father's name. "If there were more than one daughter, they were numbered."[12]

In Judaism, women were legally the property of men, as was the case in most patriarchal societies. The last of the Ten Commandments lists the wife among the objects of property that are not to be coveted. Besides the cultural influence on the Jewish woman, the Jewish tradition was largely shaped by a religious interpretation of legal impurity. According to the Torah, women were *legally* impure during times of menstruation and childbirth. The legal impurity incurred through childbirth was so serious that it required a rite of purification.

The Hebrew Scriptures reveal a concern about physical, moral, and legal impurity. While the concept of legal impurity linked to biological functions may seem strange to us, it affected practically all ancient societies, including Israelite. Most of human sexual activity came under the broad umbrella of legal impurity. Since, according to the biblical understanding, women's bodies were sexually more active than men's, women were *legally* more impure than men. We read in Leviticus 12:1–5:

> The Lord said to Moses, "Tell the Israelites: When a woman has conceived and gives birth to a boy, she shall be unclean for seven days, with the same uncleanness as at her menstrual period. On the eighth day, the flesh of the boy's foreskin shall be circumcised, and then she shall spend thirty-three days more in becoming purified of her blood; she shall not touch anything sacred nor enter the sanctuary till the days of her purification are fulfilled. If she gives birth to a girl, for fourteen days she shall be as unclean as at her menstruation, after which she shall spend sixty-six days in becoming purified of her blood.

One does not need to be a genius to figure out why women were *legally* more impure than men. No doubt this Hebrew taboo reflects the many ancient tribal taboos based on the fear of blood as the source of life. Women, in the eyes of ancient cultures, were simply more wasteful of life-blood than men.

In Israelite home life women had no status apart from their husbands. They could not even lead table prayers. "The wife was obliged to obey her husband as she would a master [and]...indeed this obedience was a religious duty."[13] Where polygamy was practiced, the wife had to live with the concubines. The right to divorce a spouse belonged exclusively to the husband. The wife could not leave the house without hiding her face with two head veils, so her features could not be recognized. If she did so, her husband could put her away.[14] A father could sell his daughters into slavery, if they were under twelve years of age, and, of course, decide whom they would marry. Daughters could not refuse prearranged marriages.

In public life women were not allowed to read from the Torah at the synagogue service. They were expected to listen while hidden behind a lattice barrier. They had "no right to bear witness, because it was concluded from Genesis 18.15 that they were liars."[15] In this biblical story Sarah lies when she says she did not laugh at the Lord's announcement that she would have a son in her old age. In the Temple, wives were separated from the husbands and confined to the Court of Women. The main reason for women's exclusion from full participation in the worship of the Temple was their frequent *legal* and ritual impurity.

Philo (d. 50 C.E.), a Jewish philosopher from Alexandria, provides a helpful insight into the philosophical milieu of Jesus' times. He taught that women were inferior creatures, "that man was led by reason and woman by sensuality. Influenced by the spirit-matter dichotomy of Neo-Platonism, he viewed sex, which involved contact with matter, as evil."[16]

The Israelite priesthood was hereditary and completely dominated by males. Women were excluded by law. The elders were another male-dominated structure. The Hebrew word for elder literally meant "one who wore a beard." These elders played an important role in the political and religious life of Judaism. In the synagogue they were installed by prayer and the imposition of hands. They held the seats of honor and sometimes interpreted the Torah. They ruled the synagogues and the schools that were attached to them. Naturally, women were excluded from the office of elder.

In view of women's status in the cultural milieu of the New Testament, it is no wonder they were excluded from the team of "the twelve." Slaves didn't make it either. Besides, "the twelve" represented the twelve tribes of Israel, which Jesus was gathering together. The twelve tribes were all named after men.

In the context of the patriarchal cultures described above, the words and actions of Jesus are all the more remarkable. We see in the Gospels that women, such as Mary and Martha (Lk 10:38–42), were disciples of Jesus. In Luke 24:49 we learn that "the women had followed him from Galilee." In Luke 8:1–3 we are told that when Jesus went on his preaching mission he was accompanied by the twelve "and also some women who had been healed of evil spirits and infirmities: Mary, called Magdalene, from whom seven demons had gone out, and Joanna, the wife of Chuza, Herod's steward, and Susanna, and many others who provided for them out of their means."

Modern Scripture scholars have pointed out that Luke was not as favorable in his portrayal of women as had often been assumed. Nevertheless, in Acts 18:25 we find Priscilla instructing a man (Apollos) in the truths of the faith. She is a teacher exercising an effective ministry of the Word. John Chrysostom in his homily on Romans writes: "Apollos was an eloquent man, well versed in Scripture, but he knew only the baptism of John; this woman [Priscilla] took him, instructed him in the way of God, and made him an accomplished teacher."[17] Then, too, Tabitha (Acts 9:36) is specifically named as a disciple: "Now there was at Joppa a disciple named Tabitha."

We need to point out too that in the New Testament women are called apostles. "There is a strong fourfold gospel tradition which presents at least one woman, Mary of Magdala, as having fulfilled all the criteria of apostleship and as having exercised her apostleship at the very least in her critically important mission to the other disciples."[18] In the Pauline writings we meet Andronicus and Junias, who are "outstanding among the apostles" (Rom 16:7). The manuscript evidence is quite strong that the Junias mentioned in this verse is a woman.

We noted above (chap. 1) the importance of prophets in the churches of the New Testament. In Acts 13 they exercise a liturgical ministry, possibly presiding at the Eucharist. Their teaching ministry is attested to in many parts of the New Testament. We can mention here at least three instances when women exercise a prophetic ministry. In Acts 21:9

we see that Phillip "had four unmarried daughters, who prophesied." In 1 Corinthians 11:5 Paul writes that women who prophesied should keep their heads veiled. In Revelation 2:20 we see Jezebel, "a prophetess in charge of the church of Thyatira."

Paul's lists of charisms in 1 Corinthians 12 make no distinction with regard to gender. The gifts are given according to the measure of faith, not the sex, of the recipient. In 1 Corinthians 7:7 marriage itself is a charism. The lists of charisms in Romans and Ephesians reveal Paul's functional approach to ministry. For Paul the crucial point for the ministries is not gender, but their capacity to build up the church. Thus Paul calls women his fellow workers. Among them are Prisca, Eudia, and Syntyche (Rom 16:3 and Phil 4:3). In his own ministry Jesus, surprisingly, does not conform to the customs and conventions of Jewish society regarding women. In the very beginning of his ministry he heals Peter's mother-in-law. Later he heals the daughter of Jairus, the woman with the hemorrhage, and the daughter of the Syro-Phoenician. Finally, there can be no doubt that Jesus had a close and rather public relationship with Mary Magdalen.[19]

In all of Jesus' dealings with women the most revealing text regarding Jesus' attitude toward them is contained in John 4. This chapter gives us the touching story of Jesus' conversation with the Samaritan woman at Jacob's well. We get an insight into the event when we read: "Just then his disciples came. They marveled that he was talking with a woman, but none said 'What do you wish?' or 'Why are you talking with her?' " (v. 27). Here we see Jesus publicly flouting all the laws of Jewish propriety. More importantly, he is disobeying the Law of Moses that decreed that the Samaritan woman was *religiously* unclean and therefore to be avoided. Jesus ignored both Jewish law and Samaritan taboos. This Gospel, whenever it is proclaimed, will continue to judge the discriminatory practices of the Christian churches.

Deaconesses

We have already met Phoebe, the deaconess of Cenchreae, in Romans 16:1–2. In 1 Timothy 3:8–12, we find a listing of qualifications for deacons. In the middle of this list Paul includes some qualifications for women. While the Greek text presents some difficulties, scholars nevertheless see evidence here for the existence of deaconesses in Timothy's church at Ephesus. There may be times when "deaconess" and "widow" are interchangeable, since "deaconess" is more descriptive of function than office. We know that the duties of widows and deaconesses did overlap.

After the New Testament period the deaconess becomes a clearly identifiable minister in the church, especially in the East. Perhaps the stricter segregation of the sexes and the more widespread celebration of baptism by immersion required greater use of deaconesses. They were particularly necessary in the East for the more fulsome baptismal anointing of adult women converts. The candidate for baptism entered the pool naked. Then the deaconess plunged her into the water three times and completed the anointing with oil applied over the entire body.

> Deaconesses also performed a host of other duties: The deaconess instructed the female catechumens, acted as intermediary between baptized women and the bishop, conducted the necessary physical examination when a virgin was accused of breaking her vow, guarded the church door against entrance of women who were not members of the community and, sitting in a chair similar to the bishop's *cathedra*, presided over the women's section at liturgical gatherings. She visited the poor and sick in their homes, being especially solicitous for sick women, to whom, according to some evidence, she administered the Eucharist. It was also the task of the deaconess to prepare the bodies of the faithful for burial.[20]

It is noteworthy that before the teaching ministry became identified with the ordained male clergy deaconesses were teachers of Christian doctrine. They were listed with the clergy and, like the clergy, received their "daily wages" from the church. When they died intestate and without legitimate heirs, their possessions were given to the church to which they were attached by their ordination.[21] The *Didascalia Apostolorum*, a third-century constitution written in Syria, lays down the rule that "the deaconess must be honored as a figure of the Holy Spirit."[22]

Deaconesses were numerous in the East. When St. John Chrysostom was exiled in 404, there were forty deaconesses assigned to his cathedral of Hagia Sophia in Constantinople. Deaconesses were addressed as "venerable" and "most reverend." In the West, deaconesses were not as numerous but there is ample evidence that they existed in Gaul and Rome at least until the year 800.

In the ninth century, with the growth of monasticism, the order of deaconesses began to decline. Adult baptisms were rare. Baptism by immersion was abandoned in the West and men and women no longer sat in segregated parts of the church. Gradually, the duties of deaconesses were taken over by male deacons and subdeacons.

The question is often asked whether these deaconesses were ordained. The answer needs to be carefully nuanced. There are two problems: first, the Greek *kairotoneō* (to impose hands) had several meanings; second, the word "ordain" had a much broader and more flexible meaning before the Council of Trent. If we place "ordain" in its proper historical context, we have a strong case for concluding that deaconesses were in fact ordained. At least the ordination ceremony used for deaconesses was the same as that used for male deacons. In the ordination prayer from the rite of Constantinople we read:

> O Lord God, who does not reject women who offer themselves in accordance with the divine will to minister in thy holy places, but admittest them into the rank of ministers [leitourgoi] give the grace of thy Holy Spirit even to this thy handmaid who desireth to offer herself to thee and to fulfill the grace of the ministry as thou didst give the grace of the ministry to Phoebe.[23]

Theologians point out that deaconesses, like other clerics, received an ordination conferred by the imposition of hands and the prayer of the bishop. This ordination was celebrated in the presence of the presbyters, deacons, and deaconesses.

The *Apostolic Constitutions* (fourth century) is the largest collection of liturgical books in antiquity. Its prayer for the ordination of deaconesses is quite specific: "Do thou also look down upon this thy servant who is to be ordained to the office of a deaconess, and grant her thy Holy Spirit, that she may worthily discharge the work which is committed to her."[24] Nothing in this prayer indicates any difference between the ordination of male deacons and that of deaconesses. We can conclude, therefore, with Roger Gryson, that deaconesses received an ordination similar to that of their male colleagues.[25]

Besides exercising the power of orders as deaconesses, women have, at various times, held offices with the power of jurisdiction. When the church is seen as a society, jurisdiction is the power to rule the baptized subjects of the church. It includes legislative, judicial, and executive authority. Usually this power is given only to clerics. Joan Morris, however, has done extensive research from the viewpoint of canon law on women and jurisdiction. She provides historical evidence that the abbesses of monasteries possessed ecclesiastical jurisdiction without benefit of ordination.[26] They ranked just below the bishop but above the priest. They nominated priests for parishes and appointed chaplains. They issued faculties to offer Mass, to hear confessions, and to preach. The famous abbess Hilda was one of the signers of the synodal decrees of Whitby, England. She held jurisdiction over a double monastery of men and women.

Even aside from the question of ordination, from the viewpoint of the Catholic tradition regarding jurisdiction, there is no reason why women today, without ordination, could not be chancellors, vicar generals, vicars for religious, administrators of parishes, and even cardinals of the church. (Cardinals, as we know from history, do not need to be ordained priests.) Separating ordination, or the power of orders, from the power of jurisdiction would open up numerous offices to the ministry of women.

We saw above (chap. 3) that councils passed laws to keep women, including deaconesses, out of the sanctuary to protect the celibacy of the priests. The decline of women in ministry in the church can be attributed, at least in part, to the persistence of patriarchy, the fear of sex, the growth of celibacy in the Western church, and the growth and dominance of monasteries of men.

The Ordination of Women

A question raised with increasing frequency today pertains to the ordination of women to the priesthood. The Vatican declaration cited in the beginning of this chapter did not stop the debates about the ordination of women. Before undertaking a critical evaluation of that Vatican text, it may be helpful here to recall some of the arguments for and against the ordination of women.

Research Report: Women in Church and Society, edited by Sara Butler, summarizes the arguments against the ordination of women as follows: (1) it is the constant tradition of the church to exclude women from the ordained ministry; (2) women are complementary to men — they bring their own riches, not equality, to the upbuilding of the church; (3) even though, as noted above, Jesus challenged the customs of his day, he did not call any women to the team of the twelve; (4) the New Testament doctrine of headship justifies the leadership of men and the subordination of women (1 Cor 14:34–35); (5) the ordained priest acts in the person of the male Christ; (6) the apostles did not invite a woman to take the place of Judas; (7) there is no right to ordination; (8) it is not clear that the deaconesses in the early church were ordained; (9) Mary was not called to be an apostle; (10) in the New Testament Christ is the bridegroom and the church is the bride; therefore it is fitting that a man represent the bridegroom; (11) in the Old Testament, all priests were male; this must be God's will.[27]

The same report summarizes the arguments in favor of the ordination of women: (1) the exclusion of women on the basis of gender, apart from personal qualifications, is unjust; (2) the demands of mission and the needs of the church require a competent person and this often means woman-to-woman ministry; (3) through baptism all women already share in the priesthood of Christ; they have always baptized and, as brides, administered the sacrament of marriage; (4) many women experience a call to the priesthood; the church needs to be open to the possibility that this call is from the Holy Spirit; (5) there is a growing consensus regarding the ordination of women in the Anglican and other Protestant churches; (6) the official ministry as a sign of a non-discriminating church should represent the variety of persons being ministered to; (7) ordination of women would prevent the further alienation of women from the church and therefore would give the church more credibility on justice issues; (8) changes in other areas of church life and discipline provide a precedent for change on this issue; (9) women have a special experience of life to bring to the ministry; their ministry would enrich the church; (10) it is high time to actualize what the Scriptures say about the equality of all in Christ Jesus (Gal 3:28); (11) the ancient church provided a liturgy for the ordination of deaconesses and thus a precedent for the ordination of women.[28] To Butler's list we could add another argument, namely, that it is time for the church to make a prophetic gesture, as a sign of the reign of God where there will be no discrimination against women; it is time to lead in shaping culture rather than being shaped by it.

An Attempt at a Theological Appraisal

It is important to note that the Vatican declaration on the question of the ordination of women, issued January 27, 1977, is signed not by Pope Paul VI but by Cardinal Franco Seper, prefect, and Bishop Jerome Hammer, O.P., secretary, of the Congregation for the Doctrine of the Faith. It is not, therefore, a dogmatic definition but primarily "a prudential decision."[29]

By way of introduction we need to point out that the language of the declaration reflects the Aristotelian-Thomistic framework. Theologians note that "this particular philosophical framework no longer enjoys the privileged position it possessed in the past. There has emerged a plurality of philosophical frameworks — analytical, existential, personalist, phenomenological, processive and structuralist."[30] For these and many other reasons theologians feel the Vatican's "prudential decision" is subject to review and reconsideration. Future popes, synods, or councils could approach this question from an entirely different direction. In the meantime, the prayer and continuing discernment of all the baptized may contribute to the clarification of an extremely important issue in the church.

The declaration poses two main theological concerns: one Christological, the other sacramental. First, we will reflect briefly on one aspect of the Christology of the declaration. To do so, we need to be aware of the words used both in the New Testament and in the patristic period to describe the church's resurrection faith in the Jesus/Lord event. The Greek language used both in the New Testament and in the early councils of the church had two words for man: *anēr* and *anthrōpos*. These two words compare exactly with two Latin words for man: *vir* and *homo*. *Anēr* and *vir* mean *a* "man," "*a male* human being"; *anthrōpos* and *homo* mean "a human being." Our English word "anthropology" is derived from the Greek *anthrōpos*. It is the study, not of males, but of the origin, nature, and destiny of *the human*.

The Vatican declaration states: "The Incarnation took place according to the male sex: this is indeed a question of fact."[31] There can of course be no doubt that the historical Jesus was a member of the male sex. However, we need to understand from the viewpoint of faith what role his maleness played in the scheme of the incarnation and redemption. Remembering the distinction between the Greek word *anēr* (a man) and *anthrōpos* (a human being), we note that already in the New Testament the Christian church expressed its resurrection *faith* by transcending the maleness of the historical Jesus. In Philippians 2:7 Paul writes, Jesus, "though he was in the form of God, did not count equality with God a thing to be grasped, but emptied himself, taking the form of a servant, being born in the likeness of men [*anthrōpos*]." Clearly Paul, recalling here an early Christian hymn, teaches that Jesus became *human*. He is expressing the faith of the Philippian church. After the resurrection, Paul did not limit the mystery of the incarnation to the male gender of the historical Jesus.

In Romans 5:15 Paul once again stresses his faith in Jesus/Lord as the incarnation of the human: "For if many died through one man's trespass, much more have the grace of God and the free gift in the grace of that one man [*anthrōpos*] Jesus Christ abounded for many." It is clear in this verse that Paul presents the risen Lord as the new Adam (*anthrōpos*). Since the first Adam in the first creation was an "earth creature," sexually undifferentiated, it is the symbol for the whole human race, male and female. (In Hebrew *adama* = earth; *adam* = earth creature). So now for Paul, the second Adam in the "new creation," also sexually undifferentiated, is the symbol for the redemption of the whole human race, male and female.

In the early Christian creeds we see that the church continued to express its faith in the Christ as the embodiment of the human, male and female. Thus the Council of Nicaea (325) proclaimed its resurrection faith in the incarnation in the following words: " . . . who became incarnate, becoming human [*enanthrōpēsanta*]. . . . "[32] The Creed of Epiphanius (374) states: "who for us men and for our salvation came down, and was incarnate . . . was made man, that is, assumed the perfect man, soul and body and mind and all that is man, excepting sin. . . . "[33] The Constantinopolitan Creed (381) states: " . . . and was incarnate from the Holy Spirit and became human [*enanthrōpēsanta*]."[34] Moreover, the Council of Chalcedon (451) teaches: "Following, then, the holy fathers, we unite in teaching all men to confess the one and only Son, our Lord Jesus

157

Christ. This selfsame one is perfect both in deity and also in humanness [*anthrōpotēti*]."[35]

The main point these creeds prove is that the early church expressed its resurrection faith in the incarnation by moving beyond the limitations of the maleness of the historical Jesus. It was convinced that the Christ was the embodiment of the human, both male and female. It was for this reason that Gregory of Nazianzus and other fathers of the church could proclaim the Christological axiom: "For what was not assumed, was not healed."[36] If women are not included in the incarnation of the male Jesus, they are not redeemed and are not freed from their sins.

We know nothing about the maleness of Christ as risen except that it has reached its fulfillment. What we do know from the Scriptures and the early councils is that the early church expressed its *faith* in language indicating that Christ's maleness was no longer important for believing in the mystery of the incarnation and redemption. The church quickly moved beyond Jesus' maleness to confess its faith in Christ as an all-inclusive, human redeemer. The creeds are symbols of *faith*; they are not statements about Christ's gender.

Since the incarnation is a mystery, the early church used many different symbols and metaphors to express its faith in God becoming human. In the Hebrew Scriptures Wisdom was often personified. Like Christ, Wisdom is present with God from the beginning (cf. Prv 8:22–31). In Matthew's Gospel, written for Jews familiar with the Hebrew Scriptures, Jesus is portrayed as *Sophia* (Wisdom) (Mt 11:19). Sandra Schneiders comments: "The Jesus of early Christian faith, in short, was understood to a large extent as the child, the prophet, the emissary, and even the incarnation of Wisdom. And Wisdom, in the Old Testament, was a feminine figure."[37]

Since the early church understood Jesus through the feminine figure of holy Wisdom, it should be plain that "if Jesus reveals anything about the gender of God, it is certainly not that God is masculine!"[38]

When the New Testament, in Paul and in Acts 9:4, uses the image of the body of Christ, the metaphor refers to the risen organism of Christ's person. It means "that Christ, in contrast to Jesus, is not male, or more exactly not exclusively male. Christ is quite accurately portrayed as black, old, Gentile, female, Asian, or Polish. Christ is inclusively all the baptized."[39]

If, in our sacramental symbolism, we proclaim the incarnation and the grace of a continuing redemption through Jesus' historical maleness, we fall into reductionism. "The fact of Jesus' biological maleness," writes George Worgul, "*per se*, does not bear an *essential* significance to his mission and ministry as revealer and redeemer. The reality of incarnation demanded that Jesus be biologically human, but ... not necessarily male."[40]

158

Sacramental Signification

The second difficulty, sacramental signification, that emerges in the Vatican declaration, contains two other problems, namely: dual- or single-nature anthropology and the literal interpretation of the Thomistic axiom cited in the Vatican text: "Sacramental signs represent what they signify by *natural resemblance*."[41] The text concludes that to represent the male Christ the eucharistic presider has to be male.

We note parenthetically that Aquinas's argument against the ordination of women is also based on sacramental signification but with a different twist: "Accordingly, since it is not possible in the female sex to signify eminence of degree, for a woman is in the state of subjection, it follows that she cannot receive the sacrament of Order."[42] For Aquinas the crucial point is woman's subjection "by nature." He defends the validity of the ordination of a male slave whose state of subjection is *not* "by nature."[43]

Aquinas taught that women were in a state of subjection because he accepted Aristotle's teaching that males were active and females passive, that women were defective males. Thus he writes:

> As regards the individual, woman is defective and misbegotten, for the active force in the male seed tends to the production of a perfect likeness in the masculine sex while the production of woman comes from a defect in the active force or from some material indisposition or even from some external influence; such as that of a south wind which is moist, as the Philosopher observes.[44]

Many theologians during the scholastic period accepted this Thomistic teaching. The church, therefore, assumed that nature was organized into a hierarchy and that men were at the top of the hierarchic pyramid.

The Thomistic "natural resemblance" prompts questions first about anthropology and then about the meaning of sacramental signification. We need to reflect, therefore, on the anthropology that shapes the declaration. Sara Butler discusses the question: Is the declaration based on a "two-nature" or "one-nature" vision of humanity? A dual anthropology is based on a "two-nature" vision of humanity. In this view, each sex embodies different possibilities of being human — possibilities that are denied to the other. The role of women is *essentially* linked to motherhood; the role of men is *essentially* linked to fatherhood. Appropriate roles, functions, and activities are derived from biological characteristics. Thus leadership and complementarity are viewed as being founded in nature. This duality is inherent in nature and is part of the created order, the *divine* plan. There is a "biological determination from which psychological, sociological, religious and theological roles are derived. Neither sex can embody the fullness of the human."[45]

This "two-nature" anthropology assumes such gender polarities as rational/intuitive, structural/personal, active/receptive, generative/nutritive, and intellectual/emotional.[46] The proper roles are then extrapolated from these biological/physical characteristics. Cultural, historical, and psychological sciences are basically irrelevant. The emphasis is on the unchanging and static structure of biology. Thus men *by nature* symbolize the active church and women *by nature* the passive, receptive church.

Single-nature anthropology is based on a "one-nature" vision of humanity. Sexual differences, in this view, are accidental. Beyond the reproductive functions, *persons* are essentially the same. Traits often ascribed to men can be cultivated by women and vice versa. There is a primordial unity in human nature. There are no preordained roles or functions beyond the biological. Appropriate roles and activities can be extrapolated from personal and spiritual characteristics. The structures of human existence are within the arena of human responsibility. The roles now ascribed to the different sexes are primarily the result of historical conditioning. But such roles are subject to the dispositions of human decisions. This "single-nature" view has a more evolutionary, more dynamic understanding of human anthropology. The appropriate roles are not divine "givens" derived from biology.[47]

Now the question can again be asked in what sense "natural resemblance" applies to the eucharistic presider. If one accepts the "one-nature" anthropology then "natural resemblance" would include male and female. There would be a less biological, a less physical interpretation of the sacramental symbol. George Worgul addresses this issue:

> If the eucharistic presider symbolizes Christ, especially in speaking the words of consecration, it is the peace, love, and justice which constitute Jesus' mission and ministry and actualize his personhood as revealer and savior which attain primary signification and not Jesus' bio-physiological maleness. Likewise, if a "natural resemblance" to Christ is demanded in the priest, this resemblance should have as its proper reference gospel values and not gender.[48]

If the eucharistic presiders act "in the person of Christ," they activate the personhood, the mission, and especially the death and resurrection of Jesus. The mystery of redemption that is enacted cannot be symbolized by one gender. It transcends sex. " 'Natural resemblance' is only one small element within the whole complex which stimulates the imagination and the attainment of presence."[49]

The church teaches that the seven sacraments, including the Eucharist, are actions of the risen Christ, not of the historical Jesus.[50] Of course, the Jesus of history and the Christ of faith are one and the same. But Christ's sacramental saving activity transcends the limitations of one historical period, including the period in which Jesus was a male person on earth. In the sacraments Christ acts through the victory of the resurrection.

The New Testament is a witness that the risen Christ is often "signified" by symbols that do not "resemble" his historical male sex. To mention but a few instances: John calls Christ "the light" (Jn 1:5). In Revelation 5:6 the risen Lord is symbolized by a Lamb with seven horns (complete power) and seven eyes (complete knowledge). The Lamb of power and knowledge, as image of the risen Christ, transcends the "resemblance" of sex. In Revelation 1:8 Christ is symbolized by the *Alpha* and *Omega*, "the beginning and the end, the totality." Revelation 2:1 refers to Christ as "the one who holds the seven stars in his right hand." Finally, Revelation 2:12 presents Christ as "the one with the sharp two-edged sword." Clearly, stars and sword do not resemble Jesus' male sex.

The saints too were quite comfortable in addressing God and Christ with various titles that transcended gender. Catherine of Siena, a doctor of the church, referred to God as the "sea of peace," "ineffable fire," and "mad lover." She also addressed Christ as "the narrow gate" and as "the bridge" that links heaven to earth and divinity to humanity.[51]

It is the human/divine, risen Christ who "signifies" through the seven sacraments. In fact the church itself, with its male and female people of God, is *the* sacrament of the risen Christ. It hardly needs saying that the sacraments of this "Sacrament" have their power because of the continuing victory of Christ. Even though the risen Christ of faith is the same as the male Jesus of history, we do not need to symbolize Christ's risen state, especially not the present saving activity, through the historical maleness.

Catholics have always understood that the sacraments are the acts of Christ, not the acts of a male or female minister. Since the beginning of church history, women have baptized and proclaimed the Word. Their baptisms were efficacious because of the power of the risen Christ, not because of their gender. Pope Pius XII in his encyclical *The Mystical Body* reaffirms the sacramental principle already taught by Augustine: "Christ baptizes ... absolves, offers sacrifice."[52]

The Vatican declaration states that the "priest is a sign that must be perceptible and which the faithful must be able to recognize with ease." Later the Vatican text uses "image" instead of "sign." Worgul correctly notes that there is a "mammoth difference" between "sign" and "image." "An effective sign," writes Worgul, "need not necessarily resemble what it signifies, as in the example of smoke and fire."[53]

Throughout history the forms of sacramental signs have been shaped and reshaped by the growing understanding of the church. Vatican II's Constitution on the Sacred Liturgy called for a revision of the rites of the Mass and the sacraments to "adjust them to the requirements of our times." Signs do not continue to convey a clear, single meaning across different cultures and centuries. In other words, the meaning of signs is culturally conditioned.

In the United States, McDonald's golden arches signify Big Macs without any "natural resemblance." Then too, there is no natural resemblance between the barber pole and the act of hair-cutting. Many other human signs in our culture also effectively transcend gender. A police uniform, for instance, whether worn by a man or a woman, signifies the law and the power to issue a ticket for violation of that law. Military uniforms, worn by men or women, effectively signify rank and its inherent authority. Citizens recognize these signs "with ease."

We have to ask, therefore, how literally "natural resemblance" has to be applied to the sacramental signs. Since Vatican II a wide variety of paraliturgical symbols, specially created for a particular service, have been very effective in community celebrations. Sacramental signs, of course, if they are to remain catholic, may not become subject to arbitrary individual whims. The discernment of the church, however, could well design a "uniform" for the eucharistic presider that, whether worn by a man or a woman, would be recognized by the faithful "with ease."

Indeed, a case could be made that the sacramental symbols would be more effective if they represented the relational nature of men and women in ministry. In 1972, the Faith and Order Commission of the National Council of Churches, meeting at Marseille, addressed the problems of women in ministry:

> The relational nature in which men and women share if they are to be fully human is slighted and the resulting patterns of ministry are impoverished through a lack of engagement of the full humanity of those who serve the church. . . . The real issue is that the church is perpetuating a situation in which both men and women are diminished.[54]

In its 1973 meeting in Geneva the same Commission on Faith and Order became even more specific: "The church is entitled to the style of ministry which can be provided by women as well as that which can be provided by men. Indeed, an understanding of our mutual interdependence needs to be more widely reflected in all branches of ministry."[55] We can conclude that our sacramental symbols will continue to be distorted and mutilated until they reflect the relational male-female partnership and mutual interdependence. In the meantime, "The radiance of the Church's face shines less brightly."[56]

Healing Divisions

In faithfulness to the demands of the reign of God the church is always called to heal all divisions that wound the body of Christ. "The division between masculine and feminine, like that between sacred and profane, is false to the Gospel which calls all people together in the Spirit of Jesus in the unity of the one body."[57] All the church's ministers are called to witness to the sign of the reign of God where "there is neither male nor female" (Gal 3:27).

The Vatican declaration states that Jesus did not entrust the apostolic ministry to Mary, his mother. Mary's historical exclusion from the ministry of the twelve is cited as an argument that women cannot be ordained to the priesthood. Recent history, however, reveals that the "priesthood of Mary" won approval from both bishops and popes. In the seventeenth century the French School of Spirituality, under the leadership of Fathers Berulle and Olier, tried to develop a special spirituality for the diocesan clergy. Besides adopting a particular view of the priesthood and its ministry, this school had also proposed the title "Virgin Priest." Some members of the school applied this title to Mary in an analogical sense.[58] Just as priests bring Jesus into the world through the words of consecration, so also Mary brought Jesus into the world. Others used the title in a more literal sense to refer to Mary's participation in the priesthood of Christ.

In 1873 Pope Pius IX wrote in a private letter that Mary "was so closely united to the sacrifice of her divine Son, from the virginal conception of Jesus Christ to his sorrowful Passion, that she was called by some Fathers of the Church, the Virgin Priest."[59] "In 1906 Pius X approved and indulgenced a prayer that ended with the words: 'Mary, Virgin Priest, pray for us.' "[60] By 1916 the Holy Office had to issue warnings against some forms of devotion to Mary under the title of "Virgin Priest." Nevertheless, the Vatican declaration's argument against the ordination of women based on Jesus' exclusion of Mary, is not as strong as first appears. The church has at least once officially prayed to Mary as priest and, more importantly, encouraged Catholics to see Mary as symbol of the priesthood of the risen Christ. Mary's historical exclusion from the twelve did not prevent her from being a "natural resemblance" to Christ's priesthood.

In this ecumenical era we cannot ignore the fruitful experience of our sister churches in regard to ministry. Vatican II teaches that we are joined with these churches in the Holy Spirit who gives them "His gifts and graces." We are called to heal "the rifts" (including those in the ministry) that still divide the Christian churches. In 1975 the Faith and Order Commission of the World Council of Churches commented on the positive experience of those churches that ordained women:

> Since those who advocate the ordination of women do so out of their understanding of the meaning of the Gospel and ordination, and since the experience of the churches in which women are ordained has on the whole been positive and none has found reason to reconsider its decision, the question must be asked as to whether it is not time for all the churches to confront this matter forthrightly. Churches which ordain women have found that women's gifts are as wide and varied as men's, and that their ministry is as fully blessed by the Holy Spirit as the ministry of men.[61]

Pastoral Reflections

Women are going into the vineyard in ever-increasing numbers. This is creating tensions that in the long term are basically healthy for church. But they are also painful. It hurts when women chaplains arrive at the bedside of the dying, hear the tearful confession of repentance, and then may not pronounce the church's words of forgiveness. It hurts when a woman minister's prayer and sacramental presence brings healing to the sick but she is not allowed to anoint the patient with the church's healing oil.

It hurts when a married pastoral coordinator prepares a young couple for the sacrament of marriage over several weeks and then has to back away while an ordained priest arrives to impart the church's nuptial blessing. It hurts when a woman who has studied the Word until it burns on her tongue is forbidden to preach that Word in the eucharistic assembly. It hurts when an ordained priest suddenly takes his place with the women on the parish team because a personnel committee of male clerics has decided, without consulting the women, to assign one of their members to the parish team.

These tensions also hurt the ordained clergy. Because they are male and ordained, women sometimes see them as partners in a conspiracy to keep patriarchal power in place. Yet the priests themselves often feel voiceless and powerless. Short of a destructive "sit-down strike," they feel they cannot accomplish any change in the patriarchal system. They too are victims of an obsolete structure that no longer serves the people. Paternalistic verbal assurances from bishops are not much help. These priests feel that in spite of many years of labor in the pastoral trenches, they too have no access to the levers of change.

164

The hunger of the Catholic community for a full eucharistic celebration, with one of its own as presider, is not being met. As the years go on, the Catholic sense of faith yearning for the eucharistic celebration is gradually losing its edge. Younger generations who have never experienced the full Eucharist may soon not hunger for it. The Catholic sense of faith that yearned for Eucharist will be quite dead.

Because of this "danger of death" the search for pastoral solutions of any kind continues. Meanwhile, church structures that hinder the ministry and are not changing are having a serious negative effect on morale. Dean Hoge, who conducted research on the future of Catholic leadership, asked campus ministers what factors discouraged interest in working for the church. Forty-four percent of the women were discouraged by the fact "that the church has males in all of its top positions of leadership."[62] He concludes:

> Rules, disciplines, and procedures need to be re-examined from time to time to see if they are still serving the central mission of the church or not. If they are a hindrance and not a help, they must be adjusted.... The priest shortage is an institutional problem, not a spiritual problem, and it can be solved through institutional measures.[63]

Some Catholic women, well trained for ministry, have responded to this institutional problem by leaving their church and joining other churches where their ministry is gladly accepted. Other women have become active in promoting women's ordination in the Catholic Church. Some of these women appear to be asking for the Tridentine sacrament of holy orders from the imposed hands of an ordaining bishop. They are looking for ordination "from above." This is understandable in view of the pre–Vatican II "pipeline" understanding of apostolic succession. The assumption then was that, for *validity*, ordination had to come from a bishop standing in the line of apostolic succession. He passed on to the ordinand part of the power he himself possessed in virtue of his own ordination by another bishop in the "pipeline."

However, in view of the broader understanding of an apostolic succession of all ministers who are faithful to the apostolic teaching, women could also define ordination and priesthood "from below," i.e., from their baptismal participation in the one priesthood of Jesus Christ. Maria Harris, seeing baptismal priesthood in more functional, less ontological terms, shows how women could claim their roles in the priesthood and, in the process, reform it:

> The key roles in the priesthood are *remembering* the past through liturgy and teaching; *mediating* the presence of God through sacra-

mental activity; and *hallowing* the presence of divinity everywhere through blessing. What needs addressing in our own time is the dis-covering and claiming of these roles of remembering, mediating and hallowing for all of us. . . . In other words, each of us exercises priestly ministry every day of our lives. What we need to do is claim that as our identity, thus contributing to a reformation of the meaning of priesthood. . . . Instead of responding to the question, "Do you want to be ordained?" with a yes or no answer, I would respond with a different question: "In what is your priesthood manifested and how can you re-form it in order to make it more manifest?"[64]

Redefining the baptismal priesthood "from below," from the actual pastoral situation, requires a change of attitude. A new pastoral approach would honor the real existence of the baptismal priesthood and, at the same time, would allow that priesthood to be shaped and redefined as a pastoral response to the needs of the congregation. The bishop who ordained the Chinese woman in Hong Kong in 1944 wrote in a letter to his friends that his ordination merely confirmed the woman's priesthood, which had already proven itself for four years in an actual congregation:

On St. Paul's Day 1944 I ordained a Chinese woman as a "priest in the Church of God." . . . For four years she has been in sole charge of a congregation, and both spiritually and practically she has been a most successful pastor, both to men and women, . . . a competent, modest, sensible, quiet parish priest. . . . I informed my brother bishops that . . . I should ordain her priest. . . . The reason in this case is: (1) During war it is the only way in which nearly 100 Communicants can receive the Sacrament. . . . (2) She has amply proved (like Cornelius) that she has the pastoral charism; (3) Perhaps it is better that the ordination of women . . . should come in this way, out of need and out of gift.[65]

Some aspects of the Hong Kong solution may also be appropriate today. In many areas of the world the church is fast approaching the same "wartime" emergency, not less so because it is created by ecclesiastical law. If women, in an emergency or not, continue to exercise their baptismal priesthood, Christian communities will soon recognize the priesthood of Christ coming to new visibility in their actual ministry in behalf of their communities. They will then recognize the gift of the Spirit and confer leadership and authority upon those women who by their actions give singular witness to the priestly ministry of Christ. The outward forms of the sacraments are not frozen by the symbolism of any historical period. They can be reshaped by the people of God, in response to new pastoral needs.

The church universal could hardly deny the "breath" of the Spirit and "the unerring sense of faith" in the local community that, in response to the same Spirit, orders (ordains) its ministering women to leadership functions. Even if, *in the beginning*, such priestly leadership did not include eucharistic presiding, it would, nonetheless, be an authentic and sacramental priestly ministry. Eucharistic presiding is only one of many saving functions of Christ's priesthood. The importance of the various saving functions is not judged or measured by any kind of ecclesiastical ranking system, but by the love and sacrifice, known to God alone, which build up the church of Christ. In many parts of the world, the pastoral emergency created by the lack of full Eucharist is already so severe that the situation itself demands that the community select and ordain (order) a eucharistic presider, male or female.

Apart from eucharistic presiding and pastoral emergencies, the new Code of Canon Law already allows women to hold ecclesiastical offices and to exercise some priestly functions. Besides serving as lectors, acolytes, and ministers of the Eucharist and presiding over liturgical prayer, women may baptize and assist at marriages. They may be appointed as judges of the diocesan tribunal and serve as auditors and consultors. Finally, they may be appointed to the "pastoral care" of parishes.[66]

Women, without further delay and in large numbers, could well perform those priestly ministries that, under certain conditions, are already permitted by the code. In this way they could prevent the large-scale closing of parishes. At the same time, they could eliminate the "priestless parish," which, from the Catholic viewpoint of community and Eucharist, is a liturgical and theological monstrosity. Like the woman in Hong Kong, who was a parish priest for four years before formal ordination, these women would become the functioning priests in the so-called priestless parishes. Eventually, the people themselves would demand that some of these women, who have the pastoral charism, be ordained to the ministry of eucharistic presiding.

Shaping the priestly ministry as a pastoral response "from below" could well include the institution of a diversity of extraordinary ministers, for both men and women. We already have extraordinary ministers of the Eucharist. There is no theological reason why the local church, with an appropriate preparation and ordination, could not institute extraordinary ministers for the anointing of the sick. Baptized lay ministers have anointed the sick in the past.[67] This ancient practice could well be recovered in view of today's "wartime" emergencies in many *colonias*, barrios, hospitals, and convalescent homes, where the sick are dying in large numbers without the grace of anointing. Many women have already been trained as health care chaplains. The church could bless their fruitful ministry to the sick by allowing these women to celebrate the sacrament of anointing wherever it is needed. This could be done without further delay.

Extraordinary ministers, not unlike the existing eucharistic ministers, could also be instituted for the sacrament of marriage, again with an appropriate preparation and ordination. The many women who now prepare couples for marriage would then follow through and preside at the nuptial ceremony. The new Code of Canon Law, as noted above, already allows women to assist at marriages "where priests or deacons are lacking" (canon 1112). (This provision of the law has already been invoked in one diocese in Alaska.)

Women could also be ordained to the preaching ministry without further delay. Thousands of women have earned theological degrees with great distinction. The parish would then be blessed with the experience of feminine faith and spirituality. Of course such women would preach the homily after the Gospel, where it belongs, and not after communion as is done in some churches at present.

Understandably, many of these extraordinary ministers would need special training designed and adapted for their particular ministries. These ministries, each with an ordination ceremony shaped by gift, need, and discernment, could then be multiplied as a pastoral response to the various needs in the actual congregations. Eventually, they would go well beyond the traditional and rather narrow ministry of the seven sacraments. There are thousands of places and moments where the church is called to bring healing grace to the ailing human condition.

Often what is "extraordinary" from the viewpoint of law is already "ordinary" from the viewpoint of theology and pastoral practice. Eventually it also becomes "ordinary" from the viewpoint of law. Of course the saving grace experienced through these "extraordinary" ministries is not dependent on the determination of an ecclesiastical law. All communities and all ministries, for that matter, if they are to avoid chaos, need the law. But pastoral needs and emergencies usually precede the law. Saving grace, if it happens at all, happens in the flesh and blood of the actual pastoral situation, which the law cannot possibly foresee. Furthermore, the law of love that Jesus preached will always have the priority in pastoral care.

As the whole church continues to search for pastoral solutions, all these priestly ministers, men and women, ordinary and extraordinary, will already be working from the grassroots to reform the sacrament of the church. In its song, its prayer, its service, and its celebrations the church will gradually become a more luminous sign of the diversity of ministries and the equality of the baptized people of God. Christ may indeed wish to redeem our sinful church through sacramental clay like us.

CHAPTER NINE

Partnership

*"I ask you also, my true yokemate, to help them, for they have struggled
at my side in promoting the Gospel..." (Phil 4:3).*

Since the close of Vatican II many Christian communities have experimented with team or shared ministry. As our aging clergy die or resign, there will surely be more and more forms of collaboration in the pastoral ministries. This does not mean that "lay" ministers will be substitutes for the missing clergy, or that fewer clergy will now have more helpers. Partnership in the ministry is not a solution to the clergy shortage. The so-called vocation crisis, however, may be a blessed occasion for rediscovering the collaborative principle that is part of the very nature of the church.

Many of the experiments in partnership ministry are still in process and are undergoing the normal growing pains of new church structures. Sometimes they are in tension with pre–Vatican II pyramid structures. Before we discuss the strengths and weaknesses of these experiments it may be helpful to reflect on the theological foundation for shared ministry.

Vatican II recovered the New Testament teaching on *diakonia* (ministry) and the Pauline emphasis on charisms as they relate to the body of Christ. Besides that, the council often focused on the baptism we all share in common. Whether ordained or not, all the baptized share in the priestly, prophetic, and kingly mission of Christ. All are called to be disciples and partners in one and the same mission.

Whatever forms of shared ministry we create in the future, we can certainly find the theological rationale for a partnership ministry in the very nature of a Christian community as *essentially* a sharing community. Thus wherever Christians gather, whether for the annual Conference of

Catholic Bishops or for the monthly meeting of the parish council, they always retain their identity as a sharing community. They share the cup, the bread, the Word, the Spirit, the priesthood, and the ministry. Already in Acts we see that "the brethren devoted themselves to the apostles' instruction and to the communal life, to the breaking of bread and the prayers.... Those who believed shared all things in common" (2:42–43). Even if this scene from Acts is idyllic, it reflects the hope of the church in community.

Theological discussions about shared ministries have to begin with the assumption that a sharing community already exists. The shared ministry, like the shared bread and cup, will simply be one more sign or sacrament of a sharing community. Where the bread is not shared, there is no Christian community; where the ministry is not shared, there is no Christian community. That's simple enough. Shared ministry begins, not with a downward distribution of the pie of authority by ordained ministers, but with the recognition and celebration of the gifts of the baptized who share "all things in common," including the ministry. Of course such shared ministries will gradually include some kind of order that of necessity comes from unity with the larger church. Without such an ordering toward the larger communion, a local community would eventually become a sect, following its own "charismatic" leader. But more about that later.

The New Testament word "community" (*koinōnia*) indicates a relationship of mutuality and reciprocity. Its root meaning is "partnership," the favorite word for the giving and receiving in marriage. In the secular world the Greek *koinōnia* was often used to describe the marriage relationship between husband and wife. It is a relationship of equality in which receiving is as important as giving.

We know from Paul's letters dealing with the collection for the starving saints in Jerusalem (Rom 15:25–27) that receiving the collection from the Gentiles was a sign of the equality of Jews and Gentiles in the partnership of the Christian community. If the Jews had refused to receive the gift from the Gentiles, they would have rejected partnership. For Paul the partnership of the *koinōnia* (community) means: "(a) participate in, have a share in; (b) give a share, 'communicate' (c) fellowship, communion. The term expressed the state of the Christian relationship as well as the reciprocity inherent in the relationship: giving; receiving."[1]

Paul's insistence on the partnership of community recalls the main message of the creation account in Genesis 2:5–25. Here we see that the creation of the partnership of Adam and Eve is the main theme of the story. When Eve is presented to Adam he exclaims: "This one at last is bone from my bones" (2:23). The story proclaims the good news that humans are created to be in partnership with each other:

The creation of human sexuality represents the culminating high point of the story. It signals movement from isolation to community. . . . The potential for full self-expression comes in the context of partnership. . . .

In both creation accounts of Genesis, the story ends with the man and the woman standing in partnership. This primordial partnership is the oldest of visions, the best of God's dreams. It was to be a reminder that life is best served by mutuality, that peace is best promoted by relationships. It was a call to all people for all time to enter into partnership with each other and with the earth.[2]

In recent years "community" has been overused and diluted to the point where it has lost its rich biblical meaning. It will be up to the churches to recover its real truth. J. Robert Nelson comments:

The New Testament Greek word *koinōnia* has become virtually debased by the popularization it has received, for it has been erroneously equated with personal relations alone. But the word, with its various cognate forms, means literally "mutual participation" or "common sharing" in the goods and values which are most essential to the Christian life. Who or what is shared? According to the New Testament, especially in St. Paul's letters and the Acts of the Apostles, the members may share in a common life in the Body of Christ, in the gifts and presence of the Holy Spirit, in suffering, in money and property and food, in the mission of Gospel, and in the eucharistic bread and wine. All such sharing presupposes a large measure of common faith and love. It is pointless to suggest such matters as a sentimental and idealized formula for the local church. But the amazing thing is the fact that these aspects of *koinōnia* can still find expression in the present time.[3]

In recent years *communion* has been proposed as an ideal model for church. Pope John Paul II in his exhortation *Christifideles Laici* (Exhortation on the Laity), published January 30, 1989, uses "communion" 127 times. Evidently the pope feels this word conveys an important message. If we retain the biblical meaning of this word and do not immediately impose a hierarchic construct upon it, then we have an ecclesial reality that is rooted in eucharistic communion: admission to the Lord's table includes a measure and criterion of sharing in the social, ministerial, and disciplinary life of the local church. "The central teachings about the church," writes James Coriden, "lend strong support for and show strikingly the appropriateness of a broad sharing of decisional responsibilities in the local church."[4]

A second biblical/theological foundation for shared ministry is most certainly the Pauline image of the body of Christ (Eph 4:11–12; 1 Cor 12:12–21; Rom 12:4–8). The members of the body have different functions but work for the common good of the body. The whole image speaks of interdependence, reciprocity, mutuality, shared life, and finally a differentiation of function. The main purpose of this image is to teach the Christians of Corinth that they have their ministries in the church on the basis of their baptism and the gifts of the Spirit. Even though Paul feels some gifts are more important than others, he does not impose a ranking system upon them in a priori fashion. The most useful gift, and therefore the most important, is the one that builds up the church the most. This may be that of the administrator, the helper, the teacher, or the prophet, depending on the need of the church at a particular time for that kind of ministry. The usefulness of the Spirit's gifts is not determined by how well they do or do not fit into a church's pre-existing ranking system.

Parenthetically, with Karl Rahner we could raise the question of whether the church's hierarchic office could itself be a charism of the Spirit, ministering order, in a priori fashion, among the various ministries.[5] This is quite possible. But, that is exactly what needs to be discerned, according to Pauline or, perhaps, Ignatian criteria. Does hierarchic office build up the church? Does it foster peace among the various ministers? "But the Spirit produces love, joy, peace" (Gal 5:22). If hierarchy is an "ordering" gift of the Spirit (a possibility that cannot be ruled out), it is subject to the same discernment process applied to all the other gifts. Neither Vatican II nor the subsequent episcopal synods, so far at least, have listed as an item on their agenda: "Discernment of the Usefulness of Hierarchy." Naturally, the baptized people of God, with their own gifts of discernment (1 Cor 12:10) and "sense of faith" would contribute their own "word of wisdom" to such an agenda.

Another Pauline image pointing toward shared ministry is the "building of God" (1 Cor 3:9). Paul is fond of the idea that the various ministries given to the baptized "build up" the church. When the Scriptures speak of edification they are really speaking of upbuilding. Paul's Greek noun *oikodomē* refers to "the operation (process) of upbuilding." Paul Minear explains:

> Attention is concentrated on the process of construction and the crucial relationship between the one essential foundation and what every workman builds upon it. In other words, the image directs our minds to the continuing dramatic action on the part of both God and man, rather than to the contour of the completed house.... Stonemasons and carpenters are alike fellow workers with God.[6]

For Paul the church gets built up because the skilled builders interrelate and coordinate their gifts with each other. Just as there is no hand or foot apart from the body so there is no builder apart from the whole building process. The upbuilding process is very much dependent on the disposition and ability of the builders to coordinate their gifts with each other.

Just as Vatican II defined the church as mystery, so too Paul's image of the building has its mysterious element. Karl Barth explains:

> Whereas in ordinary construction we have an owner with its fixed and declared intention and a master builder with his corresponding plans and directions, in the upbuilding of the community there is only the Lord whose purpose and plan are concealed, or are revealed and made known only in the orders which He continually gives, so that He cannot be nailed down to any intention supposedly known to those who take part.... In this building new dispositions may be made at any time by which ... the last become first and the first last: a leading worker or overseer again dropping back into the ranks and having an important contribution to make as a laborer.[7]

Thus we see that an important function in the actual achievement of shared ministry for the upbuilding of the church is the ongoing integration and coordination of the ministers and their charisms. Barth, with an eye to the pastoral reality, observes that the ministers are not in the beginning a common organism but "a heterogeneous collection of individuals who even if they do not conflict, do not cooperate."[8] The image of the building of God points to the cooperation of the Spirit and all the "living stones." It recognizes "both the joy and the discipline of shared responsibility."[9]

A third biblical/theological foundation for shared ministry is the common discipleship of all the baptized. In their 1987 report to the Roman Synod, the American bishops' delegates expressed this idea with the word "co-discipleship."[10] They explained that "we are all disciples of Jesus Christ ... and share responsibility for carrying out His mission."[11] Without repeating chapter 1 it is sufficient to note here that all disciples, ordained or not, are called to heal, to teach, to reconcile, to visit the sick, to feed the hungry, to visit those in prison, to shelter the homeless, to make peace. All these functions are part of the baptismal vocation to discipleship. All those who share in this vocation by that very fact are involved in shared ministry. Distribution of functions is a practical, pastoral decision at the level of the local church. It is more an organizational than a theological concern.

A fourth biblical/theological foundation is the common possession of the Spirit. Without repeating chapter 2, we need to recall that the Holy Spirit is given to each of the baptized "according to the measure of faith" (Rom 12:3–4). If we take the common possession of the Spirit seriously then all the baptized already possess empowerment for shared ministry. They merely need to activate the gift of administration (1 Cor 12:28) to build the structures for sharing their ministries. These structures need to support, enable, and maximize all the community's ministries.

A fifth biblical/theological foundation for shared ministry certainly has to be the common possession of the one priesthood of Christ. "You are a chosen race, a royal priesthood" (1 Pt 2:9). In his homily to the newly baptized, the author of 1 Peter admonishes the new Christians to be "built into a spiritual house, to be a holy priesthood, to offer spiritual sacrifices acceptable to God through Jesus Christ" (1 Pt 2:5). While organizational forms for shared ministry are very necessary, they may never undermine this common priesthood of the faithful. Similarly, ordinations to different "levels" of priesthood may not depreciate this common priesthood. If shared ministry is going to witness to partnership, the baptized will have to be ordained to *functions*, not to "levels." If husband and wife are in a true partnership, they are not on different "levels."

A sixth biblical/theological foundation for shared ministry is the common mission flowing from shared baptism and confirmation. No ordinations can negate the call to ministry that proceeds from these two sacraments. Even though they are usually celebrated when the candidate are too young to understand their responsibilities, nevertheless both sacraments are oriented to mission and ministry. These "ordinations" are not bound to the time or age when they are celebrated but continue to call the recipients to the ongoing fulfillment of the responsibilities of the various stages of their adult vocation.

The seventh biblical/theological foundation for shared ministry can be called pastoral collegiality. While it is true that collegiality as defined by Vatican II applies only to bishops, one can nevertheless, by way of analogy, extend collegiality to other communions in the church. Collegiality, analogically understood, is a sign of a community breaking bread together and sharing with one another, not only their bread, but also their gifts. As sharing in one bread and one cup is the sign of our community identity, so also is the collegiality of our pastoral style.

This pastoral collegiality has been evident in the history of the church through the actual exercise of participative responsibility. Coriden lists only a few of the forms of collegiality: "the Council of Jerusalem, the elders and overseers exercising corporate guidance in the first three centuries, the universal practice of the election of bishops by clergy and people, the pattern of synodal deliberations, the participative function of religious and cathedral chapters, etc."[12] We can assume that our new

Pentecost, breathing forth new ministries, will also create new forms of pastoral collegiality.

A final model for sharing the ministries could well be the Trinity. During the Sunday liturgy we proclaim our faith in three equal Persons in one God, who exists in relationship. Even though the Persons are equal, we attribute to Them the distinct functions of creating, redeeming, and sanctifying. Diverse functions do not affect equality. Those who baptize and proclaim a Gospel in the name of the Trinity are called to image God in a triune relationship by living and working in a partnership of diverse ministries.

The Social and Societal Conditions

Besides the biblical/theological foundations already noted there are sociological and historical conditions calling for more participative decision making and ministering structures in the church. Sociologists today compile impressive data showing that Catholics conditioned by democracy and modern management systems expect to have a significant voice in the decisions that directly affect them. Paternalistic and authoritarian models, therefore, are ineffective in today's Catholic culture. If today's ministers are going to interact with today's world they need to be comfortable with participative decision making. If the ministers have no voice in the decision they will bring little energy to its implementation. In fact, they may undercut the decision in the actual pastoral situation.

Much has been written about the principle of subsidiarity. This principle was first proposed by Pope Pius XI in his encyclical *Quadragesimo Anno* (On Reconstructing Social Order). The same principle was highlighted by Pope John XXIII in his encyclical *Mater et Magistra*, 1961, and again in Vatican II's Pastoral Constitution on the Church in the Modern World.[13] As formulated by Pius XI, this principle states:

> That most weighty principle, which cannot be set aside or changed, remains fixed and unshaken in social philosophy: Just as it is gravely wrong to take from individuals what they can accomplish by their own initiative and industry and give it to the community, so also it is an injustice and at the same time a grave evil and disturbance of right order to assign to a greater and higher association what lesser and subordinate organizations can do. For every social activity ought of its very nature to furnish help to the members of the body social, and never destroy and absorb them.[14]

If we apply this weighty principle to the church we will not defer to Rome decisions that can and ought to be made by the National Conference of Bishops; we will not refer to the diocese decisions that can and ought be made in the parish. Decisions about altar girls and washing women's feet on Holy Thursday do not need to be "assigned to a greater and higher association." In many such cases ministers at the grassroots will do best to trust their pastoral sense and simply make decisions for their own communities.

Consultation as a Form of Shared Ministry

In the last twenty-five years we have seen the formation of numerous types of consultative bodies: diocesan pastoral councils, presbyteral councils, sisters' councils, lay councils, parish councils, and deanery and vicariate councils. In addition, many bishops have appointed clergy personnel boards, arbitration or grievance committees, and consultative boards for Catholic schools. Others have appointed boards or commissions to oversee finances, liturgy, family life, and peace and justice programs.

Forming a consultative body implies that shared ministry begins with shared policy-making and shared pastoral planning. If these consultative bodies are going to be an exercise in shared ministry, consultation must be serious and meaningful. Coriden warns:

> Beware of boards and councils made of papier-mâché for purpose of window dressing! Groups designated for special tasks must be allowed and encouraged to do them. The precise label given to their authority (e.g., advisory, consultative, legislative, etc.) is far less important than that their work be done well and their decisions followed. Good judgments have an intrinsic authority because of their own worth and wisdom. Groups become educated to their tasks and develop expertise by actually doing their job and being taken seriously by those who deputed them.[15]

Once the consultation process has taken root in the governance of the church it is disastrous to bypass or ignore it. To consult is to be faithful to the very nature of the church as a sharing community. To fail to consult is to betray the sign and sacrament of the church. As Coriden puts it: "To state it plainly (if a bit too categorically): every time a pastor decides alone to build a church or to change the times of Sunday Masses he acts irresponsibly.... Every time a bishop, by himself or with a few hand-picked advisors, spends large sums of diocesan money, closes a school, starts a new parish, or backs a low income housing program, he does violence to his pastoral office and fails the people he is commissioned to lead."[16]

176

It is worth recalling that most citizens today have a right to choose their own form of government. "They can elect a mayor, a city manager, a town board, a city council, or any combination of these elements. There is no one perfect and changeless system. . . . The right to decide belongs to the people."[17] There is no reason why democratic forms of civil government cannot be adapted to today's church government just as monarchic forms were adapted by the church during the Constantinian era.

Team Ministries

Besides the volunteer or part-time consultative structures mentioned above, we have seen the growth of full-time team ministries and even co-pastorates. These forms of shared ministry sometimes are seen as an effort to stretch the ministry of the clergy a little further. They will not be true to the nature of the church, however, as long as they are seen as the arms or instruments of the dwindling clergy.

Team ministry has been defined "as an authentic, cooperative effort by those called, to exercise accountability, leadership in the Christian community for the full realization of the ministry of Christ."[18] Even though these team ministries have had their growing pains, we can, even at this stage, list many advantages: teams bring about a more efficient use of the various ministries; they provide a structure for the different specializations; they inform and educate more people about the needs of the community; and finally, they witness rather effectively to community and the shared aspect of all ministry.

Some disadvantages, nevertheless, have also been noted: some people, accustomed to having one priest in charge, are confused when there is no single leader who has ultimate authority for decisions; sometimes, team members who refer the people's questions to the next team meeting are accused of being indecisive; at other times, this style of government appears inefficient, time-consuming, and expensive (copies for everybody); team members, while they are sensitive to supporting each other, do not often criticize or challenge each other. They do not hold each other accountable. For some team members accountability is seen primarily as vertical, to bishop or pope, rather than horizontal, to fellow team members and the people of God.

Commentators emphasize the need for criteria in the selection of team members. If the team is to avoid wasting its energy in internal conflicts, it needs compatibility in theology and even, to some extent, in psychological profiles. The people of God deserve quality and competence in ministry. So far the qualifications for team ministry have been poorly defined.

Various authors have noted several ingredients essential for a suc-

cessful team. These can be summarized as a shared sense of belonging,
a shared sense of achievement, shared accountability, and, of course,
shared prayer and theological reflection.[19]

Some tentative qualifications for membership on a team would seem
to be openness, listening ability, awareness of feelings in one's self and
in others, flexibility to work with others, eagerness to grow through interaction, a willingness to receive the gifts from others, and a willingness
to sacrifice individual goals for the common good when necessary and
finally *"a big, fat sense of humor."*[20]

Team ministry calls for transcendence of sexual stereotypes since the
unity of the team as community is the important reality. Division of the
team along the lines of clergy or laity, male or female, is a contradiction of
shared ministry. The team functions best when it emphasizes the unique
gifts of the members regardless of caste or gender.

Dealing with Some Problems

As we experiment with team ministries, we learn that there are different understandings of team and community. Sometimes ministers see
the team as their community. Others, especially religious, feel that the
team is a working structure and their own religious community remains
their primary community. Still others feel that the parish itself is their
main community. These different understandings need to be openly
discussed; otherwise there will be conflict and wasted energy.

Some authors have pointed out that, to keep problems to a minimum,
special criteria are required for membership on a team:

1. a peaceful acceptance of the lifestyle inherent in their own vocation;

2. a capacity to adapt with some ease to changing situations;

3. sufficient health for the vigorous demands of the apostolate and
   emotional stability to weather stress;

4. completion of ordinary education;

5. proven ability to initiate some programs;

6. a capacity to choose group goals and work for them effectively;

7. a capacity to live with the personalities of this group;

8. a capacity for mutual growth through interaction with the other
   members of the team;

9. a theological and philosophical consensus that all can work with;

10. probation for six months; a commitment of at least two years.[21]

Those who have been members of team ministries have noticed that the parishioners are very much attached to the traditional style of ministry under one pastor. Besides the entrenched habits fostered by the pyramid structure, J. Robert Nelson has described four other obstacles to shared ministry:

> These are the *inertia* felt by the congregations which are habituated to traditional manners and ways; the *reluctance* of people, who often want to find only comfort in religion, to assume the harder disciplines of self-giving which effective membership requires; the *confusion* in contemporary theology with the accompanying loss of confidence in the proximate and ultimate goals to be sought, and the consequent weakening of faith itself; and the *denominational structures* which usually inhibit local churches in their efforts to achieve needed changes.[22]

At least one author has commented that with team there seems to be a reluctance for individual members to assume responsibility. It's easier to "pass the buck."[23]

The confusion in theology, mentioned above by Nelson, can indeed be a serious problem with shared ministry. With the emergence of different models of church and parish, it is not easy for the team to reach a consensus on a specific model that translates smoothly into pastoral practice. As a result, pastoral planning can be filled with conflict. The team's energy, instead of becoming focused on common goals, gets diffused by unnecessary infighting.

Also, in this postconciliar church we have more than a remnant of the patriarchal management style. It is not unusual to find a dependent parent/child relationship operating in the team. Among other things, it may mean that "Father" takes the brunt of unpopular decisions. It is easier to hold "Father" responsible for the pastoral insensitivity of the Code of Canon Law and of diocesan policies. It can also mean that the dependent team member waits for Father to issue the orders. Nothing happens until Father says: "Go."

There is a residue of clericalism that reveals itself during the celebration of the sacraments. It is not easy for a lay member to do all the work of preparing a couple for marriage and then have to turn the couple over to "Father" for the actual celebration of the wedding. The same problem emerges in the care of the sick when the laity minister at the bedside of the dying and then must step aside while the priest takes charge of the anointing. This practice does not honor the lay team member's pastoral relationship, which is also the grace of the healing sacrament.

In practice some clergy are still threatened by what they view as an encroachment on "their" spiritual domain. If their identity is too closely linked with the spiritual ministry of the sacraments, they will sense a gap in their own ministerial identity as laity take over "their" priestly roles as ministers of the spiritual. This can create a lay-clergy tension that becomes an obstacle to shared ministry.

If we eliminate the "lay"/"clergy" labels, as suggested in chapter 7, much of this tension will vanish. But the question still remains, who on the team is in charge of the spiritual? More specifically, who is supposed to be the eucharistic presider? Part of the answer has to come from the team as a "new" governing structure in the church. Another part of the answer, it seems to me, has to come from a new theology of orders, as explained in chapter 5.

We recalled in chapter 2 that in the early church there existed a plurality of church organizations. Some churches were ruled by a committee or council of lay elders, as in Jerusalem. Others were ruled by prophets and teachers, as in Antioch. Still others were ruled by traveling apostles or by "those who are over you." It seems that prophets and teachers presided over the Eucharist where they presided over the community. In the *Didache*, we see that deacons and bishops preside when the prophets are not available.

In view of this tradition of a plurality of approaches to the ministry of eucharistic presiding, we would have to retain the option that a modern parish team, with the discernment and "Amen" of its people, could select a eucharistic presider. To maintain order in the church, such a person would first need to be ordained in some ceremony similar to that described in chapter 5. Such a person, who before ordination had a presiding function over the community, would also need some visible communion with the larger, diocesan church.

In the early church, perhaps through sociological necessity, there was a movement toward one-man rule. Gradually, as charismatics and prophets disappeared, the bishop, at first an unordained overseer, became *the* eucharistic presider. It was a natural and understandable development: first he was the presider over the community; then he became the presider over the Eucharist. This became an important norm, blessed by the early councils of the church.

In modern times, I suspect, many parishes and dioceses will also adopt the one-person rule (the overseer) of the late New Testament period (1 and 2 Tm and Titus). Still, the question remains, who will be the eucharistic presider? The theology of the early church would demand that whoever presides over the community also preside over the Eucharist. One would assume that the person presiding over the community has arrived at this leadership position because of the leadership qualities discerned by the community. The presider would be the one whom the people have discerned to have the functional competence to be a good liturgist, an effective preacher of the Word and excel in enabling all the pastoral ministries of the community.

Such a eucharistic presider would be ordained to call together a community, to continue building community, and then to celebrate it. This presider would be the public embodiment, the living symbol, of the community's goals and values. As such, the presider would be a sacrament of God's presence in the community. At the same time, he/she would be a unifying symbol who reconciled the members of the community to God and to each other. He/she would bring order and harmony into the community so that all its ministries would build up the church. This presider, in the prophetic tradition, would also extend the community's vision to include the whole human community. Finally, he/she would represent the larger institutional church.[24] Despite its human frailty, the institutional church is the visible sacrament of God's saving grace for all humankind. Neither the Eucharist nor its presider ever become the property of one community.

In the immediate future, this eucharistic presider will probably continue to be the diocesan or religious priest who is already ordained. As these priests die, the future presiders will have to come from the community's actual leaders, male or female, married or single. Presiding over the Eucharist will always remain one among many shared ministries to the community.

The problem of selecting the eucharistic presider highlights the need for structural reforms that will bring the people's gifts of discernment into the whole governing process of the church. Despite the many commendable efforts at renewal since Vatican II, the Catholic Church does not yet foster the shared ministry of broad participation in many community decisions such as judicial and arbitration boards. Presently, the bishop is the sole judge. With the exception of limited lay participation on marriage tribunals, there is no opportunity for most baptized ministers to offer their experience in adjudicating complaints through any kind of commonly accepted grievance procedures. "Lay" ministers may be vaguely aware that the new Code of Canon Law has a section on the rights of the baptized. They are rarely invited, however, to offer their judgment on the competence of those who minister (including eucharistic presiding) in their parishes. Moreover, the church structures themselves are rarely subject to review and evaluation. If shared ministry is going to have meaning, the ministers themselves need to have some voice in creating and shaping the structures that serve and extend their ministry.

One of the most ancient and useful structures in the local church is the often neglected diocesan synod. Some dioceses have not held a synod for fifty years despite the fact that the 1917 Code of Canon Law required a synod to be held every ten years (canon 237). The new Code of Canon Law (1983) stipulates that "a diocesan synod be celebrated in each of the particular churches when circumstances warrant it in the judgment of the diocesan bishop" (canon 461). Further, it asks that "lay members of the Christian faithful" be called to these synods (canon 463). During these synods "all the proposed questions are to be subject to the free discussion of the members" (canon 465). Synods are now held with greater frequency. But until they become a regular part of church life, a precious opportunity for the discernment of gifts and the shared ministry of pastoral planning will be lost.

Ecumenical Sharing of Ministries

When Pius IX convoked the First Vatican Council in 1869 he issued invitations to the leaders of the Eastern Orthodox and Protestant churches. The ecumenical climate, however, was so frosty and inhospitable that the patriarch of Constantinople returned the pope's invitation unopened. The Protestants, with the Church of England in the lead, also ignored the pope's invitations.[25]

During the pontificate of Pope Pius XII (d. 1958), there was very little ecumenical activity in the Catholic Church. In fact, in 1948 and 1954, he forbade Catholic attendance at the assemblies of the World Council of Churches at Amsterdam and Evanston. It was the ecumenical movement's own "dark night."

With the election of Pope John XXIII, however, the church opened its windows to a new and lively ecumenical dialogue. The media carried pictures of the smiling pope chatting on friendly terms with the leaders of Orthodox and Protestant churches. He invited Protestants to be auditors during the Second Vatican Council. He appointed the distinguished Cardinal Bea to lead the new Secretariat for Promoting Christian Unity. This Secretariat prepared the first schema for Vatican II's Decree on Ecumenism.

Breathing the fresh air of the decree's ecumenical openness, pastoral ministers have been much more comfortable in sharing their ministries with the ministers of other faiths. Many parish ministers now belong to the local ministerial associations; others attend ecumenical conferences dealing with the pastoral issues of AIDS, alcoholism, drug abuse, and family life. Pastoral ministers of all faiths have joined hands in community efforts to alleviate hunger, provide housing for the homeless, and support blood drives. Vatican II provided a new theological foundation for shared ministry among the various faiths because it highlighted what the faiths have in common. We can recall here, very briefly, that communions of all faiths share belief in the one God, in Jesus as the Christ, in the Holy Spirit, in the Word of God and prayer. Many churches also share a belief in some sacraments and in liturgical rites. Finally, most Christian churches have outreach programs that go beyond strictly denominational concerns. These are the common bonds that provide a foundation for shared ministry among ministers of many faiths. As a result, the way is open for all Christian ministers to witness to the shared aspect of all ministry being performed in the name of the one Jesus Christ.

Nevertheless, we have to admit honestly that there are many questions regarding ecumenical ministry that remain unanswered. The celebrated Lima Document of the World Council of Churches (1982) addressed just a few of the difficult issues that separate the various churches and their ministries:

> (1) authority; (2) the very term "priest" and its connection with Jesus; (3) the ministry of women in the Christian church; (4) the role of bishop, presbyter and deacon; (5) the fact that ordained ministry must be personal, collegial and communal; these three aspects are then applied to bishop, presbyter and deacon. In the various Christian communities there exist episcopal, presbyteral and congregational structures or systems and these need to be appreciated and to some degree be interrelated; (6) the meaning of apostolic succession . . . ; (7) ordination. . . . [26]

On the theological level, the validity of Anglican orders remains a serious problem for sharing ecumenical ministries. In 1896 Pope Leo XIII pronounced Anglican orders to be "invalid and entirely void" due to substantial defects in the rite of ordination used in the Church of England from the time of Edward IV. In 1973, however, the Anglican-Roman Catholic International Commission called for a "reappraisal of the verdict on Anglican orders in *Apostolicae Curae* (1896)."[27] Catholic theologians have raised serious questions about the credibility of Pope Leo's Commission on Anglican Orders.[28]

In spite of these difficulties, Christian ministers are called to witness to that unity that does in fact exist. We do gather in the name of the same Lord under the same Word and in the same Spirit. Certainly ministers need to witness to their common faith, hope, and charity. If the "certain rifts" mentioned in the Decree on Ecumenism are ever to be healed, then the ministers themselves "must make the first approaches" toward a mutual understanding of each other's faiths, which may, by God's grace, lead to a deeper unity. The same decree "exhorts all the Catholic faithful to recognize the signs of the times and to participate skillfully in the work of ecumenism."

We can hardly discuss shared ministry across the various Christian faiths without dealing with the question of recognition of each others' ministries. For the baptismal ministries the question of recognition is fairly simple. If the Christian churches recognize each others baptisms, as many now do, they are also committed to recognize each other's baptismal ministries. A wide spectrum of shared ministries can be initiated at the grassroots without any further permissions or discussions. This happens, for instance, when the baptismal ministers cooperate in staffing the soup kitchens and the clothing distribution centers for the poor. In the actual pastoral practice of the churches, considerable mutual recognition of baptismal ministries has already taken place.

When we begin to deal with the official ordained ministry of the various churches the problem becomes more complex. Nevertheless, we need to ask insistently to what extent the baptismal ministers at the parish level are called to move toward a mutual recognition of each other's ordained "clergy" ministries.

Since its first meeting at Lausanne in 1927, the Faith and Order Commission of the World Council of Churches has sponsored numerous theological dialogues on the mutual recognition of ministries. Considerable progress has been made in the last sixty years. Even though many problems remain, the baptized pastoral ministers can certainly incorporate into their pastoral practice whatever consensus has been achieved so far. It may be helpful to make appropriate distinctions and to clarify the various degrees in the process of recognition so that we can honestly and truthfully celebrate the unity that already exists.

In 1975 the Faith and Order Commission issued its official statement, *One Baptism, One Eucharist and a Mutually Recognized Ministry*. In it the commission distinguished four degrees or modes of mutual recognition of official ordained ministries. The first degree is that of *mutual respect*. "The minister of the other church is not simply considered as a private individual but as one who is invested with certain authority, which enables him to be the spokesman for his community. His representative character is recognized."[29]

A second degree of recognition is reached when the ecclesial nature of the other church is acknowledged: "Then the ministry, though it may not be without defects, cannot be declared to be without any spiritual significance. The ministers are seen to have been raised up by God for the equipping of his people and to be actually engaged in the task assigned to the ordained ministry."[30]

A third degree in mutual recognition is reached when the ministry of the other church "is officially acknowledged as the apostolic ministry given by Christ." In some cases such recognition could eventually lead to full communion between two churches. The churches reach the fourth stage when they accept a mutual recognition of each other's churches, including mutual recognition of their ministries. In this stage the churches agree to recognize the other church as truly being Christ's church as much as they regard themselves as such, even though their organizational structures differ. This final stage would include a common celebration of the Lord's Supper.

Needless to say, the baptismal ministers can move toward mutual recognition of the official ordained ministry with regard to the first degree of mutual respect. They could go even further and honor the ordained ministers of other faiths because they serve as sacraments of the Word, of grace, and of the Holy Spirit's saving activity.

Regarding the second degree of recognition, we must be more precise. Since Pope Leo XIII declared Anglican orders to be null and void, we need to ask whether the Reformed Churches *lack* a ministry or merely have a *deficient* ministry, in the eyes of the Roman Catholic Church. It is quite plain from the Lima Document issued by the same Faith and Order Commission in January 1982 that "Churches without episcopal succession and living in faithful continuity with the apostolic faith and mission, have a ministry of Word and sacrament as is evident from the belief, practice and life of those churches." The Roman Catholic/Lutheran Joint Commission in its 1981 report entitled *Ministry in the Church* concluded:

> If all this is done, the next step could consist of a mutual recognition that the ministry in the other church exercises essential functions of the ministry that Jesus Christ instituted in his church and, which one believes is fully realized in one's own church. This as yet incomplete mutual recognition would include the affirmation that the Holy Spirit also operates in the other church through its ministries and makes use of these as means of salvation in the proclamation of the gospel, the administration of the sacraments, and the leadership of congregations.[31]

It should be clear from the above that pastoral ministers can grant recognition to each other's ordained ministries also in the second degree of recognition. They can agree that the ministries in the other church exercise essential functions of the ministry of Jesus Christ. With Vatican II Catholic pastoral ministers can acknowledge the ecclesial nature of each other's churches with the consequence that its ministry has spiritual significance for its members even though there is no explicit assertion that the other ministry is the apostolic ministry instituted by Christ. Even though the ministry in the other church may appear to be deficient, it is not without spiritual significance.

Now the question remains whether Catholic pastoral ministers may go to the third level in their recognition of the ministries of Protestant churches. In other words, can the pastoral minister recognize in the other church not only essential *functions* of Christ's ministry, but a *"real* apostolic ministry of Jesus Christ and his Spirit, a real ministry of Word and sacrament that is fruitful in terms of faith and salvation for the members of that particular church?"[32] The precise theological question is: "May the Catholic pastoral minister recognize a non-episcopal ordained ministry, that is, a ministry which exists outside of the episcopal apostolic succession?" May a Catholic pastoral minister recognize the ordained ministry of another church without agreeing that the other church is the true church of Christ?

From the viewpoint of *present theology*, we are ready to answer this question in the affirmative. Joseph F. Eagan reviewed ten post–Vatican II dialogues on the ordained ministry in 1984. He lists the reasons for extending mutual recognition at the third level as described above:

> Compelling reasons exist for extending mutual recognition *at this time*, at least on the third level. *Now* is the acceptable time to recognize the reality of the ecumenical situation between the churches, to create the new relationships demanded, and to forge new categories to deal with the extraordinary situation of division in the body of Christ. Recognition is but ecumenical realism and justice in affirming the reality of Reformation ministry; recognition is the start of reconciliation, a way to forgive a potential sibling church and be forgiven in turn; recognition is further encouragement for Reformation churches to reevaluate and recover more of the Catholic elements lost in Reformation polemics; recognition on the Catholic side would remove the inconsistency in Vatican II's recognizing elements of church outside the structure of the Roman Catholic Church and asserting the Spirit uses these communities as means of salvation without a corresponding recognition of their ministry of Word and sacrament; recognition demonstrates that a church take seriously a "communion of communions" model of unity rather than a simple return of one church to another; recognition "would be a decisive step towards eliminating the scandal of our separation at the Lord's Supper" and would make it possible for Christians to "bear more credible testimony before the world of their fellowship in the love of Christ"; recognition "would be an important step in helping us...to arrive eventually at full mutual recognition of ministries by the acceptance of full church and eucharistic fellowship"; finally, recognition might provide that single powerful symbolic act so needed at present in the ecumenical movement.[33]

Regarding the fourth stage of mutual recognition, which recognizes the other church as the true church of Christ, we must admit that for the present too many differences remain. The churches cannot be true to their own traditions without honestly admitting their doctrinal disagreements. They cannot celebrate a unity in the truth that does not yet exist. Unity, when it comes, must be the unity willed by Christ.

We have a long way to go in building a truly collaborative model for our ministries in the churches. We might begin the process by imitating Paul, who called all his fellow laborers *synergoi*, "energy sharers" or "ministry partners." The director of religious education, the parish secretary, and the St. Vincent de Paul workers could help the cause along by calling their pastors, their bishops, and their neighboring Protestant ministers "partners in the ministry of Christ."

During times of change it helps to recall the original vision of our Christian communities. Implementing that vision, however, will be a continuing and sometimes difficult challenge:

> Collaboration or partnership ministry demands a greater depth of self-awareness; it calls us to a level of intimacy that is less dependent and more self-disclosive; it requires a commitment to emotional honesty and the willingness to deal with conflict maturely. In short, collaboration presupposes a level of integration and maturity which will make possible a true "circle of charisms."[34]

Every ship sailing out to sea and every jet winging into the sky requires the collaboration of many skills. If the people of God are to accomplish their mission and witness to community, they too must recruit and support a diversity of talents and ministries. Then, like Paul, they must "yoke" the ministers into a partnership so that together they can build "a new heaven and a new earth."

CHAPTER TEN

Be Holy

"Be holy, for I, the Lord, your God, am holy" (Lv 19:2).

We are all for spirituality. We are also for motherhood, apple pie, and lower taxes. So long as no one defines it, spirituality seems harmless enough. It costs nothing. And it's not controversial, like the ordination of women, capital punishment, or a protest at a nuclear missile site. We all got nervous in the 1960s when Father left the sanctuary and joined the marchers in Selma, Alabama. In a time of conflict and confusion it's tempting to retreat into the safe haven of spirituality. No one will criticize us. We can have our own private line to God. If we're lucky, the poor, the homeless, and the hungry won't bother us. Our spirituality can be as private as our religion.

If, however, we move out of our safe haven and try to define spirituality, we will find that the dictionary isn't very helpful. According to Webster, spirituality is "the quality or state of being spiritual." But we still can't go to K-Mart and buy it. It won't help to take a week off and look for it. We can't order it by mail through one of those "before" and "after" ads. We can't even sign up for a twelve-week spiritual aerobics course with a guarantee that we'll reach the higher echelons of spiritual fitness.

So right off, we might as well admit it: there is no "instant" spirituality, no sure-fire recipe. There are no escalators to the top of the mountain. We may have to stumble our way up. On the other hand, if we are going to embark on a journey toward spirituality, the best way to get on with it is simply to begin. Who knows, it may be an exciting trip. It will certainly be challenging. Besides, God commands us: "Be holy." And we know that the Holy One is pulling for us all the way.

One thing is certain — if ministering persons are going to be a leaven in the world, they have to be people who in their very persons, in their way of being, bring something that the world does not have or does not know it has, but desperately needs. That "something" may be a new vision, a new power, a new witness, a new "answer," or a new way of life. In spite of the welcome shift toward a more functional approach to ministry, Christian ministers may not become obsessed with mere skill and technique. "Doing" the ministry with its endless meetings and ever-increasing paperwork is not what the ministry is about. Workaholics may be useful in the office or factory. But they aren't much help in the ministry. Besides, they won't last long. If they don't pay attention to their spiritual sides, they are running hard toward burnout, disillusionment, or both. They will soon become empty "wineskins" with nothing to give.

If Christian ministers have no contact with the transcendent God, if they do not go now and then to Mount Tabor, if, finally, they cannot share an experience of the living God with others, then they have become "a noisy gong or clanging cymbal." They will not be able to do anything except add one more discordant note to the world's cacophony. Neither the church nor the world needs that kind of minister.

So we need to find out what spirituality is and, at the same time, reflect on some of the principles and methods that guide us toward a healthy spiritual life. Since in the United States individualism is endemic to our culture, we have a tendency to approach the spiritual life from the vantage point of the individual. Most American Catholics need a conversion on this particular point. True spirituality begins with God, who loves and consecrates a holy people as God's very own, fashioning this people into a community. Then that love touches the individual member of the community, which becomes the sacrament for the individual's growth in holiness.

We learn from the Scriptures that spirituality has something to do with growth in holiness. So immediately we are compelled to ask: "What is holiness?" Again, we must start with God, since God alone is the Holy One. We have to look for the answer in God's Word. Beginning with Isaiah 6:3 we find a partial answer. The seraphim proclaims: "Holy, holy, holy is the Lord of Hosts." The triple "holy" is the Hebrew superlative; God is the holiest of the holy.

Second, we know from the Bible that God, having created us in God's image and likeness, makes holiness available to us: " . . . be holy for I the Lord your God am holy" (Lv 19:2). It is plain that any holiness the minister reflects or "acquires" will be *derived* from some contact with the Holy One. For God is the only source of holiness. But, in God's goodness, purely through gracious initiative, God shares holiness with creatures like ourselves: "You are a people holy to the Lord your God; the Lord your God has chosen you to be a people for his own possession" (Dt 7:6). Holiness, then, comes to the minister first as the Holy One's gift. But the holiness of the individual minister will always remain only one piece in God's larger mosaic:

Holiness is the state to which God is drawing the whole created order. God's Spirit, operating within the very fabric of creation, presses upon the world, seeking opportunities to shape it and to form it, to direct it towards a destiny which he has in mind for it. To walk the way of holiness, for any individual Christian, is to try to "open up" to the Spirit of the Creator God, to provide a space for him to enter, so as to be charged with his energy and driven towards the goal already revealed and reached in Jesus Christ.[1]

To direct our steps into the way of holiness is to see ourselves as part of God's creative enterprise. God, who continues to create the world, seeks peace, integration, and wholeness for all of humanity. As we strive for holiness we become partners with the Holy One accomplishing the divine purpose in and for the world. The quest for holiness, therefore, cannot be confined to a search for individual integration, personal fulfillment, or even personal salvation. We are a small, often intractable, part of God's grand design.[2]

Paul understood well that holiness comes from God's creative initiative. For him it is an act of the Holy One's power. God relates to all of creation by "hallowing" or sanctifying it. In 1 Corinthians 1:2, Paul writes: "Those sanctified in Christ Jesus...." And again: "...So that in him we might become the very holiness of God" (2 Cor 5:21). In 1 Peter 1:2, we see that the newly baptized have been "sanctified by the Spirit." The baptized people chosen and sanctified become a royal priesthood, a holy nation (1 Pt 2:9–10). All these references tell us why the Scriptures, especially the Pauline letters, frequently refer to the newly baptized as "the holy ones." To give but one example from Paul, we read in Ephesians 1:15: "Therefore, I, too, hearing of your faith in the Lord Jesus and of your love for all the holy ones...." In Acts 9:13 it is reported that Saul has done evil things to the "holy ones in Jerusalem."

> Since God is the Holy One *par excellence* (Is 6:3), those consecrated to his service are called "holy." The term, applied originally to the people of Israel (Ex 19:6), and in particular to the community of the Messianic era (Dn 7:18), is especially apt for the Christians who are the new holy race (1 Pt 2:5, 9), called (Rm 1:7; 1 Col 2; Eph 1:4; 2 Tm 1:9), by their baptismal consecration (Eph 5:26), to a blameless life,... which makes them holy as God is holy. In the early Christian community it [the holy ones] becomes the usual term for the Christians....[3]

It may be helpful to note that the Greek word used in the New Testament (*hagiazō*) is an active verb, meaning "I make holy." Calling the newly baptized "the holy ones" proclaims the truth that the Creator's hallowing activity is efficacious. The Holy One is carefully sculpting the living stones for building the city of God. No wonder that on Pentecost Sunday, in the Liturgy of the Hours, all the baptized proclaim: "The Spirit of God consecrates me.... The Spirit of God sends me forth." The journey toward holiness is the Christian's ongoing response to God's magnetic holiness drawing the Christian to the Source. The vocation to holiness is a call to measure up or respond to the holiness with which God has consecrated the minister. "Holy behavior" is not a means for becoming holy; it is thankful response for "having been made holy."

God consecrates a people just as God consecrated the Sabbath, the Temple, and the Ark of the Covenant. "The holiness of consecration does not depend on or consist in personal virtue; it is an effect of having been set apart and anointed, and thus consecrated ('made sacred') for the worship and *service* of God."[4] God has ransomed us and made us a kingdom of priests "to reign on earth" (Rv 5:10). All the baptized by their rebirth and the anointing of the Holy Spirit are consecrated into a spiritual house and a holy priesthood.[5]

In the past we have often limited "consecration" to the sacrament of ordination or to the sacred words of the eucharistic proclamation. It was one way in which we expressed our faith in God's powerful sanctifying action. Yet, in view of the Scriptures just cited, we need to recover the full meaning of that word and apply it without any further conditions to the Spirit's activity mightily at work during and after the *consecration* of baptism. The baptismal consecration is not limited to the actual time of the anointing. It continues through the life of the ministers. With this truth clearly understood, we can reflect on the various principles and methods for growing in the holiness planted within us as a small seed during our baptism.

The Holiness of the Baptized

Karl Rahner tells us that the church of the future will be a church of real spirituality.[6] He is not the only theologian to call attention to the great need to care for the spiritual life of ministering persons. In the past, Catholic spirituality was largely shaped by the vows of poverty, chastity, and obedience. It was a monastic spirituality that encouraged flight from the world. It assumed that the world was evil and therefore one could pursue spirituality only after one had "escaped" from the evil attractions of the world. Included in this flight was a tendency to disvalue the body and bodiliness.

Many spiritual writers have noted that the clerical caste imposed its own model of the spiritual life on the laity.[7] Then too, spirituality, influenced by Augustine and Descartes, was often shaped by the dualism of the sacred and the secular, of soul and body, of spiritual and material. At the same time, it was not free from a semi-pelagianism that taught that we can achieve spirituality only by ascetical practices that include the aerobics of spiritual exercises. In the United States, spirituality for those who were not in a vowed religious community also became very individualistic. It was a lonely and very personal journey with "my" Jesus or "my" devotion toward "my" God.

With the emergence of a diversity of ministries of the baptized, it is more important than ever that we introduce forms of spirituality that reflect the actual life of these nonclerical ministers. The first principle in developing a new spirituality is to link the minister's call to holiness to the baptismal vocation, whatever its outward form. Writing to the newly-baptized "holy ones" of Ephesus, Paul advises: "Even as he chose us in him before the foundation of the world, that we should be holy and blameless before him" (Eph 1:4). Paul addresses the newly baptized Corinthians as "those sanctified in Christ Jesus, called to be holy" (1 Cor 1:2). It is plain that Paul links spirituality and the call to holiness to the baptismal vocation. Vatican II, in its chapter "The Call of the Whole Church to Holiness," also connects holiness with baptism: "The followers of Christ . . . are justified in the Lord Jesus, and through baptism sought in faith, they truly become the sons of God and sharers in the divine nature. In this way they are really made holy."[8]

The second principle for the development of the spirituality of the minister is to nourish the spirit on the Bread of the Word. Basically this means that ministers who would grow in their baptismal holiness need to adopt an existential openness before the Word. This means that they become vulnerable and engage in a true dialogue with God through the Word. If the spiritual life is a movement of the finite creature toward the infinite Creator, then there must be constant engagement with that Creator. With due respect for those who enjoy mystical experiences, the primary way to achieve this dialogical relationship is through the Word. Reflecting prayerfully on God's Word, hearing God's voice, is the life-blood of the spiritual life.

Achieving an existential openness before the Word is not as easy as it seems. In our print culture there is a constant tendency to reduce the Word to an "it," to an object. After all, the Word is in printed form. It's in a book. It appears to be a page to be read or studied, not a person to meet or a mystery to be experienced. In an age of fundamentalism there is also a tendency toward "bibliolatry," i.e., worshipping the Word itself rather than worshipping the God we meet through that Word.

To achieve an engagement with God through the Word we need to learn from the contemplatives to be still — and *wait*. The Word itself says: "They who wait upon the Lord shall renew their strength, they shall soar as with eagle's wings" (Is 40:31). And Goethe writes: "So,

waiting, I have won from you the end: God's presence in each element."
In a culture where the noise of the radio and the exploding images of
T.V. clamor for our attention, it's not easy to find a quiet place or a sacred
time to wait to meet the Holy One.

To encounter God through the Word we may first have to learn how to
relate to the Word as a "Thou" not as an "It." "The one primary word,"
explains Martin Buber, "is the combination I-Thou. . . . Primary words
do not signify things but they intimate relations. . . . The primary word
I-Thou can only be spoken with the whole being. The primary word I-It
can never be spoken with the whole being."[9]

To become truly present before the Word we must be convinced with
Buber that "all real living is meeting" and that "the Thou meets me."
"The relation to the *Thou* is direct," insists Buber. "No system of ideas,
no foreknowledge, and no fancy intervene between *I* and *Thou*. . . . Every
means is an obstacle. Only when every means has collapsed does the
meeting come about."[10] So the printed word as a means eventually has
to vanish.

It's risky business to become open before the Word: "This is the risk:
the primary word can only be spoken with the whole being. He who
gives himself to it may withhold nothing of himself."[11] To place ourselves before the Word as a Thou is to initiate a relationship, and it will
be a relationship that will definitely change us. It will make its demands.
Through the Word God reveals who the Holy One is. But the living God
is not an object to be gazed at. All revelation, as Buber reminds us, is
summons and sending.[12]

So if we are not disposed to be changed, or if we are not prepared to
be sent, we ought never to go before the Word. "Revelation does not pour
itself into the world through him who receives it as through a funnel;
it comes to him and seizes his whole being in all its particular nature
and fuses with it."[13] When we really encounter the Word, it burns on
the tongue. It has become a Thou. When Moses came down from Mount
Sinai, the Israelites noticed that "the skin of his face had become radiant
while he conversed with the Lord" (Ex 34:29). So it will be with all
ministers who encounter the Word as a Thou. Their faces will be radiant
from communion with the holy Fire.

The third principle for growth in the spiritual life has to be an inner
conviction about the centrality of the Jesus/Lord event. Jesus modelled
openness to God as Father. His *Abba* experience indicates that his life
was constantly oriented in familiarity and intimacy to God as "daddy"
or "papa." "It was the ground not only of his being, but of his message
and manner of life as well. Jesus' deep religious rapport with God was
the basis of his conviction that God is bent upon the good of humanity, which became the inspiration of his whole ministry of healing and
reconciliation."[14] It was Jesus' intimate relationship to God as Father

that moved Jesus to relate to others as their servant. It is not for nothing that we continue to pray in the third eucharistic prayer: "All life, all holiness comes from you, through your Son Jesus Christ our Lord." Or, in the words of Vatican II "the Lord Jesus . . . is the Author and Finisher" of holiness.

Thus, whenever private devotions to Mary or to the saints become part of the spiritual life, they have to remain relative to the Jesus Christ event. Vatican II, in revising the liturgy, insisted that "the minds of the faithful must be directed primarily toward the feasts of the Lord in which the mysteries of salvation are celebrated."[15] That is also a good principle for the spiritual life. The Jesus/Lord event, as revealed in the Scriptures, corrects and guides all devotions. Jesus/Lord will always remain the touchstone, testing the quality and genuineness of all forms of spirituality. "For no one can lay a foundation other than the one that is there, namely, Jesus Christ" (1 Cor 3:11).

A fourth principle for growth in the spiritual life has to be an ongoing disposition toward conversion or change of heart. Mark's Gospel says it plainly: "Repent [*metanoeite*] and believe in the gospel" (Mk 1:15). The Greek word for "repent" calls for a change of mind, a change of the inner person with particular reference to acceptance of the will of God by the mind. To be disposed to change our mind and attitude is to invite God to make us into the finely-tuned instrument needed to accomplish the re-creation of the world. Francis Thompson memorably describes this part of the conversion process:

> Naked I wait Thy love's uplifted stroke!
> My harness piece by piece Thou has hewn from me,
> And smitten me to my knee.[16]

To repent is to become clay in the hands of the divine potter (Jer 18:6).

The fifth principle for growth in the spiritual life has to be compassion. Spirituality can never be a flight into angelism or a flight from the pain and agony of this bent world. It is a process of identifying ever more intimately with the cross as it is revealed through the hungry and the homeless, through the victims of war, crime, drugs, AIDS, and repressive governments. True spirituality is characterized by empathy, "a feeling with" the wounded human condition. There can never be an individualistic "spirituality of evasion."[17] Growth in the spiritual life follows the blood-stained footsteps of Jesus on his way to Calvary. To seek holiness requires an ongoing union with the dying of Jesus. Christian compassion therefore is not to be a condescending pity but a journey with the fellow pilgrim who lies beaten and half-dead along the wayside (Lk 10:30).

The minister visits the sick, the poor, or the prisoner not primarily to bring a message or even to bring holy communion, but to bring

195

the compassion of presence. "Compassion is the ability to *be present* to someone else. The word 'present' is used here in a special sense. It is used to describe a relationship in which my capacity for hearing, seeing, feeling — indeed, loving — is made available to another human being if only for a moment."[18]

The sixth principle of the spiritual life is an awareness of the holiness of "everyday things." "Life," said Will Rogers, "is just one damn thing after another." Indeed, "Our lives are filled with commonness, with ordinariness, with repetition, with mundane earthiness, with everydayness."[19] We spend most of our lives shopping, waiting in line, fixing things, doing the laundry, and taking out the garbage.

Those familiar with the depth and breadth of the mind of the late Karl Rahner will not be surprised to learn that he wrote a moving meditation on "Everyday Things." In it he reflects on the grace of work, sleep, seeing, eating and laughter.[20] In so doing, he reminds us of the "little way" of St. Therese of Lisieux. He also confirms that growth in holiness is not a flight into the ionosphere.[21]

After Christ's resurrection, all of creation, including "everyday things," is holy again. The holy on earth is not limited to the temple or to the shrine. The biblical Holy Sabbath is a reminder that *all* days are holy. Time is holy and filled with encounters with the holy for those believers who have eyes to see and ears to hear. The present moment is indeed a sacrament. Jesus spent most of his life in the "humdrum" grind of the carpenter's shop; Paul worked "night and day" making tents (1 Thes 2:9). He called his work "toil and drudgery" (Greek: struggle, hardship). "Making tents meant rising before dawn, toiling until sunset with leather, knives and awls and accepting the various social stigmas and humiliations that were part of the artisans' lot, not to mention the poverty — being cold, hungry and poorly clothed."[22] Yet Paul, the tent-maker, did not hesitate to speak about a spiritualized body (1 Cor 15:44). He "boasted" about his mystical experience, "being caught up to the third heaven" (2 Cor 12:2). He was convinced that true spirituality was quite compatible with bodiliness and the drudgery of "everyday things."

Emil Antonucci has an artist's feeling for the holiness of our engagement with the workaday world:

> All human beings participate in the continuing creation of the world.... The experience of making something forms the grammar of religious experience. Without it ... our notions of God become too mental, not actual enough to inform our daily lives, and too "personal" to enable us to share the experience of God with others. Whatever God is, God is a totality, a wholeness that connects the world and ourselves.[23]

Since the incarnation, the baptized's involvement in the world of work must be fundamentally positive. In Christ, God is present in that world. It is no longer punishment for sin. Working in and with the world is the normal Christian vocation. William Droel and Gregory Pierce recall the three principles underlying the spirituality of work:

> The first aim of work is to bring creation to perfection.... The second aim ... is the completion, harmonization and realization of the worker.... The third challenge of a spirituality of work is competency. "If a man is called to be a streetsweeper," Martin Luther King, Jr. often said, "he should sweep streets even as Michelangelo painted or Beethoven composed music or Shakespeare wrote poetry. He should sweep streets so well that all the host of heaven and earth will pause and say 'here lived a great streetsweeper who did his job well.' "[24]

Perhaps ministers need to be poets who, like William Blake, see a world in a grain of sand and a heaven in a wild flower. They need to see and listen with a greater sensitivity than the rest of humankind:

> We need to pause, often, in the daily on-goings of life, pause to reflect on what is going on: the person who called by phone, the letter we received today, the beauty that is rushing past our car windows, the people we are meeting on the streets, the kiss we received and gave this morning, the illness we are experiencing today, that article in the news about that child, this or that, all stuff from our everyday lives: we need to pause to notice it, reflect on it, let it touch us, let it move us.[25]

To appreciate "everyday things" we need to learn to live in the present. The past is over and the future may not be ours. We lose the holiness of the present by focusing too much on the past or on the future. Jean Vanier calls our attention to the gift of the present:

> We should learn to rejoice in the gift that is today.... So many of us live either in the past or in the future. Young people think it will be wonderful when they get out of school; but it isn't, for they enter the world of work. So they say it will be wonderful when they marry; and so it may be, for the first weeks, until the frustrations creep in. So they say it will be wonderful once the babies arrive; but then there is screaming in the night. So they look to the time when the children grow up, and how wonderful it will be to be alone. When the children do grow up, they hang onto them. And then finally they get old and start to reminisce about how wonderful it

was in the old days, when they were young. This is how we can pass through life without living.[26]

The seventh principle of spiritual growth is contact with the Spirit, the breath of life. Paul calls it "walking according to the Spirit" (Rom 8:4). For him it means advancing toward life. Soon after Easter we celebrate Pentecost, the outpouring of the Spirit on all the baptized. Then we continue to celebrate a long Pentecostal season until Advent — evidence enough that the Spirit should play a large role in our spiritual growth and in our ministry. During the Pentecost season the church celebrates the fulfillment of Joel's prophecy: "I will pour out a portion of my spirit upon all flesh. . . . And I will work wonders in the heavens above and on the earth below" (Acts 2:17–19). "God saved us," Paul writes, "through the baptism of new birth and renewal by the Holy Spirit. This Spirit he poured out on us" (Ti 3:5–6). In the beginning God breathed life into the earth creature (Gn 2:7). That same "breath of God" continues to breathe life into the baptized ministers through the Holy Spirit. It continues to renew the ministries and make them fruitful, provided the ministers themselves are open to receive God's breath.

If, following the Eastern tradition, we emphasize the invocation of the Spirit (*Epiklēsis*) during the minister's "ordination" (commissioning) ceremony, then we are also recalling the Spirit's transforming power in relation to the minister. The Spirit who transforms the bread and the wine in the Eucharist also transforms the minister into a true servant of God. In the fourth century *Apostolic Constitutions* we see that the ordaining prelate invokes the Spirit for the ordination of a deaconess: "Do Thou now also look upon this thy servant who is to be ordained to the office of deaconess, and grant her the Holy Spirit, *that she may worthily discharge the work which is committed to her.*"[27] As the minister applies her gift to the work of the ministry, the Spirit, in virtue of ordination, continues to transform the deaconess into a worthy minister. The minister will grow spiritually if she is constantly responding to the Spirit's transforming action.

The eighth principle for growth in the spiritual life will be a reverence for "holy time" in a sometimes "unholy" day. Jesus said to his disciples: "Come away by yourselves to a lonely place, and rest a while" (Mk 6:31). He himself fled to the mountaintop to pray. No doubt, he often sought a quiet oasis along the lakes and rivers of Galilee. The Judaeo-Christian tradition has set aside one day of the week as holy not because that day of itself is holier than other days but because we humans need a constant reminder that all days and all times are holy. Unless we deliberately steal some "holy" time to commune with the *Holy One*, all our time will soon become "unholy" because we will become insensitive to, or unreflective about, the holy.

Growth toward holiness is the Holy One's work of re-creating us, after our bruising and crippling encounters with Evil. But our growth is also dependent on our human decisions. It means that we deliberately cling to our holy moments, our own Sabbath, and allow no unwarranted intrusions. Everyday things are not automatically holy. They can be a living hell. The steps on the road to holiness must be deliberate and purposeful. For example, Mary's holiness, although a gift from God, was nevertheless the object of free choice. While growth in the spiritual life is primarily God's work, it requires the continuing and sometimes very assertive cooperation of our free will. The Holy Creator yearns passionately for the holiness of creatures, but they have to come in love and freedom into the Holy One's loving embrace.

Finally, the movement toward holiness is a movement toward wholeness. It is a movement toward the integration of body and soul, of matter and spirit, of the secular and the sacred, of humankind and the world, of the immanent and the transcendent, of the self and the other. God is simplicity, not complexity; a unity, not a duality. For this reason, as God re-creates us, our spiritual lives will become more and more simple. Anne Wilson comments:

> We can choose to accept ourselves as whole people, thanking God for our senses, emotions, thought processes, and feelings; for our bodies, our minds, our souls. For it is the combination of all of these, as well as the larger Body of our communities, churches, and our world, that aid us in our spiritual maturation. A wholistic spirituality . . . would be one which perceives how the need for unity applies on every level of our lives and interactions. It is an attempt to look beyond notions of duality and see the underlying wholeness and interrelatedness of all things.[28]

Methods

In recent years more and more people in ministry have felt the urge to write a book, or at least a chapter, on spirituality. As a result, the smorgasbord of methods and guidelines has grown richer and larger. That's all to the good. In itself, it tells us there is no *one* method. At the same time, the diversity of methods available makes the decision-making process more difficult for those looking for *the* method for themselves.

The search for our method or our way begins with knowing ourselves and knowing ourselves as lovable. God had us, like Paul, in view from our mother's womb (Gal 1:15). We are indeed "wonderfully made" (Ps 139:14) with the loving care of the divine artist. We were not stamped out in a factory. We are all as different from each other and as wonderful as the stars in the heavens. Naturally, there will never be one way for all of us to spiritual growth. Our path to the Holy One is not "out there" on the smorgasbord. It is not in a book or in a saint or even in Franciscan, Ignatian, Dominican, or any other method of spirituality. Our path begins in ourselves, in the holiness of who we are. It is important, then, that we first look to ourselves to find out what God, the artist, has painted there.

There may be many ways of finding out where our path to the Holy One begins but Carl Jung has certainly been a helpful guide for our journey inward. In his *Psychological Types* (1921), he described eight basic personality types. Many spiritual writers believe that Jung's personality types have profound implications for the selection of methods for spiritual growth:

Jung developed a highly detailed yet flexible framework within which we can attempt to understand the legitimate differences among persons and the inner development they are called to. Certainly past spiritualities had no adequate way to deal with these differences. In practice, a uniform rule and prescribed spiritual exercises were often imposed in a mistaken quest for unity. We differ in our needs for food, sleep, and exercise. We vary in our capacity for solitude and social life, and in our reactions to joy and sorrow. In short, we differ in our very physical and psychic makeup and in our ways of perceiving and judging the world within and without. This means that we will be attracted to different forms of prayer and service, for our spiritual gifts will tend to build on the distinctive natural gifts we possess.[29]

Once we acknowledge the wide spectrum of diversity, we may still ask: "Where do I fit?" "What is my path?" Based on the personality research of Carl Jung, the Myers-Briggs Personality Type Indicator can be extremely helpful in getting some insight into our own spiritual path, even though it was not designed specifically as an instrument for the spiritual life.[30] Developed by Isabel Myers over a period of forty years, the type indicator presents sixteen personality types. One of these sixteen types fits each of us, *more or less*. With these different types come eight dominant characteristics or qualities, which in turn point (again, *more or less*) to our way of spiritual growth. The eight basic types are: extravert/introvert; sensing/intuitive; feeling/thinking; perceiving/judging. Most of us need the help of a counselor or spiritual director to interpret these types and apply them to ourselves.

Once we know our type, we may detect some patterns and preferences for different styles and methods for our own spiritual journeys. Charles Keating has provided a very useful service in matching personality types with spirituality. He has described the characteristics of the various personality types. Two examples may help us get the hang of it:

Intuitive introverts are first inclined to feeling or thinking spiritualities, such as Thomas à Kempis or St. Teresa of Avila. They make progress because they are following their secondary preferences of feeling or thinking. Most progress could be found in spiritualities of intuition such as Teilhard de Chardin. Extraverted thinkers may grow best with a theological orientation, a spirituality of orderly progress, such as St. Ignatius of Loyola's, or the Sulpician school of Fr. Olier.[31]

Our personality type, notes Keating, may lead us to the spirituality of St. Francis de Sales or of Thomas Merton. The examples of the saints can be a great help so long as we understand them as only one means, one method and not the end. The end will always be God. And for us the Holy One may indeed make some surprising exceptions to the spirituality of the saints who have gone before us.

Depending on our personality, both the place and the format for prayer will vary. Some ministers pray best on the riverbank uniting their prayer with the song of the birds, the gurgle of the water, and the rustling of the leaves. Others pray best in church surrounded by stained glass windows and the eucharistic presence. Still others do best with the psalms or modern poetry. Some older ministers pray best with the traditional rosary, litanies, and novenas. All may move from one format to another as the mystery of their spiritual journey unfolds.

The Tried and the True

We may indeed have our own unique path for spiritual growth. We cannot, however, simply ignore the tried and true methods used by Jesus and by the saints through the centuries. Like breathing and eating, some practices are clearly necessary to sustain a healthy growth in the spiritual life.

The first of these practices is prayer. This does not mean merely that "we say our prayers," but that we engage in a true dialogue with God. Becoming a person of prayer means that we first have to become dialogical persons. True dialogical persons are rare, but all of us have the potential. And becoming dialogical is a condition for becoming a person of prayer, for prayer is nothing more than a continuous dialogue with the Creator and creation.

This dialogue will include a prayer to recognize the calls to ministry as they come each day in the vineyard. An attitude of prayer is a readiness to be surprised at every moment by a new call from the Beloved for new service. This call will come, not with a loud thunderclap, but with the whisper of the wind. The minister who prays will, like Samuel, always be ready to say: "Speak, Yahweh, your servant is listening" (1 Sam 4:11).

The dialogical person has been described by Reuel L. Howe: "By dialogical person we mean one who by word or relationship is in communication with his environment and open to the communication that environment offers, environment in this sense including both persons and things."[32]

Dialogical persons have the following characteristics: First, they are *really* present; they do not run off on 'errands' of their own while they appear to listen to the person before them.[33]

Second, dialogical persons are open, characterized by their willingness and ability to reveal themselves to others and to hear and receive their revelation in turn. Dialogical persons, Howe notes, must be open to the meaning and influence of the dialogue itself. Many are lonely because they cannot accept the participation of others in the meaning of their lives. It's quite possible to "dialogue" with another about the weather and football without ever entering into the meaning of that other's life. Such "dialogue" may leave both partners lonely and empty.

Third, dialogical persons are disciplined. They practice a twofold discipline, first, in giving themselves totally to the dialogue and, second, in holding themselves to their own part and leaving others free to respond and initiate as they will.[34] Dialogical persons show in their dialogue that listening is always more important than speaking. True listening requires a continuous dying to our desire to enlighten the world with our wisdom or to regale an audience with our embellished exploits.

As noted above, there are various styles of prayer reflecting the wide variety of personalities and relationships with God. In our busy and overly active culture, however, meditation must have a high priority. A form of dialogue, it is the minister's sanity-saver. Ministers in our Western culture could benefit greatly from Eastern practices of meditation. The history of contemplative prayer teaches us to "own" our reflective sides. Without reflection, both our lives and ministry will soon become unbalanced. Passing frustrations will take on an importance they simply do not deserve.

If ministers are going to survive in today's church and world, they will also need spiritual direction. Only fools will be their own spiritual guides. Francis Vanderwall asks, "Who needs spiritual direction?" He answers:

> The point is that not everyone needs a particular person who regularly provides spiritual guidance. Everyone does need spiritual direction, however, in that all of us need clarifications, interpre-

tations, and suggestions for improvement in our inner lives. At certain times in one's life one feels the need to talk on an on-going basis with a particular person about spiritual matters, and at that time one may seek out someone for this guidance, but it is not something that is going to occur throughout one's life. On the other hand, spiritual direction is not to be considered something reserved for crisis times alone.... I see it as help-ful when one is taking another step forward in the life of the Spirit.[35]

Notwithstanding the superabundance of the Spirit's gifts, we can-not conclude that just anyone can serve as a spiritual director. As in all human relationships, there has to be compatibility and clear and com-fortable communication between director and directee. At the same time, the spiritual director needs certain qualities to perform the ministry of guiding another toward holiness. Vanderwall tells us that the directors must themselves be persons of prayer. They must also have the gift of discerning between the good and evil moments in a person's life. It is essential that spiritual directors be good listeners. Besides these quali-ties, spiritual directors require a certain amount of training that enables them to discern the gifts of the Spirit in another person. Finally, the di-rectors need to be aware that they are in partnership with God who is the true guide.[36]

Ignatius of Loyola, that great master of spiritual direction, conducted the Spiritual Exercises as a soul-friend: "The way in which he directed another person has much to do with friendship and a nearness to the soul of that person. 'Friendship is admiration that reverently bows to all that, in the beloved, asks for reverence; it is the reverence for God's wonders in another person.' "[37] As for the qualities of spiritual directors, Ignatius first looked for "prudence and ease in dealing with people." Second, he looked for the qualities of a physician: "Whoever deals with people in order to help them should act as an experienced physician who is not shocked and does not show repugnance however disgusting and terrible the wounds look. He has to bear the weaknesses and quirks of the patient with patience and gentleness."[38]

The relationship of the spiritual director to the directee can also be seen as that of a mentor. Throughout history we see people who are recognized for their wisdom and who have a greater capacity than others to reflect on their experience and then to share it with others. Thus we see the shaman of primitive tribes, the guru of the Hindus, and the rabbi in the Jewish community.

All these diverse cultures and traditions speak of the value of the person who listens well, can offer advice and support, helps others clarify their questions, discern options, make choices, fulfill the unique calling which is theirs. What all these traditions seem to recognize is that such a vocation of guidance involves special gifts — some inherited, some gained through a form of training or apprenticeship.[39]

While we might understand spiritual directors to be mentors, we may, according to Edward Sellner, also see them as teachers, counselors, and, at other times, as exemplars to imitate. But most importantly, the director is "a facilitator of the other person's Dream, the vision he has of himself, the life he wants to lead as an adult, the vocation or call that so many are attempting to clarify for themselves today in society and church."[40]

Another helpful "tried and true" practice for spiritual growth is the annual retreat. Not everyone will have the time or the money to escape to a retreat center. But, abstracting from the place, ministers need to be convinced of the importance of "retreat time" in their lives. They may then go to the park, to the woods, to the bedroom, to the back yard, or to the lake, for a day of pr yer, reflection, and communing with the self and God. Such disciplined 'retreat time" may save the ministers' sanity as well as their souls.

Ministers also need to belong to a praying community. Within this community they will celebrate the Eucharist, reconciliation, and all the sacramentals of the Christian tradition. They will never grow spiritually in isolation from the sacrament of their community. Thomas Merton taught this truth with the title of his book *No Man Is an Island*. Like it or not, there simply is no Lone Ranger trail to spiritual growth. Really *belonging* to (as opposed to merely *joining*) a community requires considerable sacrifice and the investment of much time and energy. If the community is not enriched by the ministers' presence and deprived by their absence, then something is wrong. The sacrament of community will not be complete without the grace of the ministers' presence. At the same time, the latter will draw some of their life and energy from the body of the community.

Another tried and true method of growth in the faith is spiritual reading. Although there is no one book that answers everyone's needs, the saints testify to the truth that spiritual reading is a great help to union with God. Spiritual directors can be very helpful in suggesting reading appropriate to our place in life's journey. As we continue to give ourselves to the "self-emptying" of ministry, we need to regularly refill the well from which we drink. Selection of books for spiritual reading, or tapes for listening, should not be decided according to the latest fad or on a whim. Life is short; good books and tapes are few. Knowing oneself will be a great help in the search. Some may find the life stories of saints to be "just the thing;" others will find their inspiration in the "Integrating Spirituality" of Bernard Lonergan.

A final requirement for spiritual growth is to practice discipline in the use of time. It is simply not true that ministers must always be available to their "customers." Again, the contemplatives have much to teach those of us who are daily immersed in activism and overwork. Thomas Merton speaks directly to this issue:

> The rush and pressure of modern life are a form, perhaps the most common form, of its innate violence. To allow oneself to be carried away by a multitude of conflicting concerns, to surrender to too many demands, to commit oneself to too many projects, to want to help everyone in everything is *to succumb to violence.* Frenzy...destroys our inner capacity for peace. It destroys the fruitfulness of our work, because it kills the root of inner wisdom which makes our work fruitful.[41]

Sometimes the church unwittingly fosters violence in the lives of its overworked volunteer ministers. This happens, for example, when the pastor keeps calling the same few parish workers who don't have the heart to say no. Sometimes their only escape is to move to another city where, understandably, they decide to hide as anonymous pagans. The violence of "too many demands" is not less destructive just because it is sponsored by the church.

Situational Spirituality

Ministers who truly believe in the incarnation will have a reverence for the grace of specific times and places, the actual situations, in their ministry. In the incarnate Christ ministry occurs when Jesus actually meets the leper, the tax collector, the Samaritan woman, and the woman caught in adultery. In the same way, it will be the actual pastoral situation that will be a grace-filled sacrament and that will shape the minister's spirituality. This grace can be experienced and received in the slums, in the prison, in the hospital, on the campus, in the classroom, and at the nuclear missile site. For this reason, we can conclude that the minister's particular situation, to some extent, gives birth to a situational spirituality.

The hospital chaplains, for instance, may shape their spirituality around basic issues like life and death. Crisis moments in the emergency room may be springboards for spiritual insight and growth. The health care ministers may fashion a special spirituality as they relate to the youth who lost both legs in a motorcycle accident. As they meet death at the bedside of their cancer patients, they may need to reflect on their feelings about their own death and the promised resurrection. At the same time, they may nourish their spirituality on the miracle of life as they rejoice with the new parents of a baby girl.

Campus ministers may find their spirituality shaped by the students' need for a mother or father figure. Uprooted from the security of their own family and hometown, students may seek some security in the campus ministers. In this situation, the ministers would need to help the student find security in new and/or deeper relationships with God and others. Meeting students who are caught in the grip of drugs and alcohol, the campus ministers may need to meditate often on the freeing power of God's grace. They may discover that their spirituality will be nourished in unscheduled bits and pieces.

Parish ministers may find their spirituality connected with more traditional forms of prayer such as rosaries and devotions. They may be challenged to integrate the more traditional spiritualities of a parish with their own experience and in turn invite their parishioners to explore new forms of worship and Christian living. Ministers need to learn how to balance the pressure of administrative details with peaceful contemplation on the ultimate, spiritual questions. Parishioners need to respect this time of seeming inactivity on the part of their ministers.

Prison ministers may find their spirituality shaped by the need to proclaim the forgiveness of the prodigal son and to invite the prisoner to be reconciled with a merciful God. They may have to reflect on the residual anger in their own lives as they minister to the anger of the prisoners who always feel "they got a bum rap." They may have to stress the healing ministry of Christ in their own lives in order to share it with the incarcerated who are wounded in hundreds of ways. They may need to learn with the prisoners how to maintain their inner freedom and dignity while working under an oppressive and demeaning system.

Those involved in retreat ministry may be called to respond to a wide variety of retreatants who are in many different places in their spiritual journeys. Such a ministry might include helping these spiritual sojourners leave their expectations at the curb and prepare themselves to be open to whatever experience God is waiting to give them. It may be the agony of a dark night of the soul or the joyful ecstasy of Mt. Tabor or, as is often the case, somewhere in the vast in-between.

Teachers may pattern their spiritual lives after Jesus the teacher. They may often find themselves proclaiming the beatitudes and walking with Jesus as he forms his disciples along the way. They may learn to deal with their own failures by "feeling with" Jesus who failed to reach the rich young man who "went away sad, for he had many possessions" (Lk 19:22), and who also failed to reach "the many" who "returned to their former way of life and no longer accompanied him" (Jn 6:66).

Ministers involved in the apostolate of peace and social justice may reflect often on the beatitude, "blessed are the peacemakers." They may find themselves encouraged by Scripture readings on the prophets, especially Amos and Jeremiah. They may find much spiritual enrichment from meditating on the lives of St. Thomas More, St. Vincent de Paul, Thomas Merton, and Archbishop Oscar Romero. They may also experience the loneliness and rejection of prophets like Jeremiah, whose message gains no followers until after his death. They may have to place special emphasis on detachment from success and from this world's esteem. Then too, they may need to learn meekness and forgiveness so they will not respond in kind to the anger they encounter in their peacemaking ministry.

The gracious God continues to call us to union with the Holy One. The Creator consecrates and sanctifies us as we respond to the divine lover. The treasury of the Christian tradition offers us many tried and true methods for growing in holiness. Our pilgrim journey to sainthood is God's unique story, written now with crooked, now with straight lines. While there is only one God, "there is one glory of the sun, and another glory of the moon, and another glory of the stars; for star differs from star in glory" (1 Cor 15:41).

CHAPTER ELEVEN

Finding Your Work and Your Place in the Vineyard

"The harvest is plenty; the laborers are few. Come with me into the Fields."[1]

Decisions! Decisions! The menu at a Chinese restaurant can be overwhelming. And the growing menu of Christian ministries can be equally disconcerting and confusing. You have heard that inner call to go into the vineyard to make this a better world. But how do you find your proper place among all the different laborers? Sometimes it may seem more like a jungle than a vineyard. Selecting one of the many ministries in Christ's vineyard calls for prayer, discernment, counsel, and common sense. The choice can be even more difficult if the ministry to which you feel called is not even on the menu! You may simply be trying to respond to a need "out there" that is begging for a Christian response. This means you have to create a totally new ministry.

Some Spiritual/Theological Principles

It may be a tough decision, but you need to be deeply involved in the actual selection or creation of your own work and place in the vineyard. If you allow the bishop, pastor, or chancery office simply to assign you a place in the "field," you could be underutilized or totally misplaced. This could result in burnout, depression, or stagnation from lack of challenge, stimulation, or engagement of all your creative talents. You need to be stretched a little to reach your full potential. Good Ol' Charlie Brown of "Peanuts" says it well: "Life is like a ten-speed bicycle. . . . Most of us have gears that we never use."[2]

If your ministry environment does not stretch you spiritually, intellectually, and emotionally, go somewhere else. The vineyard is large. On the other hand, you may decide to accept the challenge to bring about change in some aspect of the ecclesiastical system, which is not, after all, beyond redemption. And God may wish to use you and the cross of your pain as a catalyst for redeeming the system. However, if, after prayer and counsel, you decide that you have tried and failed to bring about change, find another place in the vineyard. The system may not be ready for conversion. The grace of conversion remains grace. It can't be forced. Then too you may be the wrong person; or it may be the wrong time. But don't let a rigid system or a stifling structure bury your talents in a field. This life is not a rehearsal.

Many people hunger for a vision of what they can be.[3] The baptized have many gifts to make that vision a reality. But these gifts still need to be discovered, often by a trial and error method, through experience in actual pastoral settings. That's one good way to find out who and what you can be. Such "testing the waters" to discover your gifts needs the supportive environment of a discerning community. Failure in one ministry does not mean failure in all. Someone has to be there just to say that.

All potential ministers need to be convinced, spiritually, intellectually, and emotionally, that they have a mission here on earth, a mission that is uniquely theirs. Once that has been achieved, Richard Bolles advises religious job-hunters:

a. to exercise that Talent which you particularly came to Earth to use — your greatest gift, which you most delight to use,

b. in the place(s) or setting(s) which God has caused to appeal to you the most,

c. and for those purposes which God most needs to have done in the world.[4]

Finding your work in the vineyard is not simply a private decision based on the personal discernment of a gift. It's Christ's vineyard, after all, not yours. Some voice from outside, such as that of a pastor, a teacher, a parish council, or church institution, may offer a more objective view of the actual needs of the church and its people. Such a voice would be one, and only one, factor in the total discernment process. It could help deliver you from the danger of embarking on an ego trip to serve your own needs.

To discover your personal gifts you may also need the help of a spiritual director or that of a career counselor:

The identification of talents, gifts, or skills is the province of career counseling. Its expertise, indeed its *raison d'être*, lies precisely in the identification, classification, and (forgive me) "prioritization" of talents, skills and gifts. To put the matter quite simply, career counseling knows how to do this better than any other discipline — *including* traditional religion. This is not a defect of religion, but the fulfillment of something Jesus promised: "When the Spirit of truth comes, He will guide you into all truth" (Jn 16:12). Career counseling is part (we may hope) of that promised late-coming truth.[5]

Among the theological principles guiding your vocational decision is an awareness of being *sent* on your mission. "Apostle" means "messenger," "envoy," "delegate." It is of the very nature of ministry to be an ambassador, sent by someone or by some church. We see in Matthew 10:5 and Luke 9:2 that Jesus "sends" his disciples on their mission. In fact, in sending them he gave them rather specific instructions: "Go nowhere among the Gentiles, and enter no town of the Samaritans, but go rather to the lost sheep of the house of Israel."

Paul too, along with Barnabas, is *sent* on his mission to Seleucia, a port city eighteen miles west of Antioch on the mouth of the Orontes river (Acts 13:3). This time the prophets and teachers, leaders in the community of Antioch, do the sending. We notice that Paul and Barnabas are not sent to just anywhere in the world but to a specific city, a specific place in Christ's vineyard. It is noteworthy too that this "sending" does not need to be a hierarchic sending by Peter or the twelve apostles. Clearly the community of Antioch sent and *commissioned* Paul and Barnabas. The imposition of hands in this case is not an ordination in the usual sense of the word, but a missionary mandate and blessing. E. Haenchen notes significantly: "Lucius, Symeon and Manaen (the sending prophets) have no higher rank than Barnabas and Paul."[6] This "sending" by the teachers and prophets is immediately seen as an action of the Holy Spirit (Acts 13:4). In view of this practice in Antioch it is understandable that for centuries religious communities, on the basis of their own community discernment, have sent their sisters, brothers, and priests into the vineyard on similar missions. Parish pastoral councils and parish communities who commission their DREs, teachers, and ministers to the sick are following a good biblical practice.

This "sending" does not imply blind obedience on your part. There is no virtue in simply subjecting your will to that of another. Many dependent personalities, especially among the young, would be more comfortable in passively accepting a "sending" by some religious authority. This is especially true in today's fundamentalist environment. Many young students, recently removed from the decision-making authority of their parents, are quite willing to abdicate personal responsibility and lean on some religious parent substitute for their vocational decisions. They may not follow such leaders to the horror of a mass suicide as happened in Jonestown, French Guyana, in November 1978. But, for dependent personalities the danger, in different degrees, is always present. And, unfortunately, there are always religious authorities who, unwittingly perhaps, are ready to exploit the immaturity of those unwilling to accept full responsibility for their own decisions. In the past, many young men entered the seminary because, as adolescents, they were too immature to challenge a mother who made their vocational decision for them. Other father/mother figures, hierarchic or charismatic, invoking obedience, can still do all the deciding, if ministers give them that authority.

While you search for your work in the vineyard you need to be aware that you are called by God to fulfill God's plan, will, and mission. There may be a variety of ways in which God reveals that call, often through the very talents, experience, and gifts you already possess. God may also call you through the changing needs of the community and the world. You need to be aware that God, as a jealous lover, is constantly calling the beloved, often through new needs and new situations. While the call comes from inside through faith and personal gifts, it also comes from outside through changing needs and community discernment. All these "outside" factors are part of the wider, and more difficult, obedience to which you are called.

You shape your ministry and find your place in the vineyard both through "call" and through "sending." You need to be constantly aware of these two elements in your ministry. The call to ministry is never finished in a one-time happening. It continues daily as part of God's ongoing covenant of love. As a laborer in the vineyard, you are "on call" to respond to the owner's voice from daybreak to the eleventh hour (Mt 20:1–6). Your call to continue Christ's mission is never finished. The purpose of your ministry is not *primarily* the fulfillment of your human potential, although that is often a blessed by-product, but the accomplishment of your unique role in the work of the vineyard.

Since your charisms are part of the body of some kind of church, your ministry is accountable to that believing community. As one among many laborers in the vineyard, you need to relate your labor to that of others, so you will know what is going on around you and so that your labor will become even more fruitful. You need to be accountable to those others. You also need to support and challenge them in their ministries. Scripture calls the servant to be accountable to the master. Being accountable also means that you have some responsibility for the upbuilding of the community. You will do your best work as a minister through an evolving, developing relationship to the community. Feedback, evaluation, and discernment regarding the successes and failures in your ministry are part of the process of growing in the ministry and being accountable.

For this reason your ministry has to be structured to some extent. The structure can begin "from above" and be imposed by a hierarchy; or it can begin "from below" with your gift as a baptized minister. You can assume responsibility for relating your gifts to those of others and thus structure them "from below." Neither ministry nor community can long exist apart from some kind of structure, however experimental and tentative. The forms of these structures and their usefulness will also be part of your responsibility as one minister among many. They are, to a large extent, *your* structures. They are not divine "givens." They can be familial, collegial, participative, hierarchic, or democratic. But they will always be subject to evaluation and discernment for the quality of their service to the people of God.

As a minister you are also accountable to God, the giver of gifts. You do not become the owner of God's gifts but their steward. As Jesus looked for figs on the fig tree (Mt 21:19), so God looks for fruitfulness from your ministry. This fruitfulness will be revealed through the upbuilding of your church and the reign of God.

As you work in the vineyard, you need to respond to the real needs of people as opposed to fulfilling your own needs through them. While you have your own legitimate needs, these may not become the primary object of your ministry. It is not always easy to maintain a clear distinction between one and the other. It is most important, however, that you exercise continual discernment regarding the kinds of personal needs that shape your ministry. A need to play God or to rescue everybody quickly destroys your ministry. You are not a Messiah, but only the Messiah's servant.

You need to weigh and distinguish the people's needs as they "crush" in on you. It is simply not true that the "customer" defines the ministry. The "customers" with their felt needs are quite capable of demanding that you conform to their understanding of ministry: "Ministers should stick to the Mass and the Sacraments. They should stay out of politics — the economy, abortion, war and peace." You are called to define your own ministry, not only on the basis of the people's felt needs, but especially in a faith response to the cross, the demands of the Gospel, your vocation, and the mission of Christ. The felt needs of the "customers" are not always part of Christ's mission. In fact, sometimes they may be obstacles to that mission. When Peter became an obstacle, Jesus rebuked him (Mt 16:23).

As you enter the vineyard you also need to remember that you are embarking on a *public* ministry. If you don't want to "go public," then you ought never to go into the vineyard. All ministry by its very nature has a public dimension. It takes place in a visible form in words and deeds. It is done in the name of Jesus, who publicly confronted the world's sin wherever he found it. There simply can be no Christian ministry apart from public witness.[7]

As sign and sacrament, you always represent some visible community and that too makes the ministry public. This public dimension requires a sensitivity to the effects of symbolic actions in a particular culture and society. Such actions cannot be "privatized" by a simple declaration. The image or sign value of your church always gains or loses as a result of the public aspect of your ministry. Your church, therefore, has a legitimate interest in the public form and style of your ministry. This holds true even when in a prophetic ministry you confront the church itself for its unfaithfulness to the Gospel it proclaims.

Some Psychological Principles

Ministers probably know their ministering potential through gift and experience better than anyone else. On the other hand, self-knowledge is a continuing and ongoing process. We are mysteries even to ourselves. So if our ministry is going to bear fruit to its fullest potential, we need to reflect humbly and honestly on our own personal gifts and natural talents as well as our weaknesses and deficiencies. Ministry begins then with a journey inward. This reflective process, however, will improve considerably with some outside guidance. Many instruments have been developed to reveal the major characteristics of our personalities. While it would be foolish to canonize any of them or give them more weight than they deserve, they can, nevertheless, be helpful guides in the discernment of personal gifts.

Four instruments often used today are the Myers-Briggs Type Indicator (see chap. 10), the DISC Personal Profile System, the Strong Vocational Interest Blank, and the Strong Campbell II. These instruments can at least help us discover whether we should seek a ministry relating to things, ideas, data, or people.[8] The results of these tests become a more trustworthy guide if we discuss them with a career or vocational counselor.

Are you a visionary? You may be a great help in parish planning and goal-setting. Are you interested primarily in facts and data? Why not use your talents to finalize the parish budget or direct a fund-raiser?

Are you artistic and creative? You could help create prayerful environments for worship or teach crafts to young and old alike. Are you drawn toward people? The Myers-Briggs test indicates that the INFJ types (Introvert/iNtuitive/Feeling/Judging) "have an unusually strong drive to contribute to the welfare of others and genuinely enjoy helping their fellow men.... They are themselves complicated and can understand and deal with complex issues and people."[9]

Performax Systems International, Inc., has developed an instrument known as the Personal Profile System. The work of William Marston, this system tries to analyze behavior patterns around the following four dimensions: (1) Dominance, (2) Inducement or Influence, (3) Steadiness, and, finally, (4) Compliance, thus the acronym DISC. Briefly summarized:

> The people with *dominance* tendencies have the results they want well in mind. Their messages are designed to stimulate and prod others to untested action.... Questions about the "right" action are shrugged away. People with *inducing* or *influencing* tendencies also want to shape and mold events and have an active voice. Their messages are designed to stimulate and prod others to action by working with and through people. They are interested in people and like to make people feel good about themselves.... Messages about *how* to actually accomplish a task are often deemed unimportant.... Persons with the *steadiness* tendencies are interested in the how and the why — a product orientation. They send messages which reflect their interest in maintaining a stability within themselves and the situation — between the old and the new. Messages which urge action before knowing how to do things, fall on deaf ears. Those individuals with the *compliance* tendencies reflect their product orientation when they send messages which ask the reasons for the change. "Why" is a favorite question. They have concern for doing it "right." They are receptive to messages which reassure them they are doing it correctly. Messages which ignore this tend to go unheeded.[10]

The implications for finding your place in the vineyard can be far-reaching. The personality profiles of some people indicate that they are good at working alone; others prefer a team environment. Some are good at gathering detailed information; others are given to the use of power and authority and do not bother with the time-consuming process of collecting data. The more you grow in self-knowledge, the easier it will be to discern God's will in your search for the right ministry for you.

Resources

Those who are searching for help in finding their unique place in the vineyard are often looking for something akin to career counseling with a theological and pastoral perspective. Unfortunately, "a survey of current literature on career counseling finds it lacking in one vital area, the theological dimension. . . . At this time [1989], no formal material has been written spelling out the theory and practice of adult career counseling from a pastoral perspective."[11]

But help is on the way. Richard Bolles in his classic book, *The 1989 What Color Is Your Parachute?*, has added an appendix entitled "Religion and Job-Hunting." Quite appropriately, he invites the searchers first to reflect on how they think about God and about their faith. Then he offers some helpful comments about "Finding your Mission in Life." Revised annually, the book is a practical guide for job-hunters and career-changers. In a lengthy chapter entitled "What Skills Do You Enjoy Most Using?" Bolles guides the job searchers in the discernment of their gifts, abilities, and, finally, their helping skills. These skills may involve: (1) data (information), (2) people, or (3) things. As noted above, this basic format could easily be adapted to ministry. Thus ministries involving *data* might focus on computing, copying, and analyzing; ministries involving *people* might include mentoring, instructing, supervising, and persuading. Ministries involving *things* could focus on activities such as driving, handling, operating, and feeding.

Another helpful resource is *Choosing Your Career, Finding Your Vocation*, by Roy Lewis. More theological and pastoral in tone, this book contains an excellent chapter on "Vocational Targeting," which takes the biblical call as its point of departure and then becomes very practical in laying out vocational options. It maintains a spiritual perspective as it leads the searchers through various steps in the discernment process.

Once you have a fairly clear idea about the kind of ministry you want to undertake, you will have a better understanding about the kind of training or preparation you will need. Fortunately, high quality training programs are growing rapidly. Some are based at Catholic universities and seminaries. These programs take an academic turn, often leading to a certificate or M.A. degree. Others are sponsored by individual dioceses. Still others are conducted at the parish level. Quite appropriately, there is considerable variety in content and method.

So far the best resource for finding these training programs is *Preparing Laity for Ministry*, edited by Suzanne Elsesser and published by the Bishops' Committee on the Laity and Office of Research of the National Conference of Catholic Bishops, Washington, D.C. It is a directory of 275 degree and nondegree programs available throughout the United

States. Program information is given in five categories: purpose, content, administration, participants, and opinions. The directory, the author promises, will be updated periodically.

When you are ready to apply for a paid position as a full-time minister, you can check the want ad section of the *National Catholic Reporter* or *Crux of the News*, available in many Catholic libraries.

Ministry/Match, based in Milwaukee, is a computerized, nation-wide service for the recruitment of professionals in ministry. For a small fee you can send your resume to Ministry/Match for listing in the computer. The system works like a dating service. When parishes, dioceses, or institutions, for instance, are looking for a youth minister or pastoral associate, they pay a fee for a computer search for the names and qual-ifications of those applying for positions through the service. In March 1990, there were seventeen categories of ministry available for search in Ministry/Match. For more information write to: Ministry/Match, 4125 West Ruby St., Milwaukee, WI 53209.

Before you accept a full-time position anywhere in the church be sure to read chapter 4 of Leonard Doohan's *Grass Roots Pastors*, listed in the Resources section in the back of this book. Doohan gives you very practical advice that could save you all kinds of grief. He talks about contracts, salary, pension plans, support systems, etc. In addition, he provides an excellent reflection format to help you in your discernment process.

If your discernment leads you to a part- or full-time volunteer min-istry, you will find *Invest Yourself* an excellent resource. It is a catalogue of over two hundred volunteer opportunities with agencies scattered throughout the world. Most of these agencies provide full-time volun-teers with room and board; some provide an additional small stipend. Among the agencies listed are the Jesuit Volunteers, the Christian Ap-palachian Project, and Have Mule Will Travel. Besides giving you the name, address, and phone number of each agency, *Invest Yourself* pro-vides general information about the program, the skills needed, and a contact person. The introductory pages give practical advice like the following:

Look for an agency that has clarity and specificity about:

1. Job description — work to be done, skills needed, place, dates, conditions, qualifications.

2. Entrance — application, interview, adequate time-line for processing.

3. Support system — training, supervision, peer group, rela-tions to staff.

4. Termination — preparation for re-entry into your former life as now modified by the volunteer service.

When you find an agency to your liking and begin negotiating a placement, expect and ask for a clear contract.[12]

For more information write to: *Invest Yourself*, 415 East 12th St., New York, NY 10009.

An equally helpful resource for volunteer ministers is *Let the Spirit Blow (The Response)*, published annually by the International Liaison of Lay Volunteers in Mission. The 1990 edition lists 142 mission programs and 20 associate programs. Many are sponsored by religious communities, others by various dioceses. For each program the booklet lists the requirements, the goals of the program, the type of placement, financial and living arrangements, and contact person, with address and phone number. Write to: International Liaison of Lay Volunteers in Mission, 4121 Harewood Rd. N.E., Washington, DC 20017.

If you have the time and money, you can sign up for a weekend workshop. The Life/Career Planning Center, 10526 W. Cermak Rd., Suite 111, in Westchester, IL 60154, conducts two-day workshops to help Catholic clientele plan their future. Through networking and information gathering, the directors help people of all ages find their ministry in the Catholic vineyard.

The Job Market for Ministry

Before we discuss specific ministries, it may be useful to note that the *1989 Catholic Almanac* lists 19 secular institutes with a variety of apostolates "in the world." It lists 23 special apostolates for laity, including Pax Christi, Cursillo, and Christian Family Movements. In addition, it lists over 175 associations and movements, such as the Christophers and the Beginning Experience, to help the divorced, the widowed, and the separated. So before you reinvent the wheel, find out what is already available in the ministry market.

Below is a very select menu of a few ministries available in the vineyard. The listing is designed to give you a brief glimpse of some ministries that may not be available in your own parish. You may find your ministry among those listed or you may get an idea for developing your own ministry. The list is a modest attempt to stimulate reflection and perhaps to stretch your vision. But you alone can match your own gift to the job. Addresses are current at time of publication.

1. Spiritual Direction

Description: Helping the directee advance in the spiritual life through one-on-one meetings on a regular basis; acting as mirror for the directee so as to enable him/her to reflect on life experience and God's presence therein.

Training/Preparation: Spiritual director should be familiar with the movements of the spiritual life. One's own life experience in the spiritual realm may be helpful but often a formal training program in spiritual direction is required.

For more information: (1) Institute of Formative Spirituality, Duquesne University, Pittsburgh, PA 15219 (M.A. and Ph.D.); (2) Progoff's Intensive Journal Workshops; (3) Ignatian Spiritual Exercise Retreats.

2. Retreat Ministry

Description: Presenting retreats to groups and individuals on a wide range of topics or acting as coordinator of a retreat center — scheduling retreats, coordinating in-house activities or hospitality, cooking, housekeeping, groundskeeping, maintenance.

Training/Preparation: Previous experience as a retreatant very helpful as well as education in Scripture, spiritual direction, behavioral sciences. Organizational and public relations skills.

For More Information: (1) Retreats International, University of Notre Dame, Notre Dame, IN 46556; (2) Retreat centers in your own diocese. Many host more retreats than they direct, i.e., groups bring their own leaders with them.

3. Ministry to the Divorced

Description: Helping divorced and separated deal with adjustments to single life and maintain ties with the church. May include helping people through annulment procedures. May also organize support groups and offer retreats.

Training/Preparation: Familiarity with canon law/church teaching and marriage tribunal procedures; some counselling, psychology. Personal experience with divorce may serve as an excellent preparation. Attitude: nonjudgmental, compassionate, trusting.

For More Information: (1) North American Conference of Separated and Divorced Catholics, 1100 S. Goodman St., Rochester, NY 14620; (2) The Beginning Experience, 3100 W. 41st St., Sioux Falls, SD 57105.

4. Campus Ministry

Description: Enabling college students to develop values through participation in volunteer, social justice, liturgical, and social activities. Includes counseling and working with other college departments to develop educational programs. Usually a member of a team.

219

Training/Preparation: Ability to relate to young adults. Understanding of moral, spiritual, and social development. Often an M.A. in theology or religious studies is required.

For More Information: Catholic Campus Ministry Association, 300 College Park Ave., Dayton, OH 45469. Ask for the Catholic Campus Ministry Directory.

5. Migrant Ministry

Description: Assisting migrants in obtaining necessary work residency permits, finding housing, and health care; teaching basic survival skills in an adopted culture, such as shopping, finding transportation; teaching language, budgeting, citizen rights, value of currency, etc. Legal aid; social work; religious instruction; organizing recreation, food distribution, leading prayer and Scripture groups.

Training/Preparation: Bilingual and bicultural ability to put oneself in another's shoes; familiarity with network of agencies providing services. Knowledge of laws governing migrants.

For More Information: Mexican American Cultural Center, 3019 West French Place, San Antonio, TX 78228.

6. Street Kids/Runaways

Description: Helping kids who are runaways or homeless return home or get off the streets, providing basic needs, plus training programs, counselling, health care, crisis intervention, etc.

Training/Preparation: Compassion, understanding, unconditional love, forgiveness.

For More Information: Covenant House, 440 Ninth Ave., New York, NY 10001-1607.

7. Maryknoll Lay Missioners

Description: Collaboration in Maryknoll mission work at the grassroots level, working with small communities. Need for pastoral ministers, nurse practitioners, educators, health care instructors, agriculturalists, community organizers, economists, mechanics, etc.

Training/Preparation: Orientation program; college degree required for most assignments; required professional experience.

For More Information: Kathy Wright, Maryknoll Lay Missioners, Maryknoll, NY 10545.

8. Stephen Ministries (Transdenominational)

Description: a one-to-one ministry as trained, caring church members reaching out to others in time of need; a confidential ministry, that is, a continuous, conscious effort is expended to maintain the bond of trust between the person receiving care and the caregiver; a helping relationship that focuses on the unique needs of each person and lasts as long as the needs exist; a lay ministry under the guidance and supervision of the pastor(s), church staff, and/or other leaders.

Training/Preparation: Fifty hours in a twelve-day leader's training course at centers throughout the country.

For more information: Stephen Ministries, 1325 Boland, St. Louis, MO 63117.

Besides the above resources, you may find that your own diocesan offices advertise openings for full and part-time ministries. Many diocesan newspapers also advertise positions for religious job-hunters.

It is possible that the ministry you really want is still in the future. New needs, and therefore new potential ministries, will appear all around us as we approach the third millennium. For this reason, we need to reflect on the ministries of the future.

CHAPTER TWELVE

In the Year 2000

---

*"Then I saw a new heaven and a new earth. The former heaven and
the former earth had passed away..." (Rv 21:1).*

During a time of galloping change it's foolhardy to predict the future either of the church or of the world. Nevertheless, certain trends can be detected that will almost surely continue in the decades ahead. John Naisbitt, in his popular book *Megatrends*, reports that we are living in a "time of parenthesis." "We have extraordinary leverage and influence — individually, professionally, and institutionally — *if we can only get a clear sense, a clear conception, a clear vision, of the road ahead.*"[1] Planning for the ministries of the future requires charting a course, however tentative, for that future. This course will reflect trends that are becoming clearer every day. Theologians who do their part in planning for the future have to rely, to some extent, on sociologists' findings. Since the Spirit speaks through the signs of the times, the church's ministers have to read those signs, interpret them, and then plan accordingly.

Planning for the future of the church's ministries is more important today than ever before. The late Karl Rahner noted that "humankind is *reflectively planning* its future, *compelled* to do so.... The thought that we could go back to a naive, unreflecting stage of consciousness and functioning is a nostalgic dream whose realization would have to be paid for by wiping out a large part of humanity."[2] Rahner then drew the appropriate conclusions for the church: "In the new theological and practical consciousness of humanity, the church must plan itself and its future in a new, hitherto unrealizable way."[3] The church, concluded Rahner, must be a "church of human planning, ... a world church under conditions of a world become one, a church . . . of global planning . . . of reflexive futurology."[4]

Church planning manuals are based on the principle that the church has the responsibility to discern its God-given mission and ministries and then to identify all the available resources to plan its ministries to accomplish that mission.[5] During a meeting in August 1989, the 1.3 million-member Assemblies of God church announced that it was planning for twenty thousand more ministers and five thousand more churches by the year 2000. Being guided by the Holy Spirit does not excuse us from the responsibility of planning for the future.

Charting a course for the future may be risky, but it is better than stumbling blindly from one decade into the next or being dragged into the future by forces beyond our control. The futurists may help us to see what is on the road ahead. The problems of the 1990s, according to one futurist, will include growing pollution, the drug crisis, disappearing resources, the struggle against poverty, rampant lawlessness, population pressures, and the collapsing family.[6] These problems, we can assume, will elicit a response from many Christian ministers. Attuned to the truth, they will sense that these problems are real even as politicians, to get re-elected, will pander to the pathology of denial.

As we move into the third millennium, the Christian churches of the world, according to another futurist, will experience profound changes:

> By the year 2025, Christians in the first-world countries will comprise slightly less than one-fourth of all the world's Christians. . . .
> More Christians will speak Spanish than any other language. . . .
> 50% of the world's full-time Christian missionaries will come from underdeveloped countries. . . .
> There will be significant cult movements based on charismatic personalities. . . .
> There will be considerable controversy over the emphasis to be placed on either rational or mystical approaches to faith. . . .
> Christianity in Western Europe and North America will be forced to accept the role of a minor player in shaping the societies and cultures. . . .
> The special status of the church in the eyes of governments will be all but eliminated.[7]

All these changes are bound to play a large role in shaping the church and the Christian ministries of the future.

Sociological Data

Every day it is becoming clearer that, as the Catholic Church plans for its future in the world of 2025, it will have to pay special attention to the shrinking number of clergy. Richard Schoenherr's research reveals that there will be 50 percent fewer priests in the year 2000 than in the vocational high-tide year of 1967. The departure rate for priests in the twenty-six to forty-five age bracket, according to Schoenherr, is holding steady at about 3.5 percent per year.

> In recent research, Schoenherr discovered that the number of res- ignations is commonly under-reported by dioceses to *The Official Catholic Directory*, partly because some priests resign in an un- official way and partly because a proportion of the resignees are granted leaves of absence by their bishops to think over what they want to do.[8]

Besides, the directory includes priests who are sick, absent, or retired. Schoenherr concludes that the priesthood by the year 2000 will be the preserve of a small and conservative group of older men.

The crisis of the ordained ministry is not merely a crisis of num- bers. The caliber of the young men entering the seminary raises serious questions about the ordained priesthood of the future. Richard McBrien summarizes the findings of three sociologists:

> What about the quality of the young men who do present them- selves for candidacy? The authors (Hoge, Potvin, and Ferry) ac- knowledge the impression which is abroad in the United States Catholic Church: namely, that the vocations crisis is as much qual- itative as quantitative. Here again the research is inadequate, but certain lines of many candidates' profiles do appear: dependency, immaturity, low interest in women, aestheticism, conservatism, au- thoritarianism, and preoccupation with prestige. Moreover, those seminarians who leave the seminary are more likely to exhibit a greater degree of independence and open-mindedness than those who stay.[9]

Trends and Dreams

With the decrease in the number of clergy in the active ministry, it seems clear that the Catholic Church of the future must continue to expand the ministries of the baptized. Dean Hoge concludes:

An elementary principle of all organizational life is that if you cannot find traditionally-designated people to carry out a necessary function of an organization, you hunt for substitutes. If the function is really needed, someone must be found. In the Catholic Church, if you cannot find enough priests, you hunt for other people and find ways that they can carry out the necessary functions.[10]

Hoge speaks as a sociologist looking at an organization's needs. From the viewpoint of theology, the new ministers will *not* merely be substitutes for the missing clergy. It is the thesis of this book that the shortage of priestly ministries is a blessed occasion for discovering and supporting the ministries of all the baptized. As Horace wrote: *Carpe diem*, "Seize the time."

Committed Christians who are both able and willing to "carry out the necessary functions" will be available in great numbers in the church of the future. "By the 1990s," writes Eugene Kennedy, "one may anticipate that psycho-social realities will favor once again a search for transcendence through lives of service rather than strategies of self-improvement.... Men and women will be ready for a call to service in the ministerial work of the church."[11] In a poll taken in 1980 Gallup discovered that 7 percent of American Catholics over the age of eighteen would be interested in either the full-time ministry or in some other form of religious work as a career.[12]

A study completed by the archdiocesan pastoral council of Cincinnati noted the need for evaluating present programs and planning for the ministries of the future. It concludes:

(1) A pilgrim people of God requires the ongoing assessment of the needs of the community; (2) the future of ministry necessitates a critical review and evaluation of existing programs of preparation for ministry; (3) efforts are still needed to increase the openness to the continuing evolution of the diversity of ministries and ministers.[13]

It is becoming clearer every day that in the future ministries will not be concentrated in the church. More and more of the baptized will find themselves ministering in the workaday world of the business people, the bus drivers, the lawyers, and the laborers. Permanent deacons have already carried the ministry beyond the walls of the church. Moreover, many dioceses are actively supporting social and educational ministries as well as public health care ministries in their communities.

Some of today's trends in the development of ministry can be expected to continue. We can anticipate new ministries in the areas of preaching, theology, teaching, physical and psychological healing, social reconciliation, peace-making, family life, communications, counseling, government, international development, the arts, and domestic celebration.

Surely there will be an increase of ministries by and to minorities. Ministry will become more professional and will include more women. Ministers will continue to serve in marriage encounter, cursillo, and the charismatic renewal. There will be an increasing diversity and more adaptability in the churches. The present declericalization of the ministry is bound to continue. Ministers will be more mobile because of the increasing mobility of society itself. More and more ministers will have a part-time ministry, e.g., teaching a religious education class in the evening after working at the post office during the day. The rate of vocational change will continue to be high. Greater responsibilities and positions of leadership will be entrusted to ministers at earlier ages.

In the future we will see a greater use of commitment to ministry for limited terms, i.e., three, six, ten years. "Only mothers die too soon," said Cardinal Darmojuwono upon retiring. "Politicians and bishops don't step down soon enough. I think a younger man can do a better job: he is more mobile and he'll understand the young."[14] In his retirement the cardinal served as an assistant parish priest in the same parish where he began his ministry forty years earlier. He recommended this course of action to other bishops. The Peace Corps approach of a two-year commitment may well become more common for Christian ministers.

Dean Hoge, in a study of Catholic college students, reports that there would be an increase in vocations to the priesthood if they could be priests for a specified period of time. After celibacy, "a life-long commitment" is the second most important deterrent to a religious vocation.[15] This factor cannot be ignored in planning the ministries of the future. More and more dioceses have already instituted a process for assigning clergy for a definite term of office. No doubt this trend will continue. At least one American bishop accepted appointment to a diocese on the condition that he could resign after ten years. He then returned to the parish ministry.

Ecclesiastical Perestroika

The ministries of the future will require some new church structures. Walbert Buhlmann predicts that the structures of the future will be decentralized and pluriform.[16] They will incorporate more democratic procedures that honor the experience of lay ministers and bring them into the decision-making process of the church. Without such restructuring it is likely that the "lay" ministers will leave the Catholic Church and offer their gifts to other churches in the ecumenical Christian communion. The harvest in the reign of God is always larger than any particular church.

The aging clerical machinery will have to be replaced with new structures. In fact, there will have to be a real and thorough ecclesiastical *perestroika*. A radical, as opposed to cosmetic, restructuring, however, if it is to be effective, must come "from below," from the little people. Restructuring "from above," as Peter Drucker notes, rarely succeeds.[17] Neither the Roman curia nor the hierarchy will ever be successfully restructured "from above." Those who wait for that wait in vain. If the East Germans had waited for reform "from above," they would still be waiting, behind the Wall.

For centuries we have been conditioned to expect leadership, vision, and direction to come "from above." So we find it hard to accept the realism that no lasting structural change will come down "from the top." Leonard Doohan concludes: "I see no likelihood that the future direction and vision of the church will filter down to the people from somewhere high up in the structure, rather, it will percolate up from the grass roots dedication and experience of the laity."[18] The baptismal ministers will make a serious mistake if they invest their emotional energy in nursing expectations that structural reform will come "from above." It won't.

The little people, even in the church, do have power. They can and do withhold their contributions. They can organize and use the media to express their concerns. "Call to Action," based in Chicago, has issued a pastoral letter calling for an end to celibacy and the ordination of women. The authors, "as committed laity, religious and clergy," also claim "their responsibility to participate in the selection of their local bishops."

Today's Roman curial system of congregations was put in place by Pope Sixtus V in 1587 in his apostolic constitution *Immensae Aeterni Dei*. Over the centuries popes and councils have tried to reform this system from above. The latest effort comes from Pope John Paul II in the decree *Pastor Bonus* (1989). In a rather thorough evaluation of this latest reform document, James Provost concludes: "It is not enough to leave the reform of the curia in the hands of the curia itself; as with any institution, there are many vested interests which hinder effective reform or renewal."[19] Those who wear the crown of power do not voluntarily set it aside.

Meanwhile, the old church structures, built with the lumber of the Roman empire, continue to rot and crumble. They have become dead weight on the backs of the laborers. They sap the strength and drain the morale of those who would proclaim the good news of the kingdom. New ministers will have to learn not to invest themselves, their time or energy, in structures that are clearly obsolete. Freed from a useless burden, they will have more energy to minister in a truly pastoral way to the needs of today. In the process, they will build the foundations for new structures that will truly serve the people. Unless the baptized ministers themselves reject the old structures "from below" and then build the new ones, their own ministries will suffocate under the rubble of the old.

There is at least a possibility that a total restructuring of the church, even "from below," will eventually produce some kind of hierarchy. Service institutions, such as hospitals and universities, operate with a structured hierarchy. The salary scale and titles like dean and vice president will quickly reveal it. New employees, if they expect to survive in the system, learn to respect its hierarchy.

These "secular" hierarchies, however, are designed to serve their clientele, the patients and the students. If they do not do so, the officers at the top will soon be replaced. They are organized more on the basis of function and competence than on power. And that's an important difference. "Secular" hierarchies have to provide quality service to their consumers or the institution will not survive. In the church, on the other hand, bishops remain agents of the pope; priests remain instruments of the bishop. They get their power "from above." Even if these hierarchic leaders provide poor service in preaching, administration, or pastoral care, the people, the clients, do not have the structures to select and install replacements.

Since the Gregorian Reform the church has built a Berlin Wall between the sacred and the secular. Clerics on the side of the sacred often make the decisions and then announce them to the laity on the other side. The real church structures remain on the clerical side, while the laity often deal with window-dressing.

On the clerical side, priest personnel or assignment commissions sometimes fall into institutionalized cronyism. Composed only of clerics, they appoint their friends to vacant parishes without consulting the "lay" ministers or the parishioners. The only leadership qualification the new pastor may possess is that he did not commit the sin of matrimony. He may be a woman-hater, drug or alcohol dependent, a poor preacher, and theologically illiterate. But he arrives in the parish because his clerical friends, with the bishop approving, have assigned him there. Psychologists and personnel or management consultants cannot serve on these assignment commissions, because they do not belong to the clergy. The people in the parish who pay the bills and have the gift of discernment usually have no voice in the assignment of clergy.

There is no theological reason why, at the death or resignation of the parish leaders, including the priests, the people could not engage in a discernment process and then form a search committee to choose their successors. After prayerful discernment, this committee could determine qualifications, advertise the position, interview prospective candidates, and then select nominees for a larger discernment process. If the successful candidate is not already ordained to the appropriate leadership function, he or she could be ordained by the community with a ceremony similar to the one outlined in chapter 6. Already in 1972 Karl Rahner taught that the local community had a right to have its chosen leader recognized by the diocese through ordination.[20] The diocese, as a sign of unity, could send a representative to bless and confirm the new pastoral leaders in their leadership function.

The same procedure could be used at the death or resignation of the bishop. The search committee, after prayerful discernment, could draw up a list of qualifications and competencies needed in the diocese at that particular time. After advertising the position, a list of final candidates could be prepared. This list would not be limited to single men or women. Nor would it be limited to those men or women whose only qualification is loyalty to the pope in such matters as birth control and the ordination of women. The committee would first look for qualified candidates within its own diocese. After a thorough and prayerful consultation with all the people, the selection would be announced. Then the people would be invited to proclaim their "Amen" of acceptance in an appropriate ordination ceremony, similar to the one outlined in chapter 6. All these "new" structures become possible as soon as the people of God recover the ancient system in which ordination was not seen as a transfer of power from above.

The church will also need new structures to deal with pastoral problems like priestless Sundays, the ordination of homosexuals, the politics of abortion, selection of leaders, the ordination of women, the care of the environment, racial and sexual discrimination, and meaningful liturgical rites for blacks and Hispanics. Neither the papal nuncio nor the National Conference of Catholic Bishops can continue to address these problems apart from the great numbers of ministers laboring in the field. If they do, the bishops' "solution" will remain at the top of the pyramid and the problem will remain in the pastoral trenches.

Every three years an episcopal synod gathers in Rome, often to make policy decisions for the "lay" ministers scattered throughout the world. Sometimes they decide family life matters without allowing a meaningful consultation of the "sense of the faith which characterizes the People as a whole." Andrew Greeley speaks to this issue:

> The greatest problem the Church as an organization faces is the pervasive human temptation to canonize as essential relationship patterns that evolved to meet the needs of one era but no longer respond to the needs of the present era.... The Church, like all human organizations, will continue to have a structure, for structure is nothing more than established patterns of relationships....
> A structureless community is as much a contradiction as would be an ocean without water.... It is the purpose of all institutional

structures to serve the welfare of the human persons who belong to them.... The particular style of organizational structure depends to some extent on the culture in which an organization finds itself and the challenges that it must meet.[21]

To date, the bishops' synod has not developed a consultative process suited to the North American culture, that actually influences the synod's final results. That must happen in the future if the synod is ever to become an effective church structure. Participants in the process must feel that their participation has helped to shape the final outcome.

Ministries cannot flourish without the support of flexible structures. They cannot exist by themselves because they need to be ordered (ordained) to the upbuilding of the church. They also need to establish patterns of relationship with all the other ministries. The new structures which develop will need to reflect the life, the culture, and the experience of the local church that supports them as part of its life in community.

Decentralization

An important goal for the ministries of the future will be a greater decentralization of the church. Missionaries to Third World countries have discovered that a new nationalism is emerging. This means "a return to one's own culture, one's own language, one's own history, with a somewhat exaggerated but understandable emphasis on national identity."[22]

One futurist foresees a continuing growth in nationalism in the future with the result that there will be an "increasing desire of peoples all over the world to be in charge of their own social organizations." By the year 2025, according to Samuel Dunn, local administrative control of almost all church and missionary programs will be in the hands of local officials.[23] Elements of the local culture will be celebrated in the liturgy and the churches will be governed in a manner indigenous to that culture.

An experienced missionary pleads for decentralization of the church of the missions:

What we are facing is not merely an intracultural difficulty within the church, but a challenge from all the cultures of the world outside the church. We have to make possible the New Testament life and reality of those "new and young and particular churches" of Vatican II. Such a reality cannot come to be in a severely centralized church.[24]

What these modern missionaries advocate is the implementation of a principle proclaimed in Vatican II's Dogmatic Constitution on the Church. This document extols the local churches with a special emphasis on the ancient patriarchal churches:

> By divine Providence it has come about that various churches established in diverse places by the apostles and their successors have in the course of time coalesced into several groups, organically united, which, preserving the unity of faith and the unique divine constitution of the universal Church, enjoy their own *discipline*, their own *liturgical usage*, and their own *theological and spiritual heritage*. Some of these churches, notably the ancient patriarchal churches...have begotten others as daughter churches.... This variety of local churches with one common aspiration is particularly splendid evidence of the catholicity of the undivided church.[25]

So far the Catholic Church has not incorporated this splendid Vatican II teaching into its pastoral practice.

One of the megatrends in the American culture is the shift from centralization to decentralization.[26] In the political world we have noticed that during elections people have considerable interest in the politics of local issues, such as redlining, crime-stopper programs, nuclear waste disposal, housing for the elderly, and preservation of historic sites. These issues elicit a response from the people because they sense they can actually do something about them. National issues, on the other hand, often seem to be beyond their sphere of influence.

To reverse the centralizing tendencies that began in the church with Gregory VII, ministers need to build from the bottom up. They need to own their situation and take responsibility for it — priestless liturgies, voicelessness, and powerlessness, etc. "Power," writes John Naisbitt, "that is bestowed from the top down can be withdrawn if the donor's priorities change. Successful initiatives hammered out at the local level have staying power. Local solutions are resistant to top-down intervention."[27]

Examples of decentralization in the church, effective since Vatican II, are the various national conferences of bishops. The Latin American bishops conferences have been especially creative in initiating a shift in ecclesiology toward the local church in their meetings at Medellín and Pueblo. The U.S. Conference of Catholic Bishops took the initiative in consulting the people in preparing the pastoral letters on peace, the economy, and the concerns of women for church and society. Decentralization in the church still has a long way to go before it reaches the grassroots in the diocesan and parish structures.

The young Third World churches have taken the initiative in giving concrete form to liberation theology. "They believe that a *local theology is an important prerequisite for a local church.*"[28] Third World theology is distinguished by three special features: it is ecumenical, dialogical, and tolerant. Surely this new theology will provide an impetus for the development of a local church with its own discipline, liturgical usage, and spiritual heritage. Eventually, as these local churches assume greater responsibility for their own structures and pastoral decisions, they will move the universal church toward greater decentralization.

An overly centralized church government, relying on religious power from above, simply will not work in the new pluralistic world. In today's society a wide variety of institutions perform functions that formerly were carried out by families in the home. Seventy-five years ago practically all babies were born in the home. Today they are all born in the maternity ward of the hospital. The child-care center, the health care system, and the schools have taken over many family functions. Peter Drucker reflects on the implications of this shift:

> The new institutions are not based on power. They are based on function.... Pluralism is nothing new. Indeed, most societies throughout history were pluralistic. But there is a crucial difference between any earlier pluralism and the present one. All earlier pluralisms were based on *power*. The present one is based on *function*.... The new pluralist organization of society has no interest in government and governance.... The new institutions speak their own language, have their own knowledge, their own career ladder, and, above all, their own values.[29]

A centralized church government, based on a pyramid power system, will never reach these new institutions from outside. The latter are concerned with their products, the cured patient, the satisfied customer. Formerly the church could reach the family through its power base at the parish level. But the new institutions are not responsive to that kind of power because they are powered by specialized functions. The church of the future will be able to reach these pluralist institutions only from inside on the basis of function, not power.

Another megatrend especially evident in this hemisphere is the emphasis on lived experience. With the rapid growth of the behavioral sciences, Christians will continue to assign more value to their own experience than to the pronouncements of authority figures. Liberation theology, for instance, begins with feeling, then moves to reaction, and then to action.[30] Rather than relying primarily on abstract norms and eternal principles, modern culture is much more empirical, inductive rather than deductive. "Lived experience" will be the ultimate test of the relevance of churches and religion. Perhaps the most powerful example of this trend is the widespread disregard of Pope Paul VI's encyclical on birth control whereby many couples give the priority to conscience and to lived experience. The implications for ministry are that ministers will simply work out their own definitions of ministry through their own personal experience when making vocational decisions. In the United States this process, rightly or wrongly, will get considerable help from the individualism that powerfully shapes the American culture, including its Christian population.

A trend with serious implications for future ministry is the development of new criteria for the ministry of the baptized. In recent years over 275 training programs have been developed to prepare laypeople for pastoral ministry. Some are degree programs; others are certificate or nondegree programs.[31] In the future there will continue to be an emphasis on qualifications and the development of ministerial skills. Good will, while helpful, is simply not enough. The people of God deserve quality ministry, and in our North American culture they will demand it. The primary purpose of these programs will be to produce competent and skilled ministers. But they will also be a means of screening out incompetent ministers. With the help of these training programs the local church will be prepared to assume responsibility for the quality of its own ministries.

The research and planning department of the Maryknoll Sisters has already developed criteria for persons seeking a new ministry in the area of justice. They require that these ministries: (1) enable the fulfillment of basic needs (food, water, housing, clothing, and education); (2) enable the fulfillment of human rights (social, economic, political, cultural, and religious) within the context of a given culture; (3) allow people to participate in decisions that affect them; (4) promote local leadership; and (5) foster faith and spiritual values.[32]

Another trend or process that will shape the ministries of the future will be a greater use of the diocesan synod. As noted earlier, the 1917 Code of Canon Law required each diocese to hold a synod at least every ten years. The synod recognizes the right of the diocesan community to decree what is good for the diocese. Since Vatican II the diocesan synod has been overhauled and thus renewed. This postconciliar structure may at times still be in tension with the canon law definition of the bishop as the sole legislator of the diocese. Nevertheless in France, in 1989, some twenty diocesan synods had just ended or were underway. Sixty percent of the participants were laypeople. The most popular issues that surfaced during these assemblies were the role of the parish, poverty, young people, and catechesis. In November 1989, the diocese of Toledo, Ohio, held a synod assembly that included two thousand participants with eight representatives, nearly all laity, from its 165 parishes.

While the synod is an old structure in the church, it is one that can be fired up with new life "from below." An updated understanding of the synod that incorporates the unique gifts and wide experience of numerous "lay" ministers will help this structure once again to serve the upbuilding of the church. Eventually state and regional synods, with large numbers of the ministers of the baptized, will assume greater responsibility for the pastoral problems that are unique to their own geographical areas. Texas, for instance, with its large Hispanic population, has pastoral concerns that are quite different from those of Pennsylvania.

A trend sure to accelerate in the future is the growth of priestless parishes. In 1982, there were 21,608 parishes without a resident priest in France. In the United States, at least seventy dioceses have priestless parishes with a total of 193 faith communities headed by either a woman religious, a deacon, a layperson, or a religious brother. In the priestless parishes where Sunday services were held, 139 women religious were authorized to lead the prayer; 96 laywomen functioned in a similar manner.

One consequence of this growth of parishes led by laity and women religious is that the clergy will no longer be exclusively in charge of the sacred. There will also be less control over these nonordained ministers. The Eucharist will no longer be controlled by the clergy. There will be more and more Word ministries. There will also be a greater use of "extraordinary" ministers for the administration of the sacraments.

An obvious trend for the future will be less secrecy concerning the inner workings of the church. With the magic of the media we have entered the global information society. Our culture demands access to all facts and figures. In our modern society, a church obsessed with secrecy will appear increasingly quaint, a remnant of a bygone era. Besides, shared decision-making will simply require sharing all available data. Participation in the decision making process will be essential to win the cooperation of those who will be expected to implement the decision. Besides, even the simplest member of the people of God may have part of the wisdom needed to discern God's will. St. Benedict, in chapter 3 of his rule, advised his abbots to consult even the youngest members of the monastery before making an important decision, because these too could help discover God's holy will.[33]

An organizational trend that will shape the ministries of the future will be a clearer determination of job descriptions, time commitments, salary scales, and benefits. Surely in our mobile society, ministers will be given portable retirement plans so that they can work outside their own diocese and still retain the benefits accrued. Nonclerical grievance procedures will have to be developed for simple and more frequent use.

Assuredly, there will be an increase in the number of women in the ministries of the future. The National Council of Churches reports that the number of women ordained to full ministry increased from 10,470 in 1977 to 20,730 in 1986. In the 188 dioceses and archdioceses in the United States, 82 women administered priestless parishes in 38 dioceses in 1989; women served as chancellors in 17 dioceses; and women held the position of diocesan superintendent of schools in 59 dioceses.[34]

The trend toward inculturation of ministries will certainly increase in the years ahead:

> Up to Vatican II, complete uniformity reigned in the Catholic Church: the same catechism everywhere, the same Latin liturgy everywhere, everywhere the same centrally monitored church discipline.... As long as the church lived in a European cultural setting, that was more or less acceptable. But today when the church lives in six continents, each having its own political, cultural, and ecclesial consciousness, the church there must not merely be accommodated in exterior things, but radically "incarnated" into these cultures.[35]

African-American and Mexican-American Catholics are leaving the Roman Catholic Church by the thousands due to a lack of inculturation. These rich heritages of faith cannot be truly expressed through the formal and rigid forms of worship shaped by Roman-European rites. An instinct of faith tells these Catholics that the Gospel does not require them to become Roman in order to practice the Christian religion. Unless the church implements the theology of inculturation, thousands of potential ministers will be lost to the Catholic Church. There will have to be more movement toward inculturation similar to the Africanization of the liturgy of Zaire. This liturgy is not merely a translation of the Roman eucharistic ritual but is an adaptation enriched with the experience of the African world of nature, tradition, and symbolism.

Fundamentalism is a fact of life. It is a trend that will grow stronger in the years ahead. The ministers of the future will have to deal with it in one way or another. A fundamentalist church in South Barrington, Ill., draws five to six thousand former Catholics every weekend. It converts four to five hundred Catholics each year. The pastor estimates that 40 to 50 percent of his parishioners are former Catholics.[36]

Fundamentalism's appeal continues to be community, hospitality, emotion in worship; and ministers who come from the community. Radio and television also attract many Catholics to the evangelical churches. As they move to the sunbelt, they find that their neighbors are evangelicals. Soon they are attending Bible classes with them and joining their faith community. This trend will continue to be a challenge to all Catholic ministers. It could even produce a worldwide Catholic examination of conscience about "what we have failed to do."

The movement of ministries into the political arena is another dimension of ministry that is bound to grow in the future. In Guatemala, a priest runs for the office of president; in Prague, Cardinal Tomasek endorses a candidate for the presidency, calling him a "fighter for justice and truth." Surely "lay" ministries will continue to move in the same direction. In San Antonio COPS (Communities Organized for Public Service), organized in the early 1970s, is a grassroots lay Christian organization that focuses on neighborhood needs. It has tackled such issues as flood control, water distribution, urban planning, capital construction, street improvement, air quality improvement, and financial development. Since the laity are more involved in the political world they will be more comfortable in ministering in their own milieu.

The church has always been in politics in one form or another. Today, however, there is a greater awareness that Jesus' own ministry had its political side. For this reason, the ministry of *every* baptized Christian, according to Kenan Osborne, is also political. The Christian ministry is directed not only to the church community but also to the world at large. Sometimes involvement in the political structures can almost be required if the Gospel teaching is to be preserved. When in doubt, we need only remember, with the children of the Holocaust, the painful experience of Germany under the Third Reich.[37]

A trend that will gather greater momentum in the future is the movement toward a more missionary orientation in the ministries. Eugene Hemrick reports that "between 1975 and 1982 the number of inquiries about lay mission programs increased from 300 to 3,200."[38] Father Anthony Bellagamba, the executive director of the U.S. Catholic Mission Association, notes this new trend and the problem it creates:

Most future missionaries may be lay missionaries. . . . For every two or three inquiries we have about joining a missionary order, we have ten or twelve about going out as a lay missioner. The vocations are there, but *we don't recognize them because they are different from what we want or expect.*[39]

Another trend that will surely grow stronger in the years ahead will be ministries to the environment. Marshall McLuhan's Global Village has arrived. The radioactive fallout from Chernobyl contaminates the potatoes in Germany. People everywhere are becoming more aware that we must care for our Garden of Eden. Whether the issue is acid rain, destruction of forests, waste management, or ozone depletion, Christians must be involved in the preservation of God's holy creation. The more the baptized ministers become aware that their ministry is not confined to the sanctuary of the sacred the more they will move into the so-called secular world. Environmental issues will become so serious that they will have no other choice.

The future will also see more ministers in the areas of justice and peace. There will be more awareness that war is insane and that, if there is to be peace, there have to be peace-*makers*. There will be more Dorothy Days, Peter Maurins, Dan Berrigans, and Tom Gumbletons. As these prophets die, their disciples will continue their ministry of peace-making.

The emergence of "unofficial" ministries in the local church is another trend that will gain ground in the years ahead. The people, as highly-motivated disciples and keenly aware of their baptismal anointing, will simply respond to the needs when and where they see them. Thus, ministry will grow "from below." Eventually, sooner rather than later, these ministries will also be ordered (ordained) toward the up-building of their emerging churches. In the process, they will fill the word "ordination" with new meaning. Small groups will select and then ordain (order) their own members to various functions as needed.

In the future there will be a growing number of seniors ministering to the communities. Clearly, we are living longer. By 1990 the average life expectancy in the U.S. had climbed to 74.7. By the year 2000 the forty-five to fifty-five-year-olds will increase by 46 percent and the seventy-five year olds by 26.2 percent. By 2025, 20 percent of the U.S. population will be over sixty-five. The graying of America will bring tremendous opportunities along with difficult challenges.[40]

We are also retiring earlier. Military personnel can retire with generous benefits after only twenty years of service, or at forty years of age. Federal civil servants can retire after thirty years of service, or in their early fifties, with full pensions. In 1987 there were more than three hundred thousand retired federal civil servants. Many firms and companies offer attractive incentives to their employees to encourage early retirement.

Many who "retire" begin part- or full-time second and third careers, doing what they always dreamed of doing. The American Association of Retired Persons (AARP) provides many resources for the "retired" who are searching for a retirement career.[41] The potential vocations to ministry from this age group are practically limitless. So far, however, the churches have not recruited these vocations in any serious way. They are still holding out for the traditional vocations to the priesthood, brotherhood, and sisterhood. In the meantime, the rich experience of these more mature and very valuable vocations goes untapped. This will change as the so-called vocation crisis becomes even more serious.

As we conclude our reflections on the megatrends that will shape the ministries, we need to recall that the future, as always, will bring both the good and the bad, the helpful and the harmful. Christian ministers, clinging to the Gospel of the reign of God and prayerful discernment, will need to separate the wheat from the weeds. They will need to search for the "hidden wisdom" of God revealed through the Spirit (1 Cor 2:6–10). They cannot uncritically accept everything the future brings and then shape their ministries accordingly. Holding fast to their identity as the salt of the earth, they need to actively shape the future. As God's "co-workers" for the reign of God, they will often have to take a prophetic, countercultural position. The mystery of evil will continue to reign until the final victory of the reign of God. The scams of the future will be more sophisticated, more technological, but they will still be scams. Our faith teaches us that the power of grace will overcome the power of evil, but the dark pages of history warn us against a naive optimism about the future.

There will indeed be "a new heaven and a new earth." But it will take the willing hands of a growing contingent of baptismal ministers to bring it about. The church will need a "clear vision of the road ahead" and an openness to the frightening risks of the future. With our rapid pace of change, the churches do not have the time to indulge in a romantic retreat into nostalgia or to hanker for the institutional securities of the past.

The people of God do not need to fear. With steadfast faith, they can walk resolutely into the year 2000, for Yahweh will travel with them: "And a fire shone within the cloud by night, for all the House of Israel to see. And so it was for every stage of their journey."

Notes

Introduction

1. John J. Ziegler, "Who Can Anoint the Sick?" *Worship* 61 (January 1987): 34–38; see also Joseph Martos, *Doors to the Sacred* (Garden City, N.Y.: Doubleday, 1982), 374–75.

2. David C. Leege and Joseph Gremillion, *Notre Dame Study of Catholic Parish Life* (Notre Dame, Ind.: University of Notre Dame, 1984), Report No. 1, 5.

3. John Naisbitt, *Megatrends* (New York: Warner Books, 1982), 252.

Chapter 1: From Moses to Jesus

1. Paul Heinisch, *Theology of the Old Testament* (Collegeville, Minn.: Liturgical Press, 1955), 324–27.

2. Ibid., 325–26.

3. St. Augustine, *The City of God* (Baltimore: Penguin Books, 1972), Book XX, 9, 915.

4. Thomas O'Meara, *Theology of Ministry* (New York: Paulist Press, 1983), 31.

5. *The Jerusalem Bible* (Garden City, N.Y.: Doubleday, 1966), note f, 267.

6. O'Meara, *Theology of Ministry*, 26.

7. Walter Kasper, *Jesus the Christ* (New York: Paulist Press, 1976), 76.

8. O'Meara, *Theology of Ministry*, 28.

9. Ibid., 29.

10. L. Boff, "Salvation in Jesus Christ and the Process of Liberation," *Concilium* 96 (New York: Herder and Herder/Seabury, 1974), 80–81.

11. Jon Sobrino, *Christology at the Crossroads* (Maryknoll, N.Y.: Orbis Books, 1976), 47.

12. Bernard Cooke, *Ministry to Word and Sacrament* (Philadelphia: Fortress Press, 1976), 45.

13. Oscar Cullmann, *The Christology of the New Testament* (Philadelphia: Westminster Press, 1959), 13–43.

14. Elizabeth Tetlow, *Women and Ministry in the New Testament* (New York: Paulist Press, 1980), 51.

241

15. Donald Senior, *Jesus* (Dayton, Ohio: Pflaum Press, 1975), 98.

16. Pope John Paul II, "Pastoral Action Asked on Penance," *Origins* 18 (1988): 87.

17. John McKenzie, *Dictionary of the Bible* (Milwaukee: Bruce Publishing Co., 1965), 651.

18. Ibid.

19. Gregory Norbet, O.S.B., Weston Priory, from the recording, *Locusts and Wild Honey*, 1973.

20. Joseph A. Fitzmyer, S.J., "The Letter to the Romans," *Jerome Biblical Commentary* (Englewood Cliffs, N.J.: Prentice-Hall, 1968), 2:331.

21. Jon Sobrino, S.J., *Christology at the Crossroads* (Maryknoll, N.Y.: Orbis Books, 1976), 48.

22. Gustavo Gutiérrez, *We Drink from Our Own Wells* (Maryknoll, N.Y.: Orbis Books, 1983), 92.

23. O'Meara, *Theology of Ministry*, 29.

24. Edward Schillebeeckx, *The Church with a Human Face* (New York: Crossroad, 1985), 24.

25. Avery Dulles, *Models of the Church* (Garden City, N.Y.: Image Books, 1987), 207.

26. Senior, *Jesus*, 60.

27. J. B. Lightfoot, ed., "Epistle of St. Ignatius to the Romans," *The Apostolic Fathers* (Grand Rapids, Mich.: Baker Book House, 1970), 77.

28. Dulles, *Models of the Church*, 225.

Chapter 2: From Jesus to Paul

1. The diocese of Lansing, Mich., has an "Office for Lay Ministers." It is responsible for preparing laypeople for ministry in three areas: (1) academic study, (2) ministerial skills, and (3) spiritual formation.

2. Walter Abbott, S.J., ed., *The Documents of Vatican II* (New York: Herder and Herder, 1966), 27.

3. Ibid., 26.

4. James Hastings, ed., "Election," *Dictionary of the Bible* (New York: Scribner and Sons, 1963), 239.

5. Joseph A. Fitzmyer, S.J., "The First Epistle of Peter," *Jerome Biblical Commentary* (Englewood Cliffs, N.J.: Prentice-Hall, 1968), 2:362.

6. Raymond Brown, *The Churches the Apostles Left Behind* (New York: Paulist Press, 1984), 81.

7. Ibid., 100.

8. H. Richard Niebuhr, *The Purpose of the Church and Its Ministry* (New York: Harper and Brothers, 1956), 64.

9. Lynn Rhodes, *Co-creating* (Philadelphia: Westminster Press, 1987), 106–7.

10. Preface, Sundays in Ordinary Time, No. I.

11. Preface, Sundays in Ordinary Time, No. VIII.

12. Thomas O'Meara, *Theology of Ministry* (New York: Paulist Press, 1983), 52.

13. Ibid., 52.

14. Richard Dillon and Joseph A. Fitzmyer, S.J., *Jerome Biblical Commentary* (Englewood Cliffs, N.J.: Prentice-Hall, 1968), 2:185.

15. Bernard Cooke, *Ministry to Word and Sacrament* (Philadelphia: Fortress Press, 1976), 45.

16. Ibid., 61.

17. Elizabeth Tetlow, *Women and Ministry in the New Testament* (New York: Paulist Press, 1980), 72.

18. Alexander Souter, ed., *A Pocket Lexicon to the Greek New Testament* (New York: Oxford University Press, 1966), 83.

19. Tetlow, *Women and Ministry in the New Testament*, 71.

20. Abbott, *The Documents of Vatican II*, 22.

21. Hans Küng, *The Church* (New York: Sheed and Ward, 1967), 188.

22. Clement of Rome, *Early Christian Writings* (Baltimore: Penguin Books, 1968), 20.

23. O'Meara, *Theology of Ministry*, 67.

24. See André Lemaire, *Les ministères aux origines de l'Eglise* (Paris: Les Editions du Cerf, 1971), 50, 51.

25. Ibid., 51.

26. Ibid., 54–55.

27. James Dunn, *Unity and Diversity in the New Testament* (Philadelphia: Westminster Press, 1977), 107.

28. Ernst Haenchen, *The Acts of the Apostles* (Philadelphia: Westminster Press, 1971), 261.

29. Ibid., 263.

30. For a more extensive explanation of both the secular and religious meanings of these Greek words consult *The Theological Dictionary of the New Testament*, Gerhard Kittel and Gerhard Friedrich, eds. (Grand Rapids, Mich.: William B. Eerdmans, 1985), vols. 2, 4, 7, and 8.

31. Sean Freyne, *The World of the New Testament* (Wilmington, Del.: Michael Glazier, 1980), 5.

32. Hans von Campenhausen, *Ecclesiastical Authority and Spiritual Power in the Church of the First Three Centuries* (Stanford, Calif.: Stanford University Press, 1969), 77.

33. Raymond Brown, *The Churches the Apostles Left Behind* (New York: Paulist Press, 1984), 33.

34. Raymond E. Brown, *The Community of the Beloved Disciple* (New York: Paulist Press, 1979), 99–100.

35. Raymond Brown, in his *The Churches the Apostles Left Behind*, sees seven different models of church in the New Testament.

36. Dunn, *Unity and Diversity in the New Testament*, 108.

37. Küng, *The Church*, 347.

38. Edward Schillebeeckx, *The Church with a Human Face* (New York: Crossroad, 1985), 56.

39. Roger Gryson, *The Ministry of Women in the Early Church* (Collegeville, Minn.: Liturgical Press, 1976), 4.

40. Küng, *The Church*, 396.

41. Gryson, *The Ministry of Women in the Early Church*, 9–10.

42. André Lemaire, *Les ministères aux origines de l'Eglise* (Paris: Les Editions du Cerf, 1971), 110.

43. Richard P. McBrien, *Ministry* (San Francisco: Harper & Row, 1986), 11.

44. Anton Houtepen, *Minister? Pastor? Prophet?* (New York: Crossroad, 1981), 33.

45. "Biblical Commission Report: Can Women Be Priests?," *Origins* 6 (1976): 92–96.

Chapter 3: From Ignatius to Gregory VII

1. See Andrew M. Greeley, *The Making of the Popes 1978* (Kansas City, Kans.: Andrews and McMeel, 1978). The book's subtitle is "The Politics of Intrigue in the Vatican."

2. Maxwell Staniforth, trans., *Early Christian Writings* (Baltimore: Penguin Books, 1968), 67.

3. J. B. Lightfoot, trans. and ed., "Epistle of St. Ignatius to the Philadelphians," *The Apostolic Fathers* (Grand Rapids, Mich.: Baker Book House, 1956), 79.

4. Paul Johnson, *A History of Christianity* (New York: Atheneum, 1979), 89.

5. Ibid., 45.

6. William A. Jurgens, trans., "Letter to the Philadelphians," *The Faith of the Early Fathers*, no. 7, 1 (Collegeville, Minn.: Liturgical Press, 1970), 1:23.

7. Henry Chadwick, *The Early Church* (Baltimore: Penguin Books, 1967), 49.

8. Robert Kraft and Gerhard Krodel, eds., *Orthodoxy and Heresy in Earliest Christianity* (Philadelphia: Fortress Press, 1971), 64 and 70.

9. Joseph Martos, *Doors to the Sacred* (Garden City, N.Y.: Doubleday, 1982), 467.

10. Walter Abbott, S.J., ed., *The Documents of Vatican II* (New York: Herder and Herder, 1966), 40.

11. Quotations from the *Didache* come from the translation of William Jurgens in *The Faith of the Early Fathers* (Collegeville, Minn.: Liturgical Press, 1970), 1:4.

12. Ibid., 5.

13. Ibid.

14. Ibid.

15. Ibid., 166.

16. Ibid., 168.

17. Bernard Cooke, *Ministry to Word and Sacrament* (Philadelphia: Fortress Press, 1976), 544.

18. Jurgens, *The Faith of the Early Fathers*, 1:168.

19. Edward Benson, *Cyprian: His Life, His Time, His Work* (London: Macmillan, 1897), xxv.

20. Ibid., xxvii and xxviii.

21. Ibid., 43.

22. Chadwick, *The Early Church*, 120.

23. Jurgens, *The Faith of the Early Fathers*, 1:231.

24. Ibid., 240.

25. Edward Schillebeeckx, *The Church with a Human Face* (New York: Crossroad, 1985), 145.

26. Jurgens, *The Faith of the Early Fathers*, 1:228.

27. Chadwick, *The Early Church*, 48.

28. Jurgens, *The Faith of the Early Fathers*, 1:234.

29. Ibid., 230.

30. *The Fathers of the Church*, trans. Rose Donna (Washington: Catholic University of America, 1964), 51:43.

31. "The Veiling of Virgins," cited in Benson, *Cyprian: His Life, His Time, His Work*, 20.

32. Benson, ibid., 20. This quotation comes from Tertullian's semi-Montanist period. However, E. Schillebeeckx makes a strong case that "Tertullian did not make his statement under the influence of Montanism." See *The Right of the Community to a Priest* (New York: Seabury Press, 1980), 109. Henry Bettenson in his *Documents of the Christian Church* (London: Oxford University Press, 1967), 71, observes that Tertullian during his orthodox days reproached heretics because "they endue even the laity with the functions of the priesthood."

33. Pierre van Beneden, "Haben Laien die Eucharistie ohne Ordinierte Gefeiert? Zu Tertullians 'De exhortatione castitatis'" 7, 3 *Archiv. fur Liturgiewissenschaft* 29 (1987): 31–46.

34. Benson, *Cyprian: His Life, His Time, His Work*, 39.

35. Johnson, *A History of Christianity*, 59.

36. Jurgens, *The Faith of the Early Fathers*, 229.

37. Ibid., 221.

38. Ibid., 227.

39. J. A. Baker, trans., *Ecclesiastical Authority and Spiritual Power in the Church of the First Three Centuries* (Stanford, Calif.: Stanford University Press, 1969), 266.

40. Johnson, *A History of Christianity*, 60.

41. Chadwick, *The Early Church*, 127.

42. Johnson, *A History of Christianity*, 76–77.

43. Ibid., 78.

44. Edward Schillebeeckx disagrees: "Historical criticism has definitely shown canon 33 of the Spanish Council of Elvira has nothing to do with the Council" (*The Church with a Human Face*, 241).

45. Rose Donna, trans., *The Fathers of the Church*, 58:127.

46. Pheme Perkins, *Reading the New Testament* (New York: Paulist Press, 1978), 121.

47. Johnson, *A History of Christianity*, 114.

48. Ibid.

49. William Herr, *Catholic Thinkers in the Clear* (Chicago: Thomas More Press, 1985), 39.

50. Edward Schillebeeckx, *Celibacy* (New York: Sheed and Ward, 1968), 27. For a more detailed description of the Encratites see Peter Brown, *The Body and Society* (New York: Columbia University Press, 1988), 92–101.

51. Schillebeeckx, *Celibacy*, 30.

52. Brown, *The Body and Society*, 171.

53. Jurgens, *The Faith of the Early Fathers*, 1:256.

54. Charles Hefele, *A History of the Christian Councils*, trans. William Clark (Edinburgh: T. & T. Clark, 1894), 435.

55. Siricius, *To Humerius*, as found in Peter Harkx, *The Fathers on Celibacy* (De Pere, Wisc.: St. Norbert Abbey Press, 1968), 38–39.

56. James Mohler, S.J., *The Origin and Evolution of the Priesthood* (Staten Island, New York: Alba House, 1970), 95, n. 12.

57. Schillebeeckx, *Celibacy*, 29.

58. Brown, *The Body and Society*, 169, n. 47.

59. Henry Lea, *The History of Sacerdotal Celibacy in the Christian Church* (New York: University Books, 1966), 45.

60. Charles Hefele, *A History of the Councils of the Church*, trans. William Clark (Edinburgh: T. & T. Clark, 1895), 4:419.

61. Ibid., 205.

62. Giovanni Domenico Mansi, ed., *Sacrorum Conciliorum Nova et Amplissima Collectio* (Graz: Akademische Druck-U Verlagsantalt, 1960), *Concilia XIX*, col. 610 (my translation). For "weaker sex" the Latin text has *infirmitatis* (weakness) and *imbecillitatis* (weakness, imbecility, feebleness).

63. Marvin Vincent, *The Age of Hildebrand* (New York: Christian Literature Co., 1896), 74.

64. H.J. Schroeder, ed., *The Disciplinary Decrees of the General Councils* (St. Louis: B. Herder Book Co., 1937), 180.

65. Ibid., 192.

66. Ibid., 201.

67. The Greek preposition *dia*, in this Matthean text can be translated "on account of," or "by reason of," especially when, as is the case here, it is followed by the accusative case.

68. Dean Hoge, *Future of Catholic Leadership* (Kansas City, Mo.: Sheed and Ward, 1987), 124.

Chapter 4: From Gregory VII to John Paul II

1. Ephraim Emerton, trans., *The Correspondence of Gregory VII* (New York: Columbia University Press, 1932), Intro., xv.

2. Marvin Vincent, *The Age of Hildebrand* (New York: Christian Literature Co., 1896), 67.

3. Paul Fournier, "The Roman Canonical Collections of the Period of Gregory VII," *The Gregorian Epoch* (Boston: D. C. Heath, 1964), 21.

4. Kenan Osborne, O.F.M., *Priesthood* (New York: Paulist Press, 1988), 190.

5. Helmut T. Lehman, ed., *Luther's Works*, vol. 36 (Philadelphia: Muhlenburg Press, 1959), II, 116.

6. For more detailed description of the theology of the Reformers as it shaped the ministry, see Osborne, *Priesthood*, 219–47.

7. H. J. Schroeder. trans., *Canons and Decrees of the Council of Trent* (St. Louis: B. Herder Book Co., 1941), 162–63.

8. Ibid., 163.

9. Jean Galot, *La nature du caractère sacramentel* (Paris: Desclée de Brouwer, 1958), 38.

10. Schroeder, *Canons and Decrees of the Council of Trent*, 163.

11. Ibid.

12. Ibid., 162.

13. Walter Abbott, S.J., ed., *The Documents of Vatican II* (New York: Herder and Herder, 1966), 54.

14. Schroeder, *Canons and Decrees of the Council of Trent*, 176

15. Thomas O'Meara, *Theology of Ministry* (New York: Paulist Press, 1983), 185.

16. Edward Schillebeeckx, *The Church with a Human Face* (New York: Crossroad, 1985), 158.

17. Donald Attwater, ed., "Gallicanism," *A Catholic Dictionary* (New York: Macmillan, 1961), 205.

18. Abbott, *The Documents of Vatican II*, 27.

19. William J. Rademacher, *An Evaluation of the Teaching on Episcopacy in Chapter Three of Vatican II's Constitution on the Church* (Dubuque, Iowa: The Aquinas Institute, 1973), 75.

20. Abbott, *The Documents of Vatican II*, 30.

21. *Acta Apostolicae Sedis* 57 (1965): 34.

22. Abbott, *The Documents of Vatican II*, 57.

23. Giovanni Magnani, "Theology of Laity and Theological Status," in *Vatican II: Assessment and Perspectives*, ed. René Latourelle (New York: Paulist Press, 1988), 1:601–2.

24. Piero Antonio Bonnet, "The *Christifideles* as Human Protagonist," in *Vatican II: Assessment and Perspectives*, 553.

25. "Christifideles Laici," *Origins* 18 (1989): 568.

26. See *The Jerusalem Bible* (Garden City, N.Y.: Doubleday, 1966), 215, note g.

27. Osborne, *Priesthood*, 340–42.

Chapter 5: The Church and Its Ministries

1. John H. Westerhoff III, *Will Our Children Have Faith?* (New York: Seabury Press, 1976), 89–91. See also James W. Fowler, *Stages of Faith: The Psychology of Human Development and the Quest for Meaning* (San Francisco: Harper & Row, 1981).

2. Walter M. Abbott, S.J., ed., *The Documents of Vatican II* (New York: Herder and Herder, 1966), 15.

3. Karl Rahner, *The Church and the Sacraments* (New York: Herder and Herder, 1963), 21.

4. Edward Schillebeeckx, *Christ the Sacrament of the Encounter with God* (New York: Sheed and Ward, 1963), 51.

5. Thomas Hart, *To Know and Follow Jesus* (New York: Paulist Press, 1984), 139.

6. See Thomas O'Meara, *Theology of Ministry* (New York: Paulist Press, 1983), 159.

7. Richard McBrien, *Ministry* (San Francisco: Harper & Row, 1987), 7.

8. *Faith and Order Paper*, no. 111 (Geneva: World Council of Churches, 1982), 21.

9. Ibid.

10. McBrien, *Ministry*, 11–12.

11. O'Meara, *Theology of Ministry*, 142.

12. Ibid., 136.

13. Ibid., 141.

14. "Envisioning the Future of Mission and Ministries," *Origins* 19 (November 9, 1989): 381.

15. Leonardo Boff, *Ecclesiogenesis* (Maryknoll, N.Y.: Orbis Books, 1986), 58.

16. Ibid., 58.

17. Abbott, *The Documents of Vatican II*, 50.

18. David Power, *Gifts That Differ* (New York: Pueblo Publishing Co., 1980), 139–40.

19. Yves Congar, "My Pathfindings in the Theology of Laity and Ministries," *Jurist* (1972:2): 180.

20. O'Meara, *Theology of Ministry*, 198.

21. John Coleman, "A Theology of Ministry," *The Way* 25 (January 1985): 13.

22. John D. Zizioulas, *Being as Communion* (Crestwood, N.Y.: St. Vladimir's Seminary Press, 1985), 215–16.

23. Power, *Gifts That Differ*, 145.

24. Ibid., 147.

25. Ibid.

26. John Bligh, *Ordination to the Priesthood* (New York: Sheed and Ward, 1955), 77.

27. Ibid., 76.

Chapter 6: Ministering in a Sinful Church

1. Walter M. Abbott, S.J., ed., *The Documents of Vatican II* (New York: Herder and Herder, 1966), 350.

2. Ibid., 346.

3. Johannes Feiner, "Commentary on the Decree," *Commentary on the Documents of Vatican II* (New York: Herder and Herder, 1968), 2:100.

4. Ibid.

5. Ibid., 101.

6. Karl Rahner, *Theological Investigations* (Baltimore: Helicon Press, 1969), 6:271–72.

7. Francis Sullivan, *The Church We Believe In* (New York: Paulist Press, 1988), 81–82.

8. Hans Küng, *The Church* (New York: Sheed and Ward, 1967), 322.

9. Ibid., 322–23.

10. Leonardo Boff, *Church: Charism and Power* (New York: Crossroad, 1986), 84 and 86.

11. Letter to *National Catholic Reporter*, September 1, 1989, 24.

12. Carroll Stuhlmueller, C.P., *Biblical Meditations for the Easter Season* (New York: Paulist Press, 1980), 158.

13. Elizabeth Beverly, "A Silence That Is Not Hollow," *Commonweal* 116 (September 22, 1989): 493 (italics mine).

14. *The Pope Speaks* 33 (1988): 144.

15. Michael Novak in *America* 160 (January 28, 1989): 56.

16. Hugo Rahner, "The Church, God's Strength in Human Weakness," in *The Church* (New York: P. J. Kenedy & Sons, 1963), 9.

17. Thomas Aquinas, *The Summa Theologica*, trans. Fathers of the English Dominican Province (New York: Benziger Bros., 1947), q. 33, art. 3 and 4, 2:1335–36.

18. Emil Brunner, *The Misunderstanding of the Church* (Philadelphia: Westminster Press, 1953), 107.

19. See William J. Rademacher, *The New Practical Guide for Parish Councils* (Mystic, Conn.: Twenty-Third Publications, 1988), 64.

20. Karl Rahner, *The Dynamic Element in the Church* (New York: Herder and Herder, 1964), 44.

21. Rademacher, *The New Practical Guide for Parish Councils*, 64–65.

22. Gotthold Hasenheuttl, *Charisma: Ordnungsprinzip der Kirche* (Freiburg: Herder, 1969), 238 (italics mine).

23. Yves Congar, "Reception as an Ecclesiological Reality," *Election and Consensus in the Church*, ed. Giuseppe Alberigo and Anton Weiler (New York: Herder and Herder, 1972), 45.

24. Francis Sullivan, S.J., *Magisterium* (Mahwah, N.J.: Paulist Press, 1983), 111.

25. Abbott, *The Documents of Vatican II*, 29.

26. Congar, "Reception as an Ecclesiological Reality," 62.

27. Edward Schillebeeckx, "The Christian Community and its Office-Bearers," *The Right of the Community to a Priest*, ed. Edward Schillebeeckx and Johann-Baptist Metz (New York: Seabury Press, 1980), 121.

28. See especially Richard Lucien, ed., *Vatican II: The Unfinished Agenda* (New York: Paulist Press, 1987), and Kenan Osborne, O.F.M., *Priesthood* (New York: Paulist Press, 1988), 337–42.

29. See *Proceedings of the Thirty-Sixth Annual Convention*, vol. 36, Catholic Theological Society of America, June 10–13, 1981; Leonardo Boff, *Ecclesiogenesis* (Maryknoll, N.Y.: Orbis Books, 1986); Leonard Doohan, *Laity's Mission in the Local Church* (San Francisco: Harper & Row, 1986); Karl Rahner, *The Shape of the Church to Come* (New York: Seabury Press, 1972).

30. Abbott, *The Documents of Vatican II*, 50.

31. Joseph Komonchak, "Ministry and the Local Church," in *Proceedings*, Catholic Theological Society of America, 36:56.

32. Avery Dulles, *Models of the Church* (Garden City, N.Y.: Image Books, 1978), 47.

33. Ibid.

34. Evelyn Whitehead, "The Structure of Community: Toward Forming the Parish as a Community of Faith," *The Parish in Community and Ministry*, ed. Evelyn Whitehead (New York: Paulist Press, 1978), 42.

35. See Leonardo Boff, *Ecclesiogenesis*, 5.

36. Gregory Baum, *New Horizon* (New York: Paulist Press, 1972), 141–42.

37. Ibid.

38. Joseph Fichter, "The Church: Looking to the Future," *America* 160 (March 4, 1989): 192

39. Boff, *Church: Charism and Power*, 125–26.

40. Alfred T. Hennelly, S.J., "The Grassroots Church," in *Proceedings*, Catholic Theological Society of America, 34:185.

41. Ibid.

42. *Ministries/Communities*, no. 56, 1988/2 (Brussels: Pro Mundi Vita, 1988), 17.

43. Karl Rahner, "Theology of the Parish," *The Parish from Theology to Practice*, ed. Hugo Rahner, trans. Robert Kress (Westminster, Md.: Newman Press, 1968), 28–29.

44. Karl Rahner, *The Shape of the Church to Come* (New York: Seabury Press, 1974), 108.

45. Ibid., 109.

46. Rosemary Haughton, "The Emerging Church," *The Way* (January 1982): 32.

47. Ibid., 33.

48. Ibid., 36–37.

49. Boff, *Ecclesiogenesis*, 23–30.

50. T. Howland Sanks, "Forms of Ecclesiality: The Analogical Church," *Theological Studies* 49, no. 4 (December 1988): 703.

51. Boff, *Ecclesiogenesis*, 23.

52. Ibid., 24.

53. Ibid.

Chapter 7: The Sacrament of the Human

1. Quoted in John A. Sanford, *Healing and Wholeness* (New York: Paulist Press, 1977), 92.

2. Quoted by Paul Johnson in *A History of Christianity* (New York: Atheneum, 1979), 347.

3. Dermot Lane, *The Reality of Jesus* (New York: Paulist Press, 1975), 137.

4. Karl Barth, *Church Dogmatics*, vol.1, *The Doctrine of God* (Edinburgh: T. & T. Clark, 1956), 151.

5. Gerald O'Collins, *What Are They Saying about Jesus?* (New York: Paulist Press, 1983), 7.

6. Lane, *The Reality of Jesus*, 140.

7. See Piet Schoonenberg, *The Christ* (New York: Herder and Herder, 1971), 94.

8. Ibid., 96.

9. D. M. Baillie, *God Was in Christ* (London: Faber and Faber, 1956), 153.

10. Norman Pittenger, *Christology Reconsidered* (London: SCM Press, 1970), 75.

11. Ibid., 138.

12. *The Documents of Vatican II* (New York: Herder and Herder, 1966), 57.

13. Lane, *The Reality of Jesus*, 140.

14. Roy Lewis, *Choosing Your Career, Finding Your Vocation* (New York: Paulist Press, 1989), 31 and 46.

15. Joseph Zinker, *The Creative Process in Gestalt Therapy* (New York: Vintage Books, 1977), 47–48.

16. Karl Barth, *Evangelical Theology: An Introduction* (New York: Holt, Rinehart and Winston, 1963), 64.

17. Lewis, *Choosing Your Career, Finding Your Vocation*, 111–23.

18. Erik Erikson, *Identity: Youth and Crisis* (New York: W. W. Norton, 1968), 96.

19. See William Bridges, *Transitions* (Menlo Park, Calif.: Addison-Wesley, 1980), 90–150.

20. T. S. Eliot, *Four Quartets* "Little Gidding" (New York: Harcourt, Brace, 1943), 38.

21. Bridges, *Transitions*, 134–50.

22. See Jerry Edelwich, *Burn-out* (New York: Human Sciences Press, 1980); Dr. Herbert J. Freudenberger, *Burn-out* (Garden City, N.Y.: Doubleday, 1980); Ayala M. Pines and Elliot Aronson, *Burnout* (New York: Free Press, 1981); G. Lloyd Rediger, *Coping with Clergy Burnout* (Valley Forge, Pa.: Judson Press, 1982).

23. Edelwich, *Burn-out*, 14.

24. Pines and Aronson, *Burnout*, 15.

25. G. Lloyd Rediger, 15–16. Ministers are invited to take their own burnout test on pp. 17–18.

26. Ibid., 22.

27. *Origins* 18 (January 18, 1989): 499–501 (italics mine).

28. Edelwich, *Burn-out*, 42.

29. Pines and Aronson, *Burnout*, 48.

30. Edelwich, *Burn-out*, 21.

31. See Pines and Aronson, *Burnout*, 124–29.

32. Charles J. Keating, *The Leadership Book* (New York: Paulist Press, 1978), 10.

33. Ibid., 40–43. See also Thomas Gordon, *L.E.T: Leader Effectiveness Training* (New York: Wyden Books, 1977).

34. William J. Rademacher, *The New Practical Guide for Parish Councils* (Mystic, Conn.: Twenty-Third Publications, 1988), 156–57. Bernard Swain in his book *Liberating Leadership* (San Francisco: Harper & Row Publishers, 1986), describes four pastoral leadership styles: sovereign, parallel, semi-mutual, and mutual. In an appendix he provides a helpful summary of the main characteristics of each style. As a church management consultant, he offers practical advice for the development of leadership skills in the postconciliar church. See also Douglas McGregor, *The Human Side of Enterprise* (New York: McGraw Hill, 1960).

35. Keating, *The Leadership Book*, 60–61.

Chapter 8: The Ministry of Women

1. *Pittsburgh Press*, February 12, 1989, B8.
2. Ibid.
3. *National Catholic Reporter*, March 10, 1989, 4.
4. *Newsweek*, February 13, 1989, 59.
5. Peter Hebblethwaite, "Little Known Mariavite History ..." *National Catholic Reporter*, July 1, 1983, 10–11.
6. Sara Butler, ed., *Research Report: Women in Church and Society* (Mahwah, N.J.: Catholic Theological Society of America, 1978), 12.
7. Gerda Lerner, *The Creation of Patriarchy* (New York: Oxford University Press, 1986), 239.
8. Adam in this section of the creation account is still an "earth creature," sexually undifferentiated. It does not become a *male* person until the creation of Eve. However, history treated Adam as male and so he became the father of patriarchy. See Fran Ferder and John Heagle in *Partnership* (Notre Dame, Ind.: Ave Maria Press, 1989), 41.
9. Elisabeth M. Tetlow, *Women and Ministry in the New Testament* (New York: Paulist Press, 1980), 9–11.
10. Ibid., 10.
11. Ibid., 16.
12. Ibid., 17.
13. Joachim Jeremias, *Jerusalem in the Time of Jesus* (Philadelphia: Fortress Press, 1975), 369.
14. Ibid., 359–60.
15. Ibid., 374.
16. Ibid., 24.
17. See Roger Gryson in *The Ministry of Women in the Early Church* (Collegeville, Minn.: Liturgical Press, 1976), 81.
18. Ibid., 119.
19. Carolyn M. Grassi and Joseph Grassi, *Mary Magdalene and the Women in Jesus' Life* (Kansas City, Mo.: Sheed and Ward, 1986), 7.
20. A. M. McGrath, *Women and the Church* (Garden City, N.Y.: Image Books, 1976), 61.
21. Gryson, *The Ministry of Women in the Early Church*, 73.
22. Ibid., 41.
23. Richard Nolan, ed., *The Deaconate Now* (Washington: Corpus Books, 1968), 152.
24. See Gryson, *The Ministry of Women in the Early Church*, 62.
25. Ibid., 120.
26. Joan Morris, *The Lady Was a Bishop* (New York: Macmillan, 1973), 76.
27. These arguments are listed in greater detail in Butler, *Research Report: Women in Church and Society*, 18.
28. Ibid., 17.
29. George S. Worgul, Jr., "Ritual, Power, Authority and Riddles," *Louvain Studies* 14 (January 1989): 49.
30. Dermot A. Lane, *The Reality of Jesus* (New York: Paulist Press, 1975), 110.

31. *Origins* 6, no. 33 (February 3, 1977): 522.

32. John H. Leith, ed., *Creeds of the Churches* (Garden City, N.Y.: Doubleday, 1963), 31.

33. Joseph Neuner, S.J., and Heinrich Roos, S.J., *The Teaching of the Catholic Church* (New York: Alba House, 1967), 426.

34. Leith, *Creeds of the Churches*, 133.

35. Ibid., 35.

36. *The Later Christian Fathers*, trans. Henry Bettenson (New York: Oxford University Press, 1970), 108.

37. Sandra Schneiders, *Women and the Word* (New York: Paulist Press, 1986), 53.

38. Ibid., 56.

39. Ibid., 54.

40. Worgul, "Ritual, Power, Authority and Riddles," 52.

41. The reference is to the Fourth Book of Thomas Aquinas's Commentary (*Scriptum*) on Peter Lombard's Sentences, *Distinctio* 25, q. 2, quaestiuncula 1 ad 4 (italics mine).

42. Thomas Aquinas, *Summa Theologica* (Supplement), trans. Fathers of the English Dominican Province (New York: Benziger Bros., 1947), 3:2698.

43. Ibid., 2700.

44. Thomas Aquinas, *Summa Theologica*, 1:466.

45. Butler, *Research Report: Women in Church and Society*, 37.

46. Ibid., 34.

47. Ibid., 32–34.

48. Worgul, "Ritual, Power, Authority and Riddles," 54.

49. Ibid., 47.

50. Edward Schillebeeckx, *Christ the Sacrament of the Encounter with God* (New York: Sheed and Ward, 1963), 47–89. See also A. M. Roguet, *Christ Acts through Sacraments* (Collegeville, Minn.: Liturgical Press, 1954), 11–35.

51. *Catherine of Siena: The Dialogue*, trans. Susan Noffke (New York: Paulist Press, 1980), 64, 264, and 273.

52. *Acta Apostolicae Sedis* 25 (1943): 218.

53. Worgul, "Ritual, Power, Authority and Riddles," 46.

54. See Conrad Gromada in "The Lima Document," unpublished Ph.D. dissertation, Duquesne University, 1988, 1:103.

55. Ibid.

56. Walter Abbott, S.J., ed. *The Documents of Vatican II* (New York: Herder and Herder, 1966), 348.

57. Veronica Brady, "Women in Ministries," *The Way, Supplement* 53 (Summer 1985): 90–91

58. See William Thompson, *Berulle and the French School* (New York: Paulist Press, 1989), 95 n. 21.

59. Michael O'Connor, *Theotokos: A Theological Encyclopedia of the Blessed Virgin Mary* (Wilmington, Del.: Michael Glazier, 1986), 293.

60. Ibid.

61. *One Baptism, One Eucharist and a Mutually Recognized Ministry* (Geneva: World Council of Churches, 1978), 45.

62. Dean Hoge, *The Future of Catholic Leadership* (Kansas City, Mo.: Sheed and Ward, 1987), 192.

63. Ibid., 215 and 216.

64. Maria Harris, "A Discipleship of Equals: Implications for Ministry," in *A Discipleship of Equals: Towards a Christian Feminist Spirituality*, ed. Francis A. Eigo (Villanova, Pa.: Villanova University Press, 1988), 167.

65. *Ministry and Community*, no. 43, 1985/1 (Brussels: Pro Mundi Vita, 1985).

66. See Felix Bernard, "Do Women Lack Rights in the Catholic Church?" *Theology Digest* 36 (Spring 1989): 17.

67. See Joseph Martos, *Doors to the Sacred* (Garden city, N.Y.: Doubleday, 1982), 374–75, and John J. Ziegler, "Who Can Anoint the Sick?" *Worship* 61 (January 1987): 34–38.

Chapter 9: Partnership

1. Keith F. Nickle, *The Collection* (Naperville, Ill.: Alec R. Allenson, 1966), 123.

2. Fran Ferder and John Heagle, *Partnership: Women and Men in Ministry* (Notre Dame, Ind.: Ave Maria Press, 1989), 45.

3. J. Robert Nelson, "Ecumenical Considerations in Shared Responsibility," *Chicago Studies* 9 (Summer 1970): 162.

4. James Coriden, "Shared Authority: Rationale and Legal Foundation," *Chicago Studies* 9 (Summer 1970): 175.

5. Karl Rahner, *The Dynamic Element in the Church* (New York: Herder and Herder, 1964), 44.

6. Paul Minear, *Images of the Church in the New Testament* (Philadelphia: Westminster Press, 1960), 49–50.

7. Karl Barth, *Church Dogmatics* (Edinburgh: T. & T. Clark, 1958), vol. 4, 2, 631.

8. Ibid., 635.

9. Minear, *Images of the Church in the New Testament*, 176.

10. Cardinals John May and Joseph Bernardin, Archbishop Rembert Weakland, and Bishop Stanley Ott, "What We Have Seen and What We Will Say," *America* 157 (September 5, 1987): 103.

11. Ibid.

12. Coriden, "Shared Authority: Rationale and Legal Foundation," 174.

13. Walter Abbott, S.J., ed., *The Documents of Vatican II* (New York: Herder and Herder, 1966), 300.

14. *Two Basic Social Encyclicals* (New York: Benziger Brothers, 1943), 139–41.

15. Coriden, "Shared Authority: Rationale and Legal Foundation," 177.

16. Ibid., 172.

17. Ibid., 173.

18. Vincent Hatt, "The Team Approach to Service and Leadership," *The Living Light* 12 (Spring 1975): 50.

19. Dody Donnelly, *Team* (New York: Paulist Press, 1977), 52–53.

20. Ibid., 70.

21. Myra Lambert and William Shields, "Criteria for Membership in Team Ministry for Priests and Sisters," *Chicago Studies* 10 (Fall 1971): 301–7.

22. J. Robert Nelson, "Ecumenical Considerations and Shared Responsibility," 163.

23. Hatt, "The Team Approach to Service and Leadership," 50.

24. For a more detailed explanation of this aspect of Holy Orders see William Bausch, *A New Look at the Sacraments* (Mystic, Conn.: Twenty-Third Publications, 1983), 256–59.

25. Christopher Butler, ed., *The Vatican Council 1869–1870* (Westminster, Md.: Newman Press, 1962), 74–75.

26. Kenan B. Osborne, O.F.M., *Priesthood* (New York: Paulist Press, 1988), 352.

27. Ibid., 347–48.

28. Ibid., 348.

29. *Faith and Order Paper*, no. 73 (Geneva: World Council of Churches, 1978), 54.

30. Ibid.

31. *Origins* 12 (1982): 303.

32. Joseph F. Eagan, "Is BEM's Call for Mutual Recognition of Ministry Realistic? Review of Ten Post–Vatican II Dialogues on Ordained Ministry," *Journal of Ecumenical Studies* 21, no. 4 (Fall 1984): 682.

33. Ibid., 686–87.

34. Ferder and Heagle, *Partnership: Women and Men in Ministry*, 127.

Chapter 10: Be Holy

1. David Conner, "Holiness, Leadership and Failure," *The Way* 29 (April 1989): 127.

2. Ibid., 128.

3. Alexander Jones, ed., *The Jerusalem Bible* (Garden City, N.Y.: Doubleday, 1966), 215, note g.

4. Francis A. Sullivan, S.J., *The Church We Believe In* (New York: Paulist Press, 1988), 71 (italics mine).

5. Ibid., 72.

6. Karl Rahner, *The Shape of the Church to Come* (New York: Seabury Press, 1972), 82.

7. See especially Elizabeth Dreyer, "Tradition and Lay Spirituality: Problems and Possibilities," *Spirituality Today* 39 (Autumn 1987), and Leonard Doohan, *The Lay-Centered Church* (Minneapolis: Winston Press, 1984).

8. Walter Abbott, S.J., ed., *The Documents of Vatican II* (New York: Herder and Herder, 1966), 67.

9. Martin Buber, *I and Thou* (New York: Charles Scribner's Sons, 1958), 3.

10. Ibid., 11–12.

11. Ibid., 10.

12. Ibid., 115.

13. Ibid., 117.

14. Thomas Hart, *To Know and Follow Jesus* (New York: Paulist Press, 1984), 62.

15. Abbott, *The Documents of Vatican II*, 169.

16. Francis Thompson, "The Hound of Heaven," *The Standard Book of British and American Verse* (Garden City, N.Y.: Garden City Publishing Co., 1932), 663.

17. Gustavo Gutiérrez. *We Drink from Our Own Wells* (Maryknoll, N.Y.: Orbis Books, 1984), 15.

18. James C. Fenhagen, *Mutual Ministry* (New York: Seabury Press, 1977), 93.

19. Bill Huebsch, *A Spirituality of Wholeness* (Mystic, Conn.: Twenty-Third Publications, 1988), 80.

20. Karl Rahner, *Belief Today* (New York: Sheed and Ward, 1967), 13–43.

21. See William Thompson, *Fire and Light: The Saints and Theology* (New York: Paulist Press, 1987), especially chap. 10, "Consulting 'Everyday' Mystics." 178–96.

22. Ronald Hook, *The Social Context of Paul's Ministry* (Philadelphia: Fortress Press, 1980), 37.

23. "Our Task Is to Create Worlds," *Commonweal* 116 (June 2, 1989): 334.

24. William Droel and Gregory Pierce, *Confident and Competent* (Notre Dame, Ind.: Ave Maria Press, 1987), 45–46.

25. Huebsch, *A Spirituality of Wholeness*, 90.

26. Jean Vanier, *Be Not Afraid* (New York: Paulist Press, 1975), 137–38.

27. Roger Gryson, *The Ministry of Women in the Early Church* (Collegeville, Minn.: Liturgical Press, 1976), 62 (italics mine).

28. Anne Wilson, "Holistic Spirituality," *Spirituality Today* 40 (Autumn 1988): 219.

29. James Arraj, "Jungian Spirituality," *Spirituality Today* 40 (Autumn 1988): 257.

30. See especially David Keirsey and Marilyn Bates, *Please Understand Me* (Del Mar, Calif.: Prometheus Nemesis Books, 1978).

31. Charles Keating, *Who We Are Is How We Pray* (Mystic, Conn.: Twenty-Third Publications, 1987), 40 and 48.

32. Reuel L. Howe, *The Miracle of Dialogue* (New York: Seabury Press, 1963), 69.

33. Ibid., 70.

34. Ibid., 78–80.

35. Francis Vanderwall, *Spiritual Direction* (New York: Paulist Press, 1981), 9.

36. Ibid., 52.

37. Paul Begheyn, S.J., "Traditions of Spiritual Guidance," *The Way* 29 (April 1989): 156.

38. Ibid., 164.

39. Edward C. Sellner, "Mid-life and Mentoring: A Pastoral Theology of Spiritual Guidance," *Chicago Studies* 25 (August 1986): 134.

40. Ibid., 135. See also Daniel Levinson, *Seasons of a Man's Life* (New York: Ballantine Books, 1978), 97–101.

41. Thomas Merton, *Conjectures of a Guilty Bystander* (New York: Image Books, 1968), 86 (italics mine).

Chapter 11: Finding Your Work and Your Place in the Vineyard

1. From the song "Come with Me into the Fields," by Dan Schutte, S.J. (Phoenix: NARL, 1971).

2. Quoted in Richard Bolles, *The 1989 What Color Is Your Parachute* (Berkeley, Calif.: Ten Speed Press, 1989) frontispiece.

3. Ibid., 345.

4. Ibid., 349.

5. Ibid., 360.

6. Ernst Haenchen, *The Acts of the Apostles* (Philadelphia: Westminster Press, 1971), 396, n. 3.

7. Thomas O'Meara, *Theology of Ministry* (New York: Paulist Press, 1983), 137.

8. Roy Lewis, *Choosing Your Career, Finding Your Vocation* (New York: Paulist Press, 1989), 65.

9. David Keirsey and Marilyn Bates, *Please Understand Me* (Del Mar, Calif.: Prometheus Nemesis Books, 1978), 170.

10. *The Personal Profile System Manual* (Performax Systems International, Inc., U.S.A. 1979), 3.

11. Lewis, *Choosing Your Career, Finding Your Vocation*, 4.

12. Susan Angus, ed., *Invest Yourself* (New York: Commission on Voluntary Service and Action, 1986), xxiii.

Chapter 12: In the Year 2000

1. John Naisbitt, *Megatrends* (New York: Warner Books, 1982), 252 (italics mine).

2. Karl Rahner, "Perspectives on Pastoral Ministry in the Future," epilogue in Walbert Buhlmann, *The Church of the Future* (Maryknoll, N.Y.: Orbis Books, 1986), 189–90.

3. Ibid.

4. Ibid., 191.

5. *Church Planning* (St. Louis: Office for Life and Worship), A-1.

6. Edward Cornish, "Whither America," *The Futurist* 24 (January–February 1990): 38–40.

7. Samuel Dunn, "Christianity's Future," *The Futurist* 23 (March–April 1989): 34–35.

8. Dean Hoge, *Future of Catholic Leadership* (Kansas City, Mo.: Sheed and Ward, 1987), 10.

9. Richard McBrien, "Commentary," *Research on Men's Vocations to the Priesthood and the Religious Life* (Washington: U.S. Catholic Conference, 1984), 76.

10. Hoge, *Future of Catholic Leadership*, 182.

11. Eugene Kennedy, *The Now and Future Church* (Garden City, N.Y.: Doubleday, 1984), 183–84.

12. McBrien, "Commentary," 75–76.

13. "An Expanded View of Ministry," *Origins* (January 15, 1987): 557.

14. "Ministries and Communities," no. 31 (Brussels: Pro Mundi Vita, 1982), 20.

15. Hoge, *Future of Catholic Leadership*, 126.

16. Buhlmann, *The Church of the Future*, 131–51.

17. Peter Drucker, *The New Realities* (New York: Harper & Row Publishers, 1989), 30.

18. Leonard Doohan, *Grass Roots Pastors* (San Francisco: Harper & Row, 1989), xii.

19. James Provost, "*Pastor Bonus*: Reflections on the Reorganization of the Roman Curia," *The Jurist* 48 (1988): 2, 529.

20. Karl Rahner, *The Shape of the Church to Come* (New York: Seabury Press, 1974), 109.

21. Andrew Greeley, "Sociology and Church Structure," *Structures of the Church*, ed. Teodoro Jimenez Urresti (New York: Herder and Herder, 1970), 26–27.

22. Buhlmann, *The Church of the Future*, 137.

23. Dunn, "Christianity's Future," 35–36.

24. Vincent J. Donovan, *The Church in the Midst of Creation* (Maryknoll, N.Y.: Orbis Books, 1989), 110.

25. Abbott, *The Documents of Vatican II*, 46 (italics mine).

26. John Naisbitt, *Megatrends* (New York: Warner Books, 1982), 97–129.

27. Ibid., 112–13.

28. Buhlmann, *The Church of the Future*, 154.

29. Drucker, *The New Realities*, 78 and 83.

30. Leonardo Boff, "The Contribution of Liberation Theology to a New Paradigm," in *Paradigm Change in Theology* (New York: Crossroad, 1989), 411.

31. See Suzanne E. Elsesser, *Preparing Laity for Ministry 1986* (Washington: United States Catholic Conference, 1986).

32. *SEDOS Bulletin* as quoted in *Ministries and Communities*, no. 49, 1986/3 (Brussels: Pro Mundi Vita, 1986), 4.

33. "The Rule of St. Benedict," Henry Bettenson, ed., *Documents of the Early Christian Church* (New York: Oxford University Press, 1967), 116

34. *Ministries and Communities*, no. 59, 1989/1, 21.

35. Buhlmann, *The Church of the Future*, 6.

36. William Bausch, *The Hands-On Parish* (Mystic, Conn.: Twenty-Third Publications, 1989), 199.

37. Kenan Osborne, *Priesthood* (New York: Paulist Press, 1988), 338 and 342.

38. Eugene Hemrick in *Ministries and Communities*, no. 60, 1989/2, 24.

39. Anthony Bellagamba in *Ministries and Communities*, no. 38, 1983/4, 29 (italics mine).

40. See Ken Dychtwald and Joe Flower, *Age Wave: The Challenges and Opportunities of an Aging America* (Tarcher, 1989).

41. See *How to Plan Successful Retirement* (Glenview, Ill.: Scott, Foresman, 1988), 55–72.

A Selected
Bibliography for
Further Study

Chapter One: From Moses to Jesus

Boadt, Lawrence. *Reading the Old Testament*. New York: Paulist Press, 1984.

Brown, Raymond, Joseph Fitzmyer, and Roland Murphy. *The New Jerome Biblical Commentary*. Englewood Cliffs, N.J.: Prentice-Hall, 1990.

Dunn, James. *Unity and Diversity in the New Testament*. Philadelphia: Westminster Press, 1977.

Miguens, Manuel. *Church Ministries in New Testament Times*. Arlington, Va.: Christian Culture Press, 1976.

Chapter Two: From Jesus to Paul

Dunning, James. *Ministries: Sharing God's Gifts*. Winona, Minn.: St. Mary's Press, 1980.

Grollenberg, Lucas, et al. *Minister? Pastor? Prophet? Grassroots Leadership in the Church*. New York: Crossroad, 1981.

Kruse, Colin. *New Testament Models for Ministry*. New York: Thomas Nelson, 1983.

Perkins, Pheme. *Reading the New Testament*. New York: Paulist Press, 1988.

———. *Ministering in the Pauline Churches*. New York: Paulist Press, 1982.

Schweizer, Eduard. *Church Order in the New Testament*. London: SCM Press, 1961.

Chapter Three: From Ignatius to Gregory VII

Bausch, William J. *Pilgrim Church*. Mystic, Conn.: Twenty-Third Publications, 1989.

Chadwick, Henry. *The Early Church*. Baltimore: Penguin Books, 1967.

Cooke, Bernard. *Ministry to Word and Sacraments*. Philadelphia: Fortress Press, 1976.

Jurgens, William. *The Faith of the Early Fathers*. Collegeville, Minn.: Liturgical Press, 1970.

Johnson, Paul. *A History of Christianity*. New York: Atheneum, 1979.

Von Campenhausen, Hans. *Ecclesiastical Authority and Spiritual Power in the Church of the First Three Centuries*. Stanford, Calif.: Stanford University Press, 1969.

Chapter Four: From Gregory VII to John Paul II

Bausch, William J. *Traditions, Tensions, Transitions in Ministry*. Mystic, Conn.: Twenty-Third Publications, 1982.

Burrows, William R. *New Ministries: The Global Context*. Maryknoll, N.Y.: Orbis Books, 1980.

Doohan, Leonard. *Laity's Mission in the Local Church*. San Francisco: Harper & Row, 1986.

McBrien, Richard. *Ministry*. San Francisco: Harper & Row, 1987.

Mitchell, Nathan. *Mission and Ministry: History and Theology in the Sacrament of Order*. Wilmington, Del.: M. Glazier, 1982.

Osborne, Kenan B., O.F.M. *Priesthood: A History of the Ordained Ministry in the Roman Catholic Church*. New York: Paulist Press, 1988.

Power, David. *Gifts That Differ: Lay Ministries Established and Unestablished*. New York: Pueblo Publishing Co., 1980.

Tavard, George H. *A Theology for Ministry*. Wilmington, Del.: M. Glazier, 1983.

Chapter Five: The Church and Its Ministries

Abbott, Walter M., S.J., ed. *The Documents of Vatican II*. New York: Herder and Herder, 1966.

Boff, Leonardo. *Ecclesiogenesis*. Maryknoll, N.Y.: Orbis Books, 1986.

Kilian, Sabbas J., O.F.M. *Theological Models for the Parish*. New York: Alba House, 1977.

Latourelle, René, ed. *Vatican II: Assessment and Perspectives*. Vol. 1. New York: Paulist Press, 1988.

O'Meara, Thomas. *Theology of Ministry*. New York: Paulist Press, 1983.

Schillebeeckx, Edward. *The Right of a Community to a Priest*. New York: Seabury Press, 1980.

———. *Church*. New York: Crossroad, 1990.

Sullivan, Francis A., S.J. *The Church We Believe In*. New York: Paulist Press, 1988.

Zizioulas, John D. *Being as Communion*. Crestwood, N.Y.: St. Vladimir's Seminary Press, 1985.

Chapter Six: Ministering in a Sinful Church

Boff, Leonardo. *Church: Charism and Power*. New York: Crossroad, 1986.
Doohan, Leonard. *Grass Roots Pastors*. New York: Harper & Row, 1989.
Leege, David, and Joseph Gremillion. *Notre Dame Study of Catholic Parish Life*. Notre Dame, Ind.: University of Notre Dame, 1984–89.
Nouwen, Henri. *The Wounded Healer*. Garden City, N.Y.: Doubleday, 1972.
Pittenger, Norman. *The Ministry of All Christians*. Wilton, Conn.: Morehouse-Barlow, 1982.
Schillebeeckx, Edward. *The Church with a Human Face*. New York: Crossroad, 1985.

Chapter Seven: The Sacrament of the Human

Bridges, William. *Transitions*. Reading, Mass.: Addison-Wesley Publishing Company, 1980.
Edelwich, Jerry. *Burn-out*. New York: Human Sciences Press, 1980.
Freudenberger, Herbert J. *Burn-out*. Garden City, N.Y.: Doubleday, 1980.
Keating, Charles J. *The Leadership Book*. New York: Paulist Press, 1978.
Levinson, Daniel J. *The Seasons of a Man's Life*. New York: Ballantine Books, 1978.
Nouwen, Henri J. M. *Creative Ministry*. Garden City, N.Y.: Doubleday, 1971.
Sammon, Sean. *Growing Pains in Ministry*. Whitinsville, Mass.: Affirmation Books, 1983.
Sanford, John. *Ministry Burnout*. New York: Paulist Press, 1982.
Whitehead, Evelyn Eaton, and James D. *Christian Life Patterns*. Garden City, N.Y.: Doubleday, 1979.

Chapter Eight: The Ministry of Women

Butler, Sara, ed. *Research Report: Women in Church and Society*. Mahwah, N.J.: Catholic Theological Society of America, 1978.
Chittister, Joan. *Women, Ministry, and the Church*. New York: Paulist Press, 1983.
Gryson, Roger. *The Ministry of Women in the Early Church*. Collegeville, Minn.: Liturgical Press, 1976.
Lerner, Gerda. *The Creation of Patriarchy*. New York: Oxford University Press, 1986.
Rhodes, Lynn N. *Co-Creating*. Philadelphia: The Westminster Press, 1987.
Tavard, George H. *Woman in Christian Tradition*. Notre Dame, Ind.: University of Notre Dame, 1973.
Tetlow, Elisabeth M. *Women and Ministry in the New Testament*. New York: Paulist Press, 1980.

Chapter Nine: Partnership

Bausch, William J. *The Hands-On Parish*. Mystic, Conn: Twenty-Third Publications, 1989.

Donnelly, Dody. *Team*. New York: Paulist Press, 1977.

Fenhagen, James, *Mutual Ministry*. New York: Seabury Press, 1977.

Ferder, Fran, and John Heagle. *Partnership Women and Men in Ministry*. Notre Dame, Ind.: Ave Maria Press, 1989.

Rudge, Peter. *Ministry and Management*. London: Tavistock, Barnes & Noble, 1968.

Sofield, Loughlan, and Carroll Juliano. *Collaborative Ministry*. Notre Dame, Ind.: Ave Maria Press, 1987.

Swain, Bernard. *Liberating Leadership*. San Francisco: Harper & Row, 1986.

Wilson, Marlene. *The Effective Management of Volunteer Programs*. Boulder, Colorado: Volunteer Management Associates, 1976.

Chapter Ten: Be Holy

Gutiérrez, Gustavo. *We Drink from Our Own Wells*. Maryknoll, N.Y.: Orbis Books, 1984.

Green, Thomas. *Weeds among the Wheat*. Notre Dame, Ind.: Ave Maria Press, 1984.

Heubsch, Bill. *Spirituality of Wholeness*. Mystic, Conn.: Twenty-Third Publications, 1988.

Jones, Cheslyn, Geoffrey Wainwright, and Edward Yarnold. *The Study of Spirituality*. New York: Oxford University Press, 1986.

Keating, Charles. *Who We Are Is How We Pray*. Mystic, Conn.: Twenty-Third Publications, 1987.

Lecky, Dolores. *Practical Spirituality for Lay People*. Kansas City, Mo.: Sheed and Ward, 1987.

Nouwen, Henri. *Reaching Out: The Three Movements of the Spiritual Life*. New York: Doubleday, 1986.

Thompson, William. *Fire and Light*. New York: Paulist Press, 1987.

Chapter Eleven: Finding Your Work and Your Place in the Vineyard

Angus, Susan. *Invest Yourself*. New York: Commission on Voluntary Service and Action (415 East 12th St. New York, NY 10009), 1986.

Bolles, Richard Nelson. *The 1989 What Color Is Your Parachute?* Berkeley, Calif.: Ten Speed Press, 1989.

Coyne, Margie, Karen Czarny, and S. Susan Winn-White. *Let the Spirit Blow*. Washington: International Liaison of Lay Volunteers in Mission (4121 Harewood Rd., N.E., Washington, DC 20017), 1989.

Dent, Barbara. *The Gift of Lay Ministry*. Notre Dame, Ind.: Ave Maria Press, 1989.

Driver, David. *Good Heart Book: A Guide to Volunteering*. Chicago: Noble Press (213 W. Institute Place, Suite #508, Chicago, IL 60610), 1989.

Elsesser, Suzanne E. *Preparing Laity for Ministry*. Washington: United States Catholic Conference, 1986.

Lewis, Roy. *Choosing Your Career, Finding Your Vocation*. New York: Paulist Press, 1989.

Rauner, Judy. *Helping People Volunteer*. San Diego, Calif.: Marlborough Publications, 1980.

Thero, Cynthia. *Can I Help?* Denver, Colo.: The Source, 1989.

Chapter Twelve: In the Year 2000

Buhlmann, Walbert. *The Church of the Future*. Maryknoll, N.Y.: Orbis Books, 1986.

———. *Dreaming about the Church*. Kansas City, Mo.: Sheed and Ward, 1987.

Dolan, Jay, et al. *Transforming Parish Ministry*. New York: Crossroad, 1989.

Donovan, Vincent J. *The Church in the Midst of Creation*. Maryknoll, N.Y.: Orbis Books, 1989.

Drucker, Peter. *The New Realities*. New York: Harper & Row, 1989.

Hoge, Dean. *Future of Catholic Leadership*. Kansas City, Mo.: Sheed and Ward, 1987.

Rahner, Karl. *The Shape of the Church to Come*. New York: Seabury Press, 1972.

Index